Costs and Benefits of VAT

Costs and Benefits of VAT

C. T. Sandford
M. R. Godwin
P. J. W. Hardwick
M. I. Butterworth

 Heinemann Educational Books

336.243
COS

336.2714
COS

Heinemann Educational Books Ltd
22 Bedford Square, London WC1B 3HH
LONDON EDINBURGH MELBOURNE AUCKLAND
HONG KONG SINGAPORE KUALA LUMPUR NEW DELHI
IBADAN NAIROBI JOHANNESBURG EXETER (NH) KINGSTON
PORT OF SPAIN

ISBN 0 435 84782 1 (cased)

First published 1981

Typeset by Northumberland Press Ltd, Gateshead, Tyne and Wear and
Printed in Great Britain by Richard Clay (The Chaucer Press) Ltd,
Bungay, Suffolk

(18/10/95)

244012

Contents

Appendices

Acknowledgements

The thanks of the authors are due to a very large number of people who have assisted in this research, and especially to those without whose help it could not have been undertaken.

On the official side we are very grateful to Customs & Excise for help in the preparation of this survey, but they are, of course, in no way committed to the views expressed or conclusions reached. Our thanks are also due to the President and Registrar of the VAT tribunals for their help.

Professor Louis Moss, of the Survey Research Centre, Birkbeck College, London, gave us the benefit of his wide experience in commenting on a draft of our questionnaire, and Professor A. R. Ilersic of Bedford College, London, has advised us on the statistical aspects of the study. Professor Ilersic, along with John F. Avery-Jones, Solicitor, and General Editor of the *Encyclopaedia of Value Added Tax*, Trevor Baldwin, MSc, FCA, Halmer Hudson, FCA, FTII, FSS, FRFA, Donald Ironside, FCA, and David Collard, Professor of Economics at Bath University, gave considerable time to reading a full draft of the study and spent a full day commenting on it. Their help improved the study enormously.

A special word of thanks is due to Dorothy Johnstone, formerly Commissioner of Customs & Excise, who has been a consultant to the study and whose unique knowledge of the administrative aspects of VAT and perceptive comments saved us from many errors of fact and infelicities of style.

We wish also to thank Dr Alan Lewis of Bath University for the assessment of the readability of some of the VAT literature, in which he acknowledges the help of Colin Harrison of Nottingham University and Donald Moyle of Edge Hill College of Education.

We gratefully acknowledge the work of Julie Hanbury, whose skill at punching cards was remarkable, and of the secretaries to the Centre, Sue Powell and especially Fenella Gabriel, who complied with unreasonable demands with skill, good humour and infinite patience.

We also much appreciate the helpfulness of officials of a number of trade associations, the West Region secretaries of the Institute of Chartered Accountants and the Association of Certified Accountants, and the VAT professional advisers who generously gave up their time to be interviewed. Not least we appreciate the help of those – nearly three thousand – who completed, with care, our lengthy questionnaire and on some of whom we inflicted a further interview.

We also gratefully acknowledge the essential contribution of the Social Science Research Council in financing the study. We hope they will consider that the money has been well spent.

Finally, we make the usual disclaimer, no less necessary for being customary. All those who have helped us bear no responsibility for the views presented or the errors which remain.

C. T. Sandford
M. R. Godwin
P. J. W. Hardwick
M. I. Butterworth

Bath University
Centre for Fiscal Studies
August 1980

Glossary of Technical Terms

Additional (or other) Exchequer costs: costs incurred by the Exchequer arising from the existence of a lag between payment of tax by a trader and its receipt by the government.

Administrative costs: costs incurred by the revenue authorities in the taxation process.

Broad-based tax: a tax applying to a very wide range of goods and services.

Cascade tax: a turnover tax collected at every stage of production with no offset for tax on purchases.

Cash flow benefit: the benefit which accrues to a third party in the process of collecting tax from the final taxpayer and withholding the money until the date on which it becomes payable to the authorities.

Commencement costs: once and for all costs incurred at the inception of a new feature of the tax system.

Compliance costs: costs incurred by taxpayers or by third parties in meeting the requirements of the tax system over and above the tax liability itself and over and above any harmful distortions of consumption and production to which the tax may give rise.

Discretionary costs: additional compliance costs which the individual may choose to incur in pursuit of reducing his tax liability.

Economies of scale: the increased efficiency arising from the possibility of greater specialisation in large units.

Eligible trader: a trader who was included in the NAS sample frame.

Exempt trader: a trader outside the VAT system.

Exemption from VAT: the position of traders who do not charge VAT on their outputs but must bear the cost of VAT on their inputs.

Higher rate of VAT: the rate applied to selected 'luxury' goods and services. (Abolished 1979.)

Input tax: VAT charged on inputs.

Inputs: goods and services supplied to a trader in the course of business.

Likert scale: a technique for measuring attitudes by means of a series of related questions.

Managerial benefit: the benefit arising in the form of improved control over the business which results from the imposition of regular record-keeping for VAT.

Mandatory costs: compliance costs incurred in direct fulfilment of legal obligations.

Marginal cost: the cost of an additional unit.

Marginal tax rate: the tax rate applying to the final unit of income received.

Mean compliance cost as a percentage of taxable turnover: compliance costs of each respondent divided by that respondent's taxable turnover; the percentages obtained are summed and divided by the number of respondents in the analysis.

Mean: the sum of all observations divided by the number of observations.

Money costs: costs of fees, correspondence, telephone, etc. caused by compliance duties.

Multi(ple)-rate tax: a tax applying different percentage rates to different commodities.

Multi(ple)-stage tax: a tax collected at more than one stage of production.

Narrow-based tax: a tax applying to a small range of selected goods and services.

Net compliance costs: (gross) compliance costs minus offsetting benefits.

Net tax payable (or repayable): tax due minus tax deductible.

Neutral taxation: taxation which does not distort patterns of production and consumption.

Operating costs: compliance costs plus administrative costs plus any additional Exchequer costs.

Opportunity costs: the cost of using resources in one particular way rather than in an alternative way.

Outlier: a value of a variable which lies outside the expected range of values.

Output tax: VAT charged on outputs.

Outputs: goods and services supplied by a trader in the course of business.

Partial exemption from VAT: occurs when a trader supplies some goods and services which are liable to VAT, and some which are not.

Partly exempt trader: a trader who supplies some goods and services which are liable to VAT and some which are not.

Payment trader: a trader whose tax due exceeds tax deductible.

Physical productivity measurement: productivity measurement through an analysis of physical inputs compared to physical outputs.

Progressiveness: the extent to which the percentage of income paid in tax increases as income increases.

Proportionality: the case in which the percentage of income paid in tax remains constant at all income levels.

Psychic costs: costs of the burden of anxiety imposed by compliance duties.

Purchase Tax: UK single stage tax collected at the wholesale stage (now abolished).

Registered trader: a trader within the VAT system.

Regressiveness: the extent to which the percentage of income paid in tax decreases as income increases.

Regular costs: costs arising from a continuing structural feature of a tax.

Repayment trader: a trader whose tax deductible exceeds tax due.

Retail sales tax: single stage tax collected at the point of sale to the final consumer.

Sector: a broad class of business type.

Selective Employment Tax: UK tax on the number and type of employees in selected industries (now abolished).

Single rate tax: a tax applied at one percentage rate.

Single stage tax: a tax collected at one stage of production.

Social costs and benefits: costs and benefits experienced by the community as a whole which arise from the operation of the tax system.

Standard error: an indication of the likely variation occurring between different samples.

Standard rate of VAT: the rate applied to most goods and services.

Tax deductible: total input tax paid by a trader.

Tax due: total output tax collected by a trader.

Taxable turnover: turnover of goods and services liable to VAT at any rate including the zero rate.

Temporary costs: costs which arise from unfamiliarity with a tax.

Time costs: value of the time spent in operating the tax system.

Time-payments index: the ratio of the amount of tax always outstanding to the annual yield of the tax.

Value Added Tax: multiple-stage tax under which registered traders may offset tax paid to their suppliers against tax collected from their customers.

Value added: the amount of increase on the price of goods or services made by a trader.

Variable: the name given to a phenomenon which takes different values.

Zero rate of VAT: a nominal tax rate of 0 per cent applied to selected 'essential' goods and services.

Glossary of Abbreviations

ADV	Discussions with professional advisers on VAT
C&E	Customs & Excise
CBI	Confederation of British Industry
CC	Compliance costs
CCAB	Consultative Committee of Accountancy Bodies
CP	Credit period
E	Exempt from VAT
EEC	European Economic Community
FOL(P)	Personal follow-up interviews to the National Survey
FOL(T)	Telephone follow-up interviews to the National Survey
GATT	General Agreement on Tariffs and Trade
H	Higher rated for VAT
HMSO	Her Majesty's Stationery Office
ICAEW	Institute of Chartered Accountants in England & Wales
IFS	Institute for Fiscal Studies
MLR	Minimum lending rate of the Bank of England
NAS	National mail questionnaire survey of VAT registered traders
NEDO	National Economic Development Office
NES	*New Earnings Survey*
PAYE	'Pay As You Earn' scheme of collecting employees' income tax
PSBR	Public Sector Borrowing Requirement
Q	Survey question number
R	Annual repayment of VAT
REP	Regional Employment Premium
S	Standard rated for VAT
SET	Selective Employment Tax
T	Annual payment of VAT
TPI	Time Payments Index
TT	Taxable Turnover
UK	United Kingdom of Great Britain and Northern Ireland
VAT	Value Added Tax
WA	Written Answers (relating to *Hansard*)
X	Exports which are zero rated for VAT
Z	Goods and services which are zero rated for VAT

Introduction

On 1 April 1973 Value Added Tax (VAT) came into effect in the United Kingdom, replacing Purchase Tax and Selective Employment Tax (SET). The introduction of VAT was a major change in tax policy, not least in its effect on the costs of operating the indirect tax system. VAT had its supporters and opponents. Two official reports, that of the Richardson Committee in 1964 (Cmnd 2300) and of the National Economic Development Office (NEDO) in 1969, had considered the case for VAT in Britain and reached rather different conclusions. But no one, not even its most fervent supporter, argued that VAT would be a simple tax for the Revenue to administer or for the trader* to cope with. VAT required both a collection and a refund mechanism. The revenue collected by Customs & Excise was only a fraction of the money which changed hands as a result of the tax. To work properly the tax needed the co-operation of some one and a quarter million traders, many of whom had little or no previous experience of working with Customs & Excise.

The introduction of VAT was preceded by an intensive period of preparation and a degree of consultation with trade associations and professional bodies which had no precedent in British indirect tax administration (Johnstone 1975). It was widely recognised that the administration costs falling on the revenue authorities would be high and that traders would face an exceptionally heavy cost of compliance, but no attempt was made to measure these costs. Indeed, before the tax was fully in operation, it would have been impossible to estimate compliance costs with any kind of accuracy. More surprisingly, despite the longer history of VAT on the Continent, little or no research appears to have been done abroad on the compliance costs of the tax; this may be partly due, however, to the relative lack of complaints abroad where VAT often replaced more numerous taxes (as in France) or complicated taxes (as in Germany).

Once VAT had begun to operate in the United Kingdom complaints about its compliance burdens were numerous, especially from small traders, though hard facts were lacking.

It thus seemed well worth while to undertake a study to try to establish the facts about the compliance and administrative costs of VAT, which might serve as a basis for policy; hence this book. After a pilot study had shown the feasibility of the enterprise, the Social Science Research Council were prepared

---

* The term 'trader', following informal Customs & Excise usage, denotes all organisations, companies, partnerships and individuals, engaged in business activities. 'Registered traders' are traders registered for VAT.

to finance a major research project at the Centre for Fiscal Studies, University of Bath. Added point has been given to the study by the increasing number of countries which have adopted a VAT or are considering its adoption, though clearly the degree of relevance of this study to other countries will depend on the form of VAT they adopt.

The pattern and scope of the book is as follows. The first two chapters provide a practical and theoretical background to the study. Chapter 1 outlines the arguments used to support the replacement of Purchase Tax and SET by VAT, describes how VAT works and draws out the implications for our study. Chapter 2 discusses administrative and compliance costs in general, and, drawing on earlier studies, provides a terminology and a theoretical framework of reference.

In Chapter 3 we describe the research programme, its objectives, methodology and components. Thereafter we are concerned with the research findings.

Chapter 4 contains estimates of the total of compliance and administrative costs, whilst Chapters 5 and 6 examine their incidence – how the burden varies as between traders and what influences may account for that variation. Chapter 7 continues the same theme, for it deals with the difficulties traders experience; such difficulties help to account for both the absolute burden of compliance and its incidence.

In the following two chapters we look at possible benefits to traders for complying with VAT – benefits to their cash flow and managerial benefits from better record-keeping; these benefits are an important offset to compliance costs for many traders. In Chapter 10 we bring costs and benefits together to assess the total and incidence of net compliance costs and of the net cost to the Exchequer of operating the tax.

A trader's attitude to VAT is partly a product of his experience of the tax, but may also be an independent variable. The level of compliance cost, the perception and realisation of benefits, and attitudes to VAT, may be related to the advice received about the tax. Chapters 11 and 12 are therefore concerned with attitudes to VAT and sources of advice, respectively.

The analysis of the survey data concludes with a chapter of case studies (Chapter 13). These studies illustrate the costs, benefits and various other features relating to compliance costs which have emerged from the research. Because the case studies relate to actual (though, of course, unidentified) firms, they may be found more readily comprehensible than the aggregated data of the preceding chapters.

Chapter 14 up-dates the study, as far as may be, by describing and taking into account the relevant changes in VAT and in the economic environment since the main survey was undertaken. Finally Chapter 15 summarises the findings and emphasises their implications for policy.

We have tried to keep the main text as free as possible of technical material so that it can be readily understood by those not well versed in either economics or statistics. Specialists are catered for in the Appendices. A glossary of those technical terms which it has been necessary to use and a glossary of abbreviations are included at the front of the book.

1 Value Added Tax in the United Kingdom

Introduction

In this chapter we describe the introduction of Value Added Tax (VAT) into the United Kingdom. We look at the arguments used to support the replacement of Purchase Tax and Selective Employment Tax (SET) by VAT. We describe the main characteristics of VAT and in particular draw attention to those aspects of the tax which bear on administrative and compliance costs. We end the chapter with a summary of events beginning with the official documents preceding the introduction of the tax and concluding with the main changes in the 1980 budget.

Why VAT?

VAT replaced Purchase Tax and SET on 1 April 1973 and the case for VAT rested in part on the deficiencies or alleged deficiencies of the taxes superseded. Let us start, therefore, by looking at these taxes.

Purchase Tax

Purchase Tax was a war-time fiscal innovation, having been introduced in 1940 on a wide range of consumer goods for the home market, but with exemptions for food, drink, services, commodities already subject to excise duties and various miscellaneous goods including essential drugs, newspapers, books and periodicals. It was levied, broadly speaking, at the wholesale stage, and charged as a percentage of the wholesale price, originally at the rates $33\frac{1}{3}$ per cent and $16\frac{2}{3}$ per cent. Subsequently the number of different rates was increased and the rates themselves raised. By 1947 there were five rates of tax, varying from $33\frac{1}{3}$ per cent to 125 per cent. Further changes took place and in 1970, when the abolition of the tax was contemplated, there were four rates, ranging from $13\frac{3}{4}$ per cent to a maximum of 55 per cent. At that time the tax was contributing some 9 per cent of central government revenue from taxation (excluding National Insurance contributions).

The multi-rate structure of Purchase Tax represented an attempt to classify goods according to their nature, the more 'luxurious' the good the higher the rate. One objection to the tax was the arbitrariness of this classification (especially as, with the passage of time, the luxuries of yesterday became the necessities of today); another was the view that such discrimination between goods distorted production patterns and consumers' preferences. The variety of rates as well as the exemptions created anomalies on the borderlines, which were a subject of complaint and, occasionally, ridicule.

In fact, many of the difficult borderlines arose from the attempt to charge tax at the wholesale stage and yet keep it off goods that were destined for business use and not for final consumption (e.g. refrigerators above a certain size were exempt because they were presumed to be primarily used by caterers while those below that size were taxed because they were presumed to be domestic). Furthermore, the tax was felt to have virtually reached its practical limits as a revenue-raiser because there were no significant additional areas of consumption goods that could be brought into its scope without involving hopelessly complicated and ineffective borderlines of that kind.

Another objection came from retailers. They had to carry tax paid stock and if goods were damaged or stolen lost the tax as well as the goods. Also, when tax rates fell, their customers expected to pay only prices reflecting the new tax rate although the goods had actually borne the old rate.

There was, of course, no necessity for Purchase Tax rates to vary as between classes of goods. It would have been possible to have had a uniform rate, which would have reduced the strength of most of the objections. But, because it was levied at the wholesale stage, Purchase Tax could not accommodate taxation of services and so could not provide uniformity across the board.

Selective Employment Tax

It was, in part, to make good this deficiency that SET was introduced in 1966. The tax required that every employer should pay to the Ministry of Social Security a weekly sum for each employee in addition to the National Insurance contribution. As originally introduced the rates were 25/- (£1.25) for a man, 12/6d (62½p) for a woman or boy under eighteen and 8/- (40p) for a girl. No payments were made by the self-employed. Employers in manufacturing activities subsequently received a refund of payments, plus a premium at the rates of 7/6d (37½p), 3/9d (18¾p) and 2/6d (12½p) respectively. A second group of industries consisting mainly of agriculture, transport, mining, quarrying and fishing received a refund but no premium. The third group, comprising construction, distribution and service industries, received no refund; it was therefore on this latter group that the impact of the tax was primarily felt.

In introducing SET the Chancellor of the Exchequer indicated (*Hansard* 3 May 1966) that he expected it to fulfil a number of purposes. It would make a substantial contribution to revenue without recourse to the traditional taxes and with less effect on the cost of living than the ordinary sales taxes. But also the Chancellor saw it as a way of improving the 'fiscal balance' by bringing services within the field of taxation, encouraging economies in the use of manpower and of providing positive encouragement to manufacturing and therefore, indirectly, to exports.

The administration of SET involved a large number of government departments but neither of the traditional revenue departments. The Treasury directed the operation. Tax was collected by the Ministry of Social Security through the

National Insurance stamps. Premiums and refunds were normally paid by the Ministry of Labour through its local offices, but in some cases (e.g. refunds to agriculture) a different department was responsible.

For administrative reasons net payment of SET related to an 'establishment' – broadly speaking a work place having a single address. If more than half the employees in an establishment were eligible for a refund (premium) it was paid in respect of all the employees; if less than half were so entitled it was paid for none.

SET was subject to a variety of changes in its short life: reduced rates for part-time workers; the addition of a Regional Employment Premium (REP); the abolition of the premium to manufacturing industry in April 1968 following Britain's devaluation of the pound in the previous November; and substantial increases in rates. The tax reached a peak revenue yield in 1969/70 when it raised over £2,000 million gross, £500 million net – just under 4 per cent of central government revenue from taxation (excluding National Insurance contributions).

Throughout its existence SET remained a controversial tax and the Conservative Party was pledged to its repeal when it came to office in 1970. It was argued against it, firstly that most of Mr Callaghan's arguments for its introduction (above) were illogical and unconvincing. The 'fiscal balance' argument was valid only for personal services (like hairdressing). SET applied to many services, like retailing and wholesaling, which were essentially part of the provision of goods, many of which carried high rates of Purchase Tax or excise duty. As regards the argument about economising in the use of labour, why only economise in services and construction? As to the promotion of exports, the tax hit some of Britain's best export earners, the invisible exports such as banking, insurance and consultancy services, and failed to benefit import savers, like agriculture.

In addition it was claimed that SET had some positive disadvantages. The rigidity of the 'establishment' basis led to an uneconomic rearrangement of the labour force amongst the establishments of large firms seeking to maximise premiums or repayments. Exemption of the self-employed encouraged the artificial development of self-employment, especially in the building industry. SET tended to cut across regional policies in that, by and large, the development areas contained an above average proportion of labour in service industries and a below average proportion in manufacturing; when redundancies were created in the service industries there were few manufacturing industries there to absorb the unemployed. Since SET was paid as a fixed sum per worker (in each category) the tax was proportionately heavier for the low paid than for the high paid; it thus may have promoted the substitution not only of capital for labour but also of skilled for unskilled labour. As a tax on a factor of production, SET had the disadvantage that it entered into production costs and therefore export prices, both of invisible exports and of the exports of goods in so far as the manufacturers had bought in services such as financial or consultancy advice. SET was also probably slightly regressive in its distributional effects.

On the other hand SET did raise substantial revenue with very low administrative and compliance costs. Subsequent research evidence also gives some credence to Mr Callaghan's view that SET raised prices less than if the same revenue had been raised by the more conventional taxes on expenditure (Reddaway 1970, 1973).

The first official body to examine the possibility of a VAT in the United Kingdom was the Richardson Committee (Cmnd 2300, 1964). The Committee, which reported before the introduction of SET, was asked to consider the replacement of either Purchase Tax or profits tax by VAT. It opposed both changes. The Committee argued that the multi-stage collection which characterised VAT would require the creation of an extensive administrative machinery; that VAT could not readily be made to differentiate between goods; and that the case for VAT as a means of promoting exports had been overstated. All turnover and sales taxes, it held, are aimed ultimately at consumer expenditure, and hence arguments for one method or another must rest largely on collection methods and flexibility, and VAT is intrinsically much more cumbersome (than Purchase Tax) as a means of consumer taxation. There is no logic, the Committee argued, in the change from an established single-stage system to a multi-stage system spread over the successive stages of production and distribution and applying not only to the finished consumer product but to all its constituents at earlier stages when the object of the tax is the final consumer product.

In the light of the dismissal of the tax by Richardson it is perhaps surprising that public opinion reversed so rapidly that VAT was in operation less than a decade later. No doubt the changes owed much to the unpopularity of SET.

The advantages claimed for VAT all related to improving the efficiency of resource use in the economy. As the Green Paper, issued by the Conservative government in 1971, expressed it: 'The existing pattern of indirect taxation in this country is open to the objection that it is selective and is based on too narrow a range of expenditure. Selective taxation gives rise to distortion of trade and of personal consumption patterns, and can lead to the inefficient allocation of resources.' (Cmnd 4621, p. 3). VAT was intended to reduce the distortion by widening the tax base, by taxing services on exactly the same basis as goods and by introducing a single rate (apart from the zero rate). The wider tax base, it was argued, would also make VAT a better instrument for managing the economy than Purchase Tax, where changes in rates intended to alter aggregate demand had fallen disproportionately on a small range of goods. Further, because VAT was collected at each stage in the chain of production and distribution, and exports were zero rated, the tax could be more readily excluded from export costs. Both Purchase Tax (to a small extent, e.g. on stationery and office equipment) and SET on all businesses save those where it was repaid, entered into export costs. VAT could therefore be expected to improve the balance of payments.*

These arguments had all gained some support from the Report of the National Economic Development Office (NEDO 1969) which set out the arguments for

---

*The export rebate, introduced in 1964 had aimed, among other things, to offset the element of Purchase Tax that entered into export costs. But it was open to international objection because it did not refund them precisely and it was abolished as 'no longer necessary' when the pound was devalued in 1967.

and against a switch to VAT and concluded 'that a VAT system has some advantages over a Purchase Tax system'. In addition, because VAT was imposed at the point of sale, and retailers could recover input tax, VAT removed the disadvantage of Purchase Tax that retailers had to carry tax paid stocks. Further, because retailers had to impose VAT on their final selling price, there was a competitive incentive to keep retail prices low, which did not exist with a Purchase Tax levied at the wholesale stage.

The broad base of VAT meant that it was a buoyant source of revenue offering scope, if desired, for a switch from direct to indirect taxation.

Although Conservative Ministers argued the case for VAT on its merits and held that they would have introduced it anyway, an essential background factor was Britain's impending membership of the EEC, which required the adoption of VAT as the Community's form of turnover taxation. (An account of some of the important features of VAT in the EEC is given in Appendix A.)

Characteristics of the United Kingdom VAT

In 1972 the Conservative government passed legislation to bring VAT into effect from 1 April 1973 in place of Purchase Tax and SET.

In principle VAT is a tax on goods and services consumed in the home market; the tax is complicated because it is collected at every stage of production and distribution. Value added is the contribution of a particular firm to the value of the product. It can be calculated either directly by taking the value of a firm's wage and salaries bill plus profits, or indirectly by subtracting the costs of materials and services (such as electricity and transport) that the firm has bought in from the value of the products it sells. Value added can be obtained by an accounting or an invoicing method. (For some of the implications of alternative methods of calculating VAT, see Appendix B.) Under the 'invoicing system' of VAT, which applies in the UK and throughout the EEC, value added is never actually calculated, but only the tax due from the taxpaying business to its suppliers and to it from its customers. A business charges VAT on the output it sells, pays tax on the materials and services it buys, and hands over to the revenue authorities the difference between output tax and input tax in each accounting period. VAT is charged on imports when they enter a country.

As introduced in 1973 the United Kingdom VAT had a standard rate of 10 per cent on all goods and services except those which were zero-rated or exempt, or were sold by exempted traders. All exports were zero-rated. When a product is zero-rated no output tax is paid, and the supplier of a zero-rated product can recover any input tax paid, either by setting it off against VAT due to Customs & Excise on positively rated products, or by means of a repayment. Foodstuffs, books and newspapers, fuel, new building and public transport, as well as exports, were all zero-rated in 1973; also, very much at the last minute, children's clothing and footwear and a limited range of foodstuffs (like confectionery, ice-cream and potato crisps) which had previously been liable to Purchase Tax were added to the list of zero-rated goods. The main motive behind the zero-rating of food, fuel, public transport and children's clothes was to limit the tax burden on the poorer members of society; the zero-rating of books presumably arose from a traditional desire to avoid a 'tax on knowledge'; whilst construction benefited because it was new investment, often in the form of tax-favoured housing.

Exempt activities in 1973 included the renting of land and buildings, insurance, postal services (where provided by the Post Office), gaming, financial services, education, medical services, burials and cremations. Traders with a turnover of under £5,000 per annum were also exempt. The grounds for exemption from the scope of VAT generally have more to do with the administrative and technical problems of applying the tax than with social or political considerations. Firstly, there is bound to be a minimum level of activity below which registration and collection are simply not worthwhile; but the limit is essentially arbitrary and other countries have much lower limits (see Appendix A).

Secondly, 'it is generally agreed that VAT is ill-suited for taxing services connected with finance' (Tait 1972). Inputs and outputs of banks and insurance companies are difficult to define and calculate under the indirect subtractive method of VAT (p. 168).

The difference between zero-rating and exemption is important and perhaps needs explanation. A trader selling zero-rated goods is normally a 'registered' trader, part of the VAT system, recovering from Customs & Excise the whole of the input tax paid on his purchases. An exempt trader (whether by virtue of the products in which he deals or because his taxable turnover is below the threshold) is outside the system; he is not a registered trader. If his purchases are subject to VAT he will have to pay tax on them and cannot recover it from Customs & Excise, though he is at liberty to raise his prices to recoup the rise in his costs. Whilst it is almost invariably an advantage to be zero-rated it is not necessarily an advantage to be exempt rather than standard-rated. A trader selling almost entirely to the general public will usually gain by being exempt, but he may find exemption a disadvantage if he is selling to registered traders in competition with registered traders: his potential customers in that case will prefer to buy from other registered traders because then they can offset input tax against their output tax, which they cannot do if they are merely paying an increased price that does not technically contain VAT. For this reason provision exists for a trader (who would otherwise have been exempt because his turnover was below the threshold) to seek voluntary registration.

When VAT was introduced certain other tax adjustments were made. A large proportion of the revenue from Purchase Tax had come from cars, which had borne considerably more tax than they would pay with a 10 per cent VAT. Because the Chancellor did not wish to forgo this revenue he introduced a special car tax of 10 per cent, levied on the wholesale value. On the other hand, Customs & Excise duties on tobacco and alcoholic drinks, etc. were reduced on the introduction of VAT to keep the overall tax revenue from them much as before.

An argument widely used by the Labour Opposition against VAT at the time of its introduction was that it would be regressive, i.e. it would bear proportionately more heavily on those with low than on those with high incomes. As we have seen, Purchase Tax had discriminated between 'luxuries' and 'necessities'.

In fact data from the Family Expenditure Survey shows that, at the time of its abolition, Purchase Tax was roughly proportional in its incidence whilst VAT emerged as slightly progressive. Thus the multi-rate structure of Purchase Tax had not succeeded in making it progressive, whilst the widespread zero-rating of VAT had given it an element of progression. It is not unlikely, however, that if Britain adopted a rate structure similar to that of most EEC countries, with a positive (if reduced) rate for foods, fuel and transport instead of a zero-rate, the tax would become slightly regressive.

A summary of the main changes in VAT since its introduction is given at the end of this chapter. We might note two of the most important points, however: the introduction of a higher rate of tax by the Labour government, which was in existence at the time of our main survey (though this rate was subsequently abolished by the Conservatives); and the raising of the exemption threshold in a series of stages.

Before looking more closely at the administrative arrangements for the tax, let us briefly examine how far the main advantages claimed for VAT worked out in practice, for there is a big difference between the theoretical advantages of a hypothetical tax and the actual advantages of a particular form of tax. The claimed advantages were a reduction in the distortion of trade and consumption, as a result of a broad and more uniform basis of taxation; a better instrument for managing the economy; no spillover of tax into costs, thus improving the balance of payments; and scope for a switch from direct to indirect taxation.

Whilst a zero rate for exports is a universal feature of a VAT, the United Kingdom is exceptional in applying zero-rating to a range of other products. Thus, although the United Kingdom VAT began with only one positive rate, the widespread zero-rating plus the range of exempt services reduced the neutrality of the tax. Moreover, as a result of the invoicing method used, the difference in effective tax rates on value added may be more than the nominal differences in tax rates because tax levied on sales at a later stage has to make up for the lack of tax at an earlier stage – the so-called 'catching up' effect (Tait 1972). Thus, if we assume a standard rate of 15 per cent applicable on sales in a restaurant, because the food inputs to the restaurant are zero-rated, tax paid by the restauranteur will be more than 15 per cent of his value added because he will charge 15 per cent on his sales but have no deduction of input tax on his principal input (for a further example see Appendix B). Clearly the existence of a higher rate further reduced the strength of the neutrality argument.

There is indeed a clash of principles between efficiency and distributive considerations. The widespread zero-rating was introduced to reduce the danger that VAT would prove regressive, and the higher rate was intended to increase its progressiveness; but both reduced the efficiency advantages that might have been gained from a more neutral tax structure.

Thus the efficiency benefits of VAT were imperfectly realised. Positive rates of VAT applied over a range of goods very little different from that of Purchase Tax which could have been set at a uniform rate. On the other hand, VAT meant that services could be taxed on the same basis as goods – impossible with a Purchase Tax levied at the wholesale stage.

VAT did provide a wider tax base for purposes of demand management, so that changes to regulate the economy might be expected to have a less drastic effect on particular industries than Purchase Tax changes. However, the much larger number of traders involved increased the cost of change, and frequent alterations in VAT rates may not be readily acceptable (see Chapter 15).

Whilst VAT was superior to Purchase Tax and especially SET in restricting the spillover of taxation into production costs, and hence export prices, it was not perfect; moreover, the benefit to the balance of payments was small. The exemption of rent, insurance, finance and postal services meant that traders with these outputs had to bear input tax (for example on furniture, fittings, telephone services, repairs and maintenance) but could not reclaim it. They could be expected to pass the tax on to their customers. Business users of these services thus have to bear some VAT costs despite the philosophy of the tax. There are considerable difficulties in taxing financial services by the indirect subtractive method; but, as Tait (1972) puts it: 'These are substantial exemptions. It might pay governments to consider the possibility of taxing the value added of such businesses on an annual base of their wages and profits (the direct additive method).' Not only would there be a revenue benefit to the government, there would be a benefit to the remainder of the business community, which is at present bearing some input tax. As for the extent of the balance of payments advantage in replacing Purchase Tax and SET by VAT, a calculation of the National Institute of Economic and Social Research just before the introduction of VAT suggested that the benefit might be only of the order of £20 million.

The final major advantage claimed for VAT was buoyancy of revenue, offering scope for a switch from direct to indirect taxes. Perhaps because Chancellors were

Table 1.1   VAT Revenue as a Percentage of Total Taxation

	VAT (£m)	Total central government taxation (£m)	VAT as % of central government revenue from taxation
1973/4	1425	17 250	8.3
1974/5	2497	22 132	11.3
1975/6	3415	28 116	12.1
1976/7	3750	32 470	11.5
1977/8	4226	36 436	11.6
1978/9	4900	40 942	12.0
1979/80	8000	50 172	15.9
1980/1[a]	12 450	61 780	20.2

[a] Budget forecasts
Source: *Financial Statement and Budget Reports*

reluctant to raise living costs and hence stimulate wage increases in an inflationary period, little or no use was made of this possibility until 1979, when Sir Geoffrey Howe unified the standard and higher rates of tax at the new high level of 15 per cent. The fact that VAT is charged at a proportional rate on sales means that it is better than Purchase Tax (levied on wholesale values) and much better than SET (at a fixed rate per worker) in maintaining its yield in real terms in times of inflation. The yield of VAT is set out in Table 1.1.

VAT Administration

The essential structure of any VAT and the particular features of VAT as adopted in the United Kingdom have vital implications for the way it is administered and the requirements imposed on registered traders. The Richardson Committee (1964) recognised the difficulties of administering a VAT (above p. 4) and the NEDO Report (1969), whilst more favourable to VAT, recorded: 'There can be little doubt that the administrative problems presented by a VAT would be considerable' (p. 5). Whatever view is taken of the advantages claimed for VAT as against Purchase Tax and SET, the costs of operating the tax are much higher.

In reply to a Parliamentary Question in 1978 (*Hansard* 22 May, col 416) on the administrative costs of Purchase Tax, SET and VAT, a Treasury Minister, Mr Robert Sheldon, gave the cost of administering Purchase Tax in 1972/3 as about £10 million and that of SET, £3 million. The cost of administering VAT in 1977/8 (the year of our survey) was about £85 million. As the Minister pointed out, both prices and administrative costs rose substantially between 1972 and 1978 and he suggested that a more meaningful comparison would be the cost per £1 of revenue collected. On this basis it cost 0.75p to collect each £1 of Purchase Tax and 2p to collect each £1 of VAT. The cost of collecting each £1 of SET was given by the Minister as about 0.5p until the halving of the rate on 5 July 1971 raised it to about 1.5p in 1972/3.

As the comment illustrates, expressing administrative cost as a percentage of revenue is liable to mislead because the measure is so susceptible to changes in tax rates and hence tax revenues; but as VAT in 1977/8 was raising a proportion of government revenue from taxation roughly the same as Purchase Tax and SET together just before their abolition was contemplated, the comparison is not an unfair one. The conclusion of the higher administrative cost of VAT is not disputable.

We have no information on costs to taxpayers of complying with Purchase Tax regulations save the vital fact that there were some 70,000 registered traders collecting Purchase Tax on behalf of the Exchequer, as against some one and a quarter million VAT registered traders.

Although SET had to be paid by all employers paying National Insurance contributions on behalf of employees (even though a majority of them recovered their payments), SET was notable for the easy method of payment. The employer simply bought an additional stamp along with the National Insurance stamp. The repayment mechanism was more cumbersome. Repayments were made by a variety of government departments (thus confusing responsibilities) and the mechanism of the tax required gross payments to the Exchequer of some four times the net tax, the difference being returned to the payers. Nonetheless, there can be no doubt that, in terms of compliance as well as administrative costs, both Purchase Tax and SET were amongst the cheapest taxes to operate.

In principle, the operation of VAT using the invoicing method requires all tax on sales and on purchases to be recorded, so that the difference can be paid to the revenue authorities. If all inputs and outputs are taxed at the same rate, then, broadly speaking, all that is necessary to calculate the tax due to the Exchequer is to take a percentage of all purchase revenues and subtract the same percentage of all sales revenues in each time period. Complications arise as a result of various rates of tax and from exemptions. As the NEDO Report (1969) put it: 'The greater the number of rates of tax, or the wider the range of exemptions, the greater the risk of anomalies and of increasing the complexity of arrangements' (p. 5).

As soon as a second rate is introduced, whether positive or zero, a straight proportion of all purchase and sales revenue will no longer do. The existence of widespread zero-rating also means that many traders pay their suppliers more VAT than they collect from their customers, and must consequently receive repayments, so that a repayment mechanism becomes necessary. If repayment traders are not to be kept waiting for an unreasonable time repayment claims and repayments need to be made frequently: thus, under the United Kingdom tax, most traders make quarterly returns but repayment traders may make monthly returns. The exemption of a wide range of services, as with the United Kingdom VAT, raises the problem of partial exemption – where part of the output of a supplier is taxable and part exempt. Input tax on supplies for taxable outputs is then properly deductible, but not on supplies for exempt outputs. However, it may be far from easy to distinguish between these inputs. Thus special rules are needed for the partly exempt trader.

Even without the complications of varied rates and a range of exemptions there would be problems with secondhand goods, such as motor cars and antiques which may have paid VAT before, and hence special schemes were introduced into the United Kingdom tax to meet this situation. Also, because many retailers sell a large number of varied items of low value, which might mean high compliance costs if the tax on each sale was separately recorded, a series of special schemes were introduced for retailers with the object of approximating the tax due to the Exchequer at less compliance cost to the trader.

It is inherent in the structure of VAT that far more revenue is paid over in tax than finds a permanent home in the Exchequer. This is not only because about one-third of the revenue received by Customs & Excise is paid out in repayments. Indeed, VAT involves less repayment than SET, where some three-quarters of gross revenue was returned. It is also because traders at each stage of production pay each other sums in tax of which only a proportion is due to the Exchequer. Thus assuming a 10 per cent VAT, a trader may collect £10,000 VAT on £100,000 value of sales in a quarter, but only pay over £3,000 to the revenue authorities because he has paid £7,000 VAT on £70,000 of materials.

The gross payments of tax by traders to each other and by consumers to traders are about four times the net revenue to the Exchequer.

Apart from making it easier to reduce spillover into production costs, the main advantage of this multi-stage procedure (as compared with a single stage retail tax) is that evasion may be less. In principle the authorities have a cross check on each trader's sales and purchases records. More important, in practice, each trader has a vested interest in ensuring that he is properly invoiced, for each trader's output tax is another trader's input tax and input tax is recoverable if properly invoiced. The exception to this self-checking procedure is sales to the consumer. At that stage opportunities for evasion are the same as those for a retail sales tax. However, because only a proportion of the revenue from a multi-stage tax like VAT is collected at the retail stage, the amount of tax at risk is much less than with a retail sales tax.

This, at any rate, is the view expounded in the Green Paper on VAT (Cmnd 4621, 1971) which stated that a retail sales tax

> at the rates that would be required, would introduce a very considerable burden of taxation at the stage at which goods or services passed to the final consumer. Experience in other countries has shown that this would present very serious difficulties of collection and control. Indeed, it is clear that a retail sales tax can be successful only if the rate is kept low. A tax at the retail stage on the scale which would be necessary if purchase tax and SET were abolished is now widely regarded as impracticable.

The Carter Commission (1966 and 1967) rejected a federal VAT for Canada on the grounds that a single stage retail tax was just as effective, while being cheaper and simpler to administer. Carter did, however, make the reservation that the documentation required under a value-added tax could reduce the scope for evasion at tax rates in excess of the envisaged 14 per cent maximum for the combined federal and state retail taxes.

The use of the invoice (rather than the accounting) method for VAT determined that Customs & Excise rather than Inland Revenue was the appropriate revenue department for administering VAT (Johnstone 1975). The experience of Customs & Excise was of direct dealings with traders and invoices rather than with accounts or accountants. The traditional Customs & Excise approach of visiting traders at their place of business was continued. Before VAT the Customs & Excise department had little or no contact with the professions, the service industries or even the retail trade; so, like the trader, the department had much to learn with VAT.

Thus, given the nature of the tax, the importance of an examination and review of the total and the incidence of administrative and compliance costs is clear.

Calendar of Events in the History of VAT in the UK

March 1964	Richardson Report, rejecting VAT, published.
August 1969	NEDO Report, more favourable to VAT, published.
March 1971	Green Paper published committing the government to introduce VAT.

March 1972	White Paper on VAT published.
27 July 1972	Finance Act, enacting VAT, became law.
1 April 1973	VAT introduced. Most commodities rated at *10 per cent*. *Zero-rated items* included exports, food (including confectionery), fuel, new construction, books and newspapers, and children's clothing. Rent, insurance, banking, education, health, postal services provided by the Post Office, gaming, burial and cremation, *exempt from VAT*. *Minimum turnover* for compulsory registration £5,000 per annum.
1 April 1974	Some changes in VAT ratings: petrol and road fuels, confectionery *standard rated*; aids for the disabled and protective clothing *zero-rated*.
29 July 1974	Standard rate reduced from 10 per cent to *8 per cent*.
18 November 1974	New higher rate of VAT, *25 per cent*, applied to petrol.
1 May 1975	Coverage of higher rate extended to most domestic electrical goods, excluding cookers, space heaters and water heaters and to furs, jewellery, boats, aircraft and most caravans.
12 April 1976	Higher rate reduced from 25 to *12.5 per cent*.
1 October 1977	Minimum turnover for compulsory registration raised from £5,000 to £7,500.
12 April 1978	Minimum turnover for compulsory registration raised from £7,500 to £10,000. Partial exemption rules relaxed. VAT return form redesigned and simplified, and certain other accounting simplifications introduced.
18 June 1979	*Higher rate of VAT abolished*, and the *standard rate* increased from 8 to *15 per cent*.
27 March 1980	Minimum turnover for compulsory registration raised from £10,000 to £13,500. Penalties for late payments increased.
1 June 1980	Lubricating oils *standard rated*.

2 Compliance and Administrative Costs

Introduction
In this chapter we take a broad look at tax compliance costs and tax administrative costs in general before concentrating in subsequent chapters on the administrative and compliance costs (and benefits) of VAT. Our purpose is to equip ourselves with a set of concepts and definitions which will be useful in our later analysis of VAT; to indicate some of the main problems associated with delineating and measuring compliance and administrative costs; and to outline the results of the (very limited) previous work in this field against which the findings of this study of VAT may be set. There is a general recognition of the importance of administrative costs, although not all the implications of these costs have been appreciated. Compliance costs, on the other hand, have tended to be neglected by the policy-makers.

Definitions and Distinctions
Relationship of Compliance and Administrative Costs
Tax compliance costs (hereafter termed compliance costs) may be defined as the costs which are incurred by taxpayers or by third parties in meeting the requirements of the tax system, over and above the tax liability itself and over and above any harmful distortions of consumption or production to which the tax may give rise. *Tax administrative costs* (hereafter termed administrative costs) are the costs incurred by the revenue authorities in the taxation process. The total of compliance plus administrative costs may be termed the *operating costs* of the tax.

There is often a trade-off between compliance and administrative costs: for instance, in the USA each income taxpayer fills in a detailed annual return and calculates his own liability, while in the UK most of this calculation is done by administrators in the Department of Inland Revenue. Similarly, the original plan was that Customs & Excise should do the annual recalculations for partly exempt traders under VAT, but since 1978 (when the partial exemption rules were eased somewhat and fewer small businesses were required to be involved with them) the partly exempt traders have had to do their own.

Clearly it should be an object of policy (subject to other policy constraints) to minimise the operating costs of any tax, and of the tax system as a whole. However, because of the relationship between administrative and compliance costs, it would be wrong to assume that minimum operating costs imply minimum administrative costs. An increase in administrative costs may be more than offset by a consequent reduction in compliance costs, with a net benefit to the whole economy.

In considering the trade-off between compliance and administrative costs it should be borne in mind that administrative costs are met from taxation and it can be assumed that they are spread across the population in accordance with government policy on the overall incidence of taxation. Compliance costs, in contrast, tend to be borne by different members of the public in a haphazard and arbitrary way. Moreover, they are more concealed and hence less subject to review. Further, the imposition of high compliance costs on some taxpayers may make them hostile, with a resulting lack of co-operation and an increase in evasion. On the other hand, taxpayers who calculate their own tax liabilities may better understand the system and feel less at the mercy of the bureaucracy.

Composition and Classification of Compliance Costs

Compliance with tax legislation may involve collecting tax revenue, accounting for it, and remitting it. To carry out these duties an understanding of the relevant laws is required. Individuals and organisations of all kinds may incur such costs. The costs are not confined to direct cash expenditures; unpaid time spent on tax compliance could have been used in other ways, and may be valued in terms of the opportunity cost of activities forgone. A psychic burden, such as anxiety, may be imposed because legislation requires individuals to perform complex duties under threat of legal penalty. Adam Smith (1776) recognised this characteristic when he wrote: 'Though vexation is not, strictly speaking, expense, it is certainly equivalent to the expense at which every man would be willing to redeem himself from it' (Vol 2, 307–9).

We can distinguish between *regular* compliance costs, *temporary* compliance costs and *commencement* costs.

Regular compliance costs arise from a continuing structural feature of a tax and continue throughout its life, e.g. the costs incurred by employers in withholding income tax from their employees and paying it to the tax authorities. Other costs are associated with changes in the tax system. Once and for all costs, like a conference fee to learn about a new tax, can be termed commencement costs. Those costs which arise from unfamiliarity with a tax, but which will subsequently tend to fall gradually during the learning process until they stabilise at the long term 'regular' level, can be termed temporary costs. Temporary costs, including commencement costs, may arise because of alterations in a tax as well as new taxes. With a new tax there is likely to be a build-up of compliance costs before the tax is implemented. With a change in tax there may or may not be a build-up depending on whether or not there was an announcement of the change which preceded the date of implementation. Figure 2.1 illustrates the pattern of compliance costs over time. Figure 2.2 illustrates the forms which compliance costs can take.

An important distinction may be drawn between the costs incurred in direct fulfilment of legal obligations – the *mandatory costs* of the tax – and the additional costs which the individual may choose to incur in order to try to reduce his tax

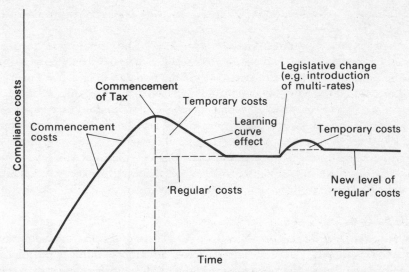

Figure 2.1   Model of changes in total compliance cost levels with a new tax (e.g.
VAT)

liability. The latter may be termed the *discretionary costs* of the tax. Some com-
mentators argue that only mandatory costs should be classified as pure costs of
compliance with tax legislation (Johnston 1961). However, it is fair to point out
that discretionary costs are an inevitable consequence of the operation of a tax.
For example, SET offered considerable scope for reducing tax liability by
incurring discretionary costs. Thus, as already mentioned (p. 3), employers could
rearrange the place of work of service employees to put them into establishments
where the majority of employees were exempt manufacturing workers; or they
could encourage employees to seek self-employed status.

The compliance effects of a tax may not be entirely detrimental. There may
be spin-off benefits; for example, stringent record-keeping requirements may force
a businessman to install an efficient financial information system which may then
cut unnecessary expenses. Further, where the authorities require a third party
to collect tax over a period of time before handing it over to the revenue
authorities, the third party gains a cash flow benefit at the expense of either the
taxpayer, or the revenue authorities, or both. Examples of collection procedures
which may benefit third parties are PAYE income taxation and Value Added
Tax (VAT). On the other hand the delay in collecting tax from the self-employed
(Schedule D tax in the UK) benefits them as compared with employees (Schedule
E taxpayers). In recognition of such benefits we need to distinguish between
(gross) *compliance costs* and *net compliance costs*, net compliance costs being compliance costs minus offsetting benefits. (As we shall see below, however, a benefit
to a taxpayer or third party may represent a detriment to the Exchequer, which
also must be taken into account.)

Besides the costs and benefits already described there may be others of a more
diffuse social kind (which we can call *social costs* and *social benefits*). Thus a cost

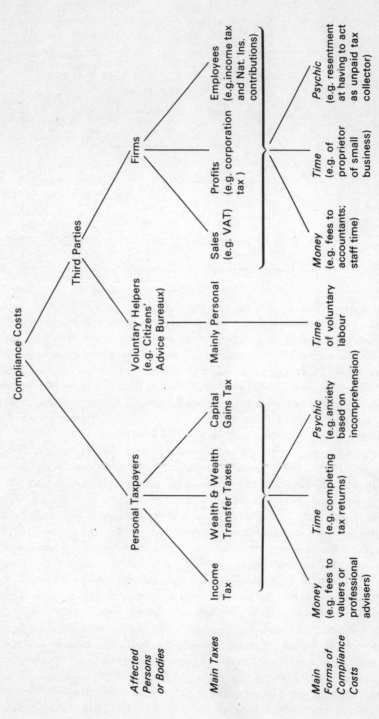

Figure 2.2 Main forms of compliance costs and affected parties. Reproduced, by kind permission of the editor, from an article in The British Tax Review by one of the authors of the present study

will be suffered by the community as a whole if, for example, a retailer discontinues a line of goods taxed at a different rate from the remainder of his sales solely in order to reduce compliance costs. There may be a social benefit where, for example, compliance with one tax provides data which restrict the evasion of another.

Composition and Types of Administrative Costs

Many of the distinctions relating to compliance costs apply equally to administrative costs of taxation. The process of learning how best to administer new legislation takes time. As with compliance costs, there are *commencement, temporary* and *regular* administrative costs. The pattern of these costs over time is similar to that of compliance costs, described in Figure 2.1. However, commencement costs are likely to start earlier than in the case of compliance costs and there will be a build-up of administrative costs before any major change.

Similarly there may be *social costs* or *social benefits* arising from the administration of a tax. Thus if rights of entry and search are given to revenue authorities and used in a heavy-handed way, there may be a social cost. On the other hand, costs incurred in the administration of one tax may provide a cross check on evasion of another and the consequent reduction of evasion may constitute a social benefit.

Other Exchequer Costs

A particular problem arises about the treatment of any financial credit which the operation of a particular tax provides to taxpayers or third parties. The benefit to the taxpayer or third party can reasonably be regarded as an offset to compliance costs. Two questions arise – should such a credit, the equivalent of a loan, be regarded as a cost to the Exchequer, and, if so, ought it to be designated an administrative cost?

There is a strong argument for regarding such a 'loan' as a cost to the Exchequer in the sense that the Public Sector Borrowing Requirement (PSBR), on which interest has to be paid, is higher than it would have been if no such 'loan' had been made. Implied in this view is the idea of a datum line or point of reference consisting of a (hypothetical) situation in which tax due by the ultimate taxpayer is paid on the due date and received by the revenue authorities on the same date. Any divergence means either a 'loan' *by* the revenue authorities or a 'loan' *to* the revenue authorities. The first raises administrative costs but reduces compliance costs; the second raises compliance costs but reduces administrative costs.

This question of the timing of tax payments is an economic aspect of taxation which, to the authors' knowledge, has never been comprehensively explored. References have often been made to the 'forced loan' which SET refund traders were required to make to the government; and the advantage of the self-employed in making later payments of income tax than employees has frequently been stressed (e.g. Barr, James and Prest 1977); but few taxes have been analysed in this way and no comparisons appear to have been made across a range of taxes. Yet relativity is the essence of tax theory and tax policy. Taxes must be compared with each other, for they can rarely be removed without being replaced. Because this aspect of taxation has received so little attention and yet may be of considerable importance, especially at a time of inflation and high interest rates, it is worth exploring more fully.

United Kingdom taxes vary considerably in the requirements for payment over time. Our examples are intended to illustrate the range rather than to be exhaustive. If we take income tax on income from work, PAYE payers have tax deducted each week or each month by their employer, who is required by law to hand over the tax to the revenue authorities fourteen days after the end of the tax month (which ends on the fifth of each month). The position of the self-employed is more complicated. Tax is payable by the self-employed in two equal instalments on the 1st of January and the 1st of July each year, based on profits made in the accounting year which ended in the tax year to the previous 5 April. However, when a trade or profession commences, the profits of one accounting year serve as the basis for two tax years. Because of this, *when incomes are unchanged from year to year* the deferment enjoyed by the Schedule D taxpayer is approximately six months or less in so far as Schedule D profits are computed on an accruals basis and receipts of income tend to lag.

If we look at some indirect taxes, we find that beer duty is charged on the quantity and gravity of 'worts' before fermentation; the duty charged in a calendar month is payable on the 25th day of the following month. It is generally reckoned that production and delivery times are such that on average the duty is paid about the time draught beer is drunk in a public house. Spirits duties are paid on withdrawal from bonded warehouse, which on average is eight to nine weeks before they are sold retail. Duties on tobacco products are payable on delivery of the products from registered premises (i.e. the manufacturer's premises), but there is an option to defer payment until the fifteenth day of the following month, provided that acceptable security is given. Hydrocarbon oil duties are paid on delivery from oil refineries or warehouses and the average time before they are sold to the public is very short, perhaps about three or four days.

Under the provisions for VAT the 'payment' trader* collects tax over a three-monthly period and is expected to pay the net tax due to Customs & Excise by the end of the following month, whilst the repayment trader submits a monthly return which Customs & Excise normally pay within a fortnight (for full details see below pp. 75–8).

We have thus a wide range of situations in which beer duty roughly accords with our datum line; income tax involves loans from the revenue; hydrocarbon oils and spirits involve loans to the revenue.

The position is illustrated in Figure 2.3 and Table 2.1, which give examples of the different situations and include a 'time-payments index' (TPI) derived by expressing the estimated size of the loan benefit from (or to) the revenue authorities as a percentage of the tax receipts. The larger the value of the index

---

* Registered traders for VAT who are not repayment traders will be termed payment traders hereafter when it is necessary to distinguish them from repayment traders.

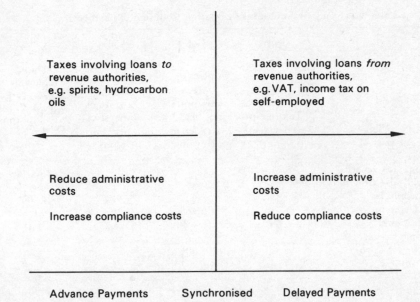

Taxes involving loans *to*
revenue authorities,
e.g. spirits, hydrocarbon
oils

Taxes involving loans *from*
revenue authorities,
e.g.VAT, income tax on
self-employed

Reduce administrative
costs

Increase administrative
costs

Increase compliance costs

Reduce compliance costs

Advance Payments   Synchronised   Delayed Payments

*Figure 2.3   Illustration of the effect on compliance and administrative costs of loans from
and to the revenue authorities*

above the datum line the larger the 'loan' from the revenue authorities per
£million collected; the larger the value below the datum line the larger the loan
to the authorities per £million collected.

The average amount of tax held by the taxpayer or third party (or received
by the revenue authorities *before* being paid by the ultimate taxpayer) is that
proportion of the annual tax paid which is equal to the length of the credit period
(or advance receipt period) in years, plus half of the collection period (in those
cases where the tax is collected over a period of time before being passed to the
revenue authorities).

The year of our survey, 1977/8, has been taken to illustrate the situation and
a rate of interest of 7 per cent (the average minimum lending rate (MLR) for
the fiscal year) has been used to calculate the benefit. The proportion of annual
tax held (Table 2.1, column 2) must be regarded as a very rough approximation,
indicative rather than exact; the TPI must be similarly regarded.

The extent of the benefit accruing to traders from delayed payments, and to
the Exchequer from advance payments, is very susceptible to the rate of inflation.
The inflation rate exercises a potent influence on the rate of interest. It also affects
the value of the delayed tax or repayment. For example, the longer the tax due
is held by the trader before being paid to the revenue authorities the less the
value of the payment in real terms to the revenue authorities. This is a simple
application of the principle that (unless the rate of inflation has been fully anticipated in a loan bargain) in times of inflation debtors gain and creditors lose.
The most marked effect is in relation to the self-employed. As we have said, when

Table 2.1 Comparison of taxes in relation to timing of payment 1977/8

	Col 1	Col 2	Col 3	Col 4
Tax (or part of tax)	Tax receipts (repayments) ($£$m)	Approximate proportion of annual tax held by trader or Revenue[b]	Benefit (at rate of interest of 7 per cent) ($£$m)	Time-payments index (TPI) $\frac{\text{col } 3}{\text{col } 1} \times 100$ (%)
Income tax on self-employed 1976 (Schedule D)	7066	0.5 ($\frac{1}{2}$)	247	*Delayed payments* 12.60
VAT (payment traders only)	6310	0.208 ($\frac{1}{8} + \frac{1}{12}$)	92	1.45
Income tax on employees 1976/7 (Schedule E)	14544	0.083 ($\frac{1}{24} + \frac{1}{24}$)	84	0.58
Beer duty	893	zero	zero	*Synchronised payments*[a] zero
Excise duty on hydrocarbon oil	2465	0.010 ($\frac{1}{96}$)	2	*Advance payments* 0.08
VAT (repayment traders only)	(2125)	0.125 ($\frac{1}{8}$)	18	0.85
Spirits duty	875	0.167 ($\frac{1}{6}$)	10	1.14

[a] Above the synchronised payments line benefits go to the taxpayer or third party (employer or trader); below the synchronised payments line, benefits go to the Exchequer (with disbenefits to the trader).

[b] The fractions in Col 2 represent the approximate proportions of a year constituting the length of the credit (or advance receipt) period plus half the collection period (where appropriate).

income is steady the Schedule D taxpayer obtains a deferment of tax of up to six months. When income is rising there is an additional deferment of tax on the increase (but not on the principal). In times of inflation additional deferment is obtained even if income is unchanged in real terms.

To return to the questions with which we began this section. Taxes vary in the periods of payment and it seems reasonable, indeed essential if realistic comparisons are to be made between taxes, to regard those taxes which provide 'loans' to taxpayers or third parties as carrying a cost to the Exchequer.

The question which then arises is: should such costs be regarded as administrative costs? There is undoubtedly a case for calling them such. They are a cost of the particular way a tax is administered. They could be reduced by changes in the methods of administration. For example if the self-employed were required to pay all tax on 1 January instead of in equal instalments in January and July, the credit benefit to them would be approximately halved. Or if VAT returns from payment traders were required monthly (as in some EEC countries) instead of quarterly, the credit benefit would be cut by 40 per cent.

On the other hand we think of administrative costs as costs which, to some extent, are within the control of the administrative departments – Inland Revenue or Customs & Excise in the United Kingdom. The departments could make recommendations to government about the time to be allowed for payments; but once these are fixed, the cost is outside their control. No improved efficiency in staff utilisation would do anything to reduce the 'loan' costs. It is thus perhaps preferable to call these costs 'additional or other Exchequer costs' rather than specifically labelling them 'administrative costs'.

Problems in the Measurement of Operating Costs
Compliance Costs
There are considerable difficulties in identifying and measuring compliance costs. For example, a taxpayer who employs an accountant may receive an unitemised bill for unravelling all his financial affairs including taxation. Clearly some proportion of this bill represents a tax compliance cost, but the amount to be allocated is a matter of judgement. It may be that non-corporate taxpayers would not produce accounts at all if they were not required by tax legislation. On the other hand a large corporation is required to publish annual accounts for the benefit of its shareholders and may in any case collect the information required for management purposes.

There is also a problem in isolating the marginal addition to costs caused by the imposition of a particular tax. Where a company has a tax department, it may be argued that the marginal cost of an additional tax is zero if the specialist tax staff can take the extra work in their stride. Alternatively the marginal cost is simply the extra labour cost incurred in cases where that labour can be accommodated within the existing office space. This line of argument may then be pursued for each separate tax which the department operates. However, clearly the costs of the department (or the overhead costs) would not have been incurred if the tax system as a whole had not existed.

There has been considerable discussion, particularly by Yocum (1961), of this problem of allocating overheads. The issue hinges on whether compliance work simply results in a more intensive use of existing facilities. If a business has to rent, heat and light additional offices solely for its tax department, the costs of such offices are clearly compliance costs. However, in many cases tax work is done within an accounting department which would continue to be needed if there were no taxation. In this case it may be argued that the overhead expenditure is independent of tax compliance, and the overhead compliance cost is zero. It may be that the percentage of overhead expenditure allocable to tax compliance work increases with the size of firm and the complexity of tax duties performed. The sole proprietor who stays at work for an extra hour every month to update his tax accounts and returns will incur minimal extra costs in heating and lighting. A larger firm may find it efficient to set up a separate accounts department, renting additional space which will be devoted to tax work for part of the time. The largest businesses may have offices maintained exclusively for tax accounting purposes.

Discretionary and mandatory compliance costs also give rise to difficulties. A business may allocate an amount of resources to tax accounting far above that necessary to comply with the law. Tax planning on a large scale is a normal feature of modern corporations. However, it has been observed (p. 15) that this expense, although tax-related, is not strictly compliance expenditure. An attempt should be made by the researcher to isolate the mandatory element in compliance costs; where this is difficult, it should be clearly stated that the estimate of compliance costs includes discretionary costs.

Another problem may arise in distinguishing between temporary, regular and once-only costs of compliance. An observer may well over-estimate the level of compliance costs if he investigates them during a period when a new tax has just been introduced, for costs will fall as the tax becomes familiar. Considerable care is needed in allocating costs to the correct category. Where a single business has incurred large legal fees in a tax dispute, this will usually be categorised as an isolated case of high costs. If, however, it emerges that, due perhaps to ill-conceived legislation, a large percentage of taxpayers are regularly in dispute with the authorities, then taking taxpayers as a whole such expenditures may be considered a regular cost of compliance.

Much of the cost of compliance arises in the form of time spent by personal taxpayers, office staff and others. It is evident that when we try to measure total compliance costs in money terms, the value assigned to such time will be a principal determinant of the total estimated cost. Unfortunately there is no general agreement on what value should be assigned to time. It seems appropriate to value the time of employees at the going rate for the relevant grade of staff (plus overheads where applicable). But even here there is a counter argument that if existing staff could have worked harder in any case, tax work is simply taking up the slack in excess staff capacity at zero cost. The problem arises because staff can only be employed in indivisible units, either part-time or full-time. For example, suppose it is assumed that appropriate staff are only available full-time, and there was work for four-and-a-half employees before the imposition of a tax. Then five staff would have been employed anyway and if the new tax compliance work required half a person's time it could be done without employing additional staff; the marginal cost would then be nil. Conversely, if the five staff were already employed to capacity, one extra person would be needed to do only the additional half a person's work. In this second instance, compliance costs would have been double the labour cost needed had labour been perfectly divisible. There seems no reason to believe that one of these situations occurs more often than the other. In practice, divisibility is increased by the possibilities of overtime and part-time work. It would therefore appear reasonable simply to assess labour compliance costs in terms of the number of hours spent on the work at the appropriate grade.

Where there is evidence of extra staff having been taken on to do tax work, or of existing staff doing this work in paid overtime, the case for valuation at the wage rate, or even at the overtime rate, is more clear cut.

A more difficult problem arises in the case of the taxpayer who does his own tax work outside normal working hours. If we take the example of the self-employed, the most straightforward approach would be to value the time they spend on tax compliance at the wage rate for those employed in a comparable occupation, though the relatively risk-free nature of employment as opposed to self-employment may mean that such an estimate will be on the low side. An alternative approach is to consider the fee which a tax adviser or book-keeper would charge to perform similar work, and use that value as the basis for costing. A further defensible approach is to use a lower value (on the grounds that the opportunity cost is lower) akin to that used in cost-benefit analysis of transport studies for travel in leisure time, where the general practice now appears to be to take one-third of the relevant wage rate (Beesley 1965).

Psychic costs of compliance are nebulous and difficult to measure. Taking Adam Smith's definition that such a cost is 'equivalent to the expense at which every man is willing to redeem himself from it', we may ask taxpayers how much they would pay to be rid of this worry; but answers to a hypothetical question of this nature may be vague or meaningless, particularly in cases where the taxpayer is not in practice in a position to off-load the work on to anyone else.

Valuing offsetting benefits may be equally difficult, especially in cases where a requirement to keep better financial records generates improved efficiency. Problems may arise concerning the proportion of taxpayers who previously kept good records, the proportion whose businesses are too simple to require, or benefit from, sophisticated accounts, and the precise value of the gain in efficiency to the remainder.

Administrative Costs

Some of the problems associated with compliance costs have their counterparts in administrative costs. For example, several taxes may be administered together, or use common services, and it may therefore be difficult to assign a realistic cost to one particular tax.

With administrative costs an apparently simple concept such as the efficiency of the tax administration gives rise to difficulties. If efficiency is measured (as it commonly is) in terms of the percentage of tax revenue absorbed by costs of administration, and the level of a tax is reduced so that it produces only half the previous revenue, the tax department's efficiency has nominally halved, although the officials may still be doing broadly the same amount of work. Conversely, on this measurement, doubling the tax yield simply by raising the existing tax rates nominally doubles the efficiency.

One alternative approach which by-passes this difficulty is that of productivity measurement through an analysis of physical inputs (e.g. man years or area of accommodation occupied) in comparison to physical outputs (e.g. number of tax returns processed). However, problems can also arise under this method. For example, the introduction of a new taxation system, whether it be a new tax or computerisation of existing tax work, may make the productivity measures useless for comparing conditions before and after the change (Dean 1976).

Some useful indications of comparative efficiency may be gained by inter-regional comparisons.

In considering efficiency of administration, a comparison of the marginal change in cost with the marginal change in revenue may be important. An increase in administrative costs in some directions may bring in more revenue than would be lost by reducing administrative costs elsewhere. This approach may yield results suggesting that more effort should be devoted to taxes which do not appear to be particularly efficient under other criteria, simply because an increase in the administrative effort on these taxes offers the best prospects for increasing revenue.

The manner in which administrative efficiency is measured in a study will depend on the context in which the problem is being considered. It may be that more than one approach is necessary to achieve useful results.

Findings of Previous Research on Compliance Costs

The bulk of research into tax compliance costs has been undertaken in the USA, where pioneering studies on the topic appeared in the mid-thirties (1).* It has been fairly well established that there are economies of scale in taxation compliance (2), (6), (7), (9), (10), (11), (12), (20), particularly where procedures can be standardised or mechanised (5). An important consequence of these economies is that compliance costs tend to be regressive, i.e. they bear more heavily on small businessmen and the self-employed than on large firms (12), (18), (20).

The compliance costs of changes in the tax system tend to be high (2), (20). Trading across tax frontiers gives rise to increased costs, as adjustment and rebating problems are met (1), (3), (5). The costs of compliance are influenced by the structure of the tax system, the way the system impinges on the particular type of firm, and the size and organisation of the firm (2), (10); they are not related in any very direct way to the amount of tax paid.

In the case of sales taxation, costs are additionally influenced by the size of an average transaction, and the number of invoices handled (9), (10), (14): where a business makes a small number of high-value transactions, little paperwork is generated and compliance costs tend to be low, whereas businesses conducting large numbers of low-value transactions have more invoicing to do, and a large volume of tax accounting is involved. If the tax system necessitates separation of invoices into non-taxable and taxable transactions, or the application of different rates of tax to different goods and services, additional costs are generated (10), (15).

Despite these references to earlier research it must be emphasised that the amount of research done on compliance costs has been limited, and the methodology has not always been rigorous. Widely varying costs have frequently

* The figures in brackets refer to the Summary Tables in Appendix C.

been observed even among taxpayers in apparently similar situations (6), (9), and the differences have not been convincingly explained. It may be that the ability, education and training of the taxpayer have an important influence. Some people may be able to cope easily with their tax affairs while others may not have the desire, the skills, or even the knowledge required for delegating such work to a competent adviser.

Some taxpayers will incur substantially higher discretionary costs than others in seeking to minimise their tax liability. Some of these may be prepared to pay large fees to professional advisers and/or spend much of their own time contesting matters with the tax authorities either on principle or because of exceptional hostility to taxation. However, no evidence to test such hypotheses has been collected.

In short, whilst the importance of the administrative costs of taxation has been generally recognised in most countries, compliance costs have been much less widely considered. Even in the USA, where most of the existing research has taken place, studies have tended to concentrate on specific sectors or particular taxes so that no general picture of the overall level and incidence of compliance costs can be built up.

If academic economists have shown little interest in compliance costs it is hardly surprising that tax policy-makers have not sufficiently considered them, even in policy discussions where compliance costs are of crucial importance. One such issue is the relative merits of self-assessment to income tax or assessment by the tax authorities. Another, as we have already indicated, is in assessing the merits and demerits of VAT.

3 The Research Programme

Introduction

In this chapter we outline the coverage of the research project – its aims, the various elements of the study and the methodology of the field work.

Objectives

The main objectives of the survey were to estimate the total compliance costs of VAT in the UK and to identify the particular areas and causes of high compliance costs.

Compliance costs had to be evaluated as far as possible in money terms, so that comparison could be made with tax revenue and with administrative costs, and the total operating costs of the tax could be calculated. Offsetting benefits accruing to registered traders were to be examined and quantified where possible, so that a figure of net compliance costs could be arrived at. Where data permitted, comparisons were to be made with other taxes.

A series of hypotheses was formulated, based on previous research (p. 24) (including the pilot study), observation and analysis about likely influences on compliance costs, and these hypotheses were to be specifically tested in the research. The principal hypotheses were that compliance costs were influenced by (1) the nature and sector of the business; (2) the size of business; (3) the number of transactions performed; (4) the number and type of VAT categories applied to inputs and outputs; (5) the length of time the business had been registered for VAT; (6) the choice of special scheme for retailers; and (7) the education and book-keeping training of small businessmen preparing their own VAT returns. Figure 3.1 illustrates the relationship of these variables to compliance costs.

To give some idea of the extent of temporary costs, information was sought on the effect of changes in VAT rates. Views were also obtained about the effects on compliance costs of the administrative changes which took place during the period of the study.

Methodology

Whilst data on administrative costs rested almost wholly on published sources, those for compliance costs could only be obtained by field work. The principal components of the empirical work are summarised in Table 3.1 and a more detailed account of each follows.

National Survey of Registered Traders (NAS)

The kernel of the research and main source of data was a national survey of

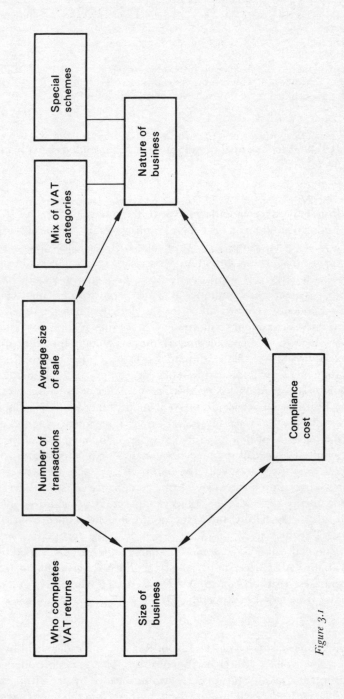

Figure 3.1

Table 3.1 Empirical work on compliance costs

Date	Activity	Abbreviation
1. Sept–Dec 1978	National survey of registered traders	NAS
2. July–Sept 1979	Follow-up interviews by telephone	FOL(T)
3. Nov 1979–Jan 1980	Follow-up personal interviews	FOL(P)
4. (Mainly) May–June 1980	Interviews with professional VAT advisers	ADV

VAT registered traders by mail questionnaire (NAS) undertaken during the last four months of 1978.

Questionnaire Contents

In order to test the hypotheses listed above the questionnaire had to be fairly long. It contained questions on the general trading sector of the business (following Customs & Excise categories, see Appendix E1) and the trader's particular activities within that sector. Questions were asked on turnover and number of employees (as measures of size), on the average size of sales and number of invoices processed and on the number of VAT categories applying to inputs and outputs. Respondents were also asked for the date they first registered for VAT and the special VAT retail or secondhand scheme they used, if any. Information on school leaving age and book-keeping training was sought from sole proprietors, partners, and directors of small companies preparing their own VAT returns.

Information on compliance costs and benefits comprised the amount and value of the time *normally* spent on VAT work per VAT period by proprietor, partner or director, by professional accounting staff, and by other staff; the money *normally* spent on fees to outside advisers for preparing VAT accounts in each VAT period, plus unusual amounts of time (and its value) spent by members of the business, and sums of money spent in the preceding year on special problems with VAT. Respondents were asked to specify the nature of any such problems.

Two alternative approaches to measuring compliance costs (considered in some detail in Chapter 4) were also the subject of questions. In addition, information was sought about the nature and value of any benefits gained from complying with the VAT regulations.

The questionnaire also asked about the sources of VAT advice used by respondents and about VAT officers' visits. An opportunity was given for an open-ended comment on these visits and on the VAT system as a whole. (A copy of the full questionnaire is included in Appendix D1.)

Sample Frame

The sample frame was based on the List of Registered Traders held by Customs & Excise, current on 31 March 1978, consisting of 1,274,000 traders classified by trade group and taxable turnover. A sample selected by size within each trade group would have been best for testing the hypotheses, but this might have revealed information from which individual traders could have been identified and would therefore have breached the confidentiality requirements of Customs & Excise. The Department therefore provided a sample matched by size, and trade group, but not by size within trade group.*

A random sample was drawn consisting of 0.75 per cent of all registered traders with a taxable turnover of less than £1 million per annum, and a 3 per cent sample of those traders whose taxable turnover was £1 million or more. The larger sampling fraction in the upper turnover range was required because of the importance of larger firms: in 1977/8 the 30,000 traders with taxable turnover above £1 million accounted for 78 per cent of total net VAT receipts.

Traders deregistered or in process of deregistering, those known to have left their registered address, and traders known to be insolvent or in the hands of a liquidator were excluded from the sample. A positive response from them was unlikely; moreover any information obtained might not relate to a sufficiently recent year. Traders registered after 31 July 1977 were excluded because many of the questions related to a full twelve-month period; this exclusion, however, had the disadvantage that it reduced the information from which to assess commencement costs and the learning effect. The traders remaining after these deletions are referred to as 'eligible traders' and the final sample size was 9,094.

When compared with the registered trader population in the year 1977/8, the number of eligible traders varied by trade group from 84 per cent eligible in financial and business services up to 95 per cent eligible in primary industries. This difference presumably reflects varying business lifespans and creates a small element of bias in two ways: firstly, commencement costs will be underestimated because the sample incorporates a bias against businesses having short lifespans; secondly, as a low eligibility rate reduces the possibility of certain groups of traders being selected, the sample is somewhat less respresentative of these groups and the results are slightly less reliable than in other groups.

Eligibility increased consistently with size, from a rate of 74 per cent for the smallest firms up to 98 per cent for the largest. It is likely that traders deregistering account for much of the low eligibility rate below £10,000 per annum turnover, though traders gone away or insolvent may also contribute towards this bias. (A full comparison of the eligible and total traders appears in Appendix E2.)

Methods Used to Ensure Confidentiality
If the sample was to be fully representative, it had to be drawn from the official VAT register. Discussions with senior officials of the Department of Customs & Excise led to an agreement, which received Ministerial approval, by which the sample could be so drawn without breaching confidentiality requirements.

The complete list of VAT registered traders classified by trade group, size of taxable turnover, and trade code, is kept on the Customs & Excise Central Unit computer at Southend. The sample was drawn from this list by the Central Unit according to the specifications laid down by the research team, subject to the

* The matching was carried out, using the chi-squared test, to within the 95 per cent confidence level.

constraint discussed on p. 28 above. However, the names and addresses were not sent to the University of Bath, but went to a direct mailing firm frequently used by the Department. The questionnaires were delivered separately to the mailing firm (which gave an undertaking not to permit the researchers to see the names and addresses), and the mailing firm then distributed the questionnaires to the addresses supplied. In this way, the research team obtained the sample without ever seeing the register of traders or the list of traders sampled.

Respondents who chose to identify themselves when they returned the questionnaires were thus the only members of the sample whose names and addresses were known to the research team. A numbered, pre-paid card was included which could be returned separately from the completed questionnaire, thereby making it impossible even for a person having access to the sample list to match the questionnaire with a particular name. However, the return of the numbered cards permitted the mailing firm to identify the respondents who did not need to be sent reminders.

The stringency of these confidentiality requirements had the unfortunate consequence that it was impossible for the researchers to seek information directly from non-respondents to test for bias in response, i.e. whether the characteristics of non-respondents differed in any significant way from those of respondents.

Response

The researchers realised that there was likely to be a poor response to a long mail questionnaire asking businessmen for confidential information on tax liability, turnover, number of invoices and terms of credit. However, there was no other feasible method of surveying a reasonably representative sample of the one and a quarter million traders. Accordingly, considerable effort was devoted to devising ways of improving response to the mail questionnaire. Letters were sent to 214 trade associations setting out the aims of the survey, asking the associations to give the survey a favourable mention in any trade journal or newsletter and to encourage members who received questionnaires to complete them.

A press release was circulated to national and local newspapers, and a gratifying number of journals published brief details of the survey.

The questionnaire itself was typeset and bound in a card cover inscribed 'University of Bath Centre for Fiscal Studies 1978. Value Added Tax. A Survey of Costs and Benefits to Businesses', with the word 'Confidential' in the top right hand corner. Great care was taken to give the questionnaire a professional finish, while ensuring that it looked sufficiently distinctive not to be confused with any official VAT literature.

The questionnaire was mailed second-class, for economy reasons, and each questionnaire was accompanied by a carefully-worded single-page letter (Appendix D2) explaining the objectives of the survey, guaranteeing confidentiality and stressing the possible simplification of the VAT system which could result from the project's success. The researchers were obliged to include with the letter a Parliamentary Question and answer which stated that the Customs & Excise

Department were co-operating with the research team in such a way that their obligations of confidentiality were maintained; and that, although the Minister hoped traders would respond, the survey was voluntary. A self-addressed, Business Reply Paid envelope was enclosed.

Following the findings of Scott (1961), two reminders were sent. Although Scott recommends intervals of ten days between mailing the questionnaire and the first reminder, and between the first and second reminders, the researchers extended this period to twenty-one days because of the vagaries of the second-class post. The initial mailing took place on 20 September 1978, and a short reminder was posted to all non-respondents on 12 October. A further copy of the questionnaire was despatched on 31 October 1978 accompanied by a second reminder letter and a photo-montage of favourable reviews of the survey taken from trade journals.

An unusual feature of the survey was that the researchers had a telephone installed so that potential respondents could telephone (reversing the charges if desired) for further information about the project or for assistance with completing the questionnaire. The special telephone was in operation from the beginning of the nationwide questionnaire mailing on 20 September 1978 until 22 November 1978. The first reminder letter (mailed 12 October 1978) emphasised the availability of the telephone advice service, which was manned at all times during office hours, and also until 8 pm on Tuesdays and Thursdays, so that those who could not telephone during the day were able to use the service. All telephone calls were carefully logged and it is probable that the telephone service led directly to the completion of at least sixty additional questionnaires (two-thirds of 1 per cent of the sample); indirectly, the knowledge that the service was available may have encouraged other respondents to tackle the questionnaire successfully.

Of the 9,094 questionnaires despatched, 2,857 completed (or partly completed) questionnaires were returned, equivalent to a response rate of 31.4 per cent.

Table 3.2 Reasons given for non-response

	Number	Per cent
Too busy, no time to complete questionnaire	68	37.0
Not interested/questionnaire too difficult	31	16.8
Ill-health or semi-retired	19	10.3
Already overworked as unpaid tax collector	18	9.8
All VAT work done by paid adviser	16	8.7
Questionnaire inapplicable to the business[a]	9	4.9
Group registration complications	6	3.3
Other reasons	17	9.2
Total	184	100.0

[a] No clear reason was given to substantiate this comment and the researchers consider that it was based on misunderstanding.

Although this response is in the range generally achieved in compliance cost surveys (see Appendix C) the research team had anticipated a somewhat better response in view of the pilot survey response rate of 46.6 per cent (Sandford *et al.* 1979). Possible reasons for the low response are given in Appendix E4.

Of the traders from whom no positive response was forthcoming, 291 (3.2 per cent of the sample) returned the questionnaires, of whom 184 gave written reasons for refusal which are set out in Table 3.2. It is perhaps noteworthy that three of the refusals commented that they were content with the VAT system.

Of the 2,857 responses to NAS, 58 were rejected as unusable because of failure to provide information on (1) type of business or business sector; (2) either on turnover or number of employees; or (3) on compliance costs.

A small number of questionnaires was rejected because, although some crucial information had been given, the remainder of the questionnaire was not completed, or was very inadequately filled in.

Table 3.3 Estimated response rates

| | Usable response | |
	Number	Per cent
(a) By sector		
Primary	451	34.8
Manufacture and utilities	395	39.0
Construction	336	27.3
Transport and communication	115	29.4
Retail	540	29.0
Wholesale and dealers	242	33.2
Financial and business services	130	41.8
Professional and scientific services	160	37.8
Miscellaneous and public services	430	24.3
Total	2799	30.8
(b) By size (taxable turnover in £000 p.a.)		
0– 9.9	395	26.3
10– 19.9	450	25.1
20– 49.9	525	22.4
50– 99.9	402	32.2
100–499.9	435	37.7
500–999.9	111	63.1
1000 and over	391	44.3
Total	2709[a]	29.8[a]

[a] 90 traders did not disclose taxable turnover.

Thus, 2,799 usable questionnaires were coded and mounted on the computer for analysis; the estimated response rates, by sector and size, are set out in Table 3.3. At a later stage, Customs & Excise provided a breakdown of the total trader population (but not of the sample) by size within sector. With the aid of this data it was possible to estimate approximate response rates by size within sector, which are recorded in Appendix E3.

Sampling Bias

Apart from the heavier weighting introduced in the sample structure in favour of large firms (p. 29). Table 3.3b reveals a bias in the response towards larger firms. Sectoral response was biased towards sectors having a heavy concentration of large firms, and against sectors with a heavy concentration of small firms, particularly miscellaneous and public services. This difference may be partly accounted for by the differences in the eligibility rates of large compared with small firms (p. 29). The later information provided by Customs & Excise made it possible to compare the size distribution of respondents within individual sectors to that of the parent population, with results that were generally satisfactory. (Appendix E5 gives the detailed comparisons and significance tests.) The information supplied by Customs & Excise made it possible to correct both for size-within-sector and between-sector bias in grossing up the data.

The question of inaccuracy in response and the general reliability of the data is considered in later chapters, especially Chapter 4. One of the principal objectives of both the personal follow-up interviews (FOL(P)) and the interviews with professional VAT advisers was to check the accuracy of the data in NAS.

Follow-up Interviews

The follow-up interviews took two forms – by telephone and on a personal basis. The first part of the personal interviews was identical to the telephone interviews but the personal interview was then developed in more depth.

Content

The telephone interviews were designed primarily to gauge the effect of the changes in the VAT system during 1978/9. The interview schedule included questions on the transitional difficulties (if any) arising from the change in VAT rates in June 1979; and on the effect on compliance work of the introduction of the new VAT form; and other changes such as modification to the partial exemption rules and the possibility of aligning the VAT year with the firm's trading year.

The personal interviews probed answers given in NAS to the questions on compliance costs; sought details of special problems; endeavoured to establish how far numbers of invoices could be taken as a proxy for value of invoices (important in establishing credit terms) and asked further questions about the transitional difficulties arising if VAT rates were frequently changed. (Copies of the FOL(T) and (P) interviewer's schedule are included as Appendix D3.)

Sample Structure

Five hundred interviews were attempted: 441 prospective interviewees were approached by telephone and 59 were asked for a personal interview. The 500 were chosen from amongst the 1,270 respondents to the national survey of registered traders who had indicated their willingness to answer further questions.

Thirty-one of the 500 persons chosen for interview were selected because they had reported special difficulties with VAT and also were within relatively easy travelling distance from Bath (120 mile radius). The remainder were chosen by random number techniques on a stratified basis to provide a representation in proportion to the number of traders in each sector and taxable turnover range.

Those selected for personal interview included the 31 respondents with special difficulties; 9 others who had made particularly interesting comments on the VAT system; and 19 who were within the Avon, Somerset and West Wiltshire areas and who could therefore be visited most easily and at least cost. Such a selection necessarily incorporates bias; in particular the heavy weighting of those with special difficulties is likely to have biased the sample towards traders with anti-VAT views and relatively high compliance costs. One of the main objects of the personal interviews, however, was to obtain an insight into the problem areas. Because the first section of the personal interview schedule was identical to that of the telephone interview, responses to the two types of interview are considered together.

Response

Fifty-five traders were eliminated from the sample for reasons indicated in Table 3.4.

Table 3.4

Telephone number unobtainable	24
Trader gone away	18
No telephone number	12
Trader no longer registered for VAT	1
Total	55

The real sample was therefore 445. One recall was attempted if the initial call was unsuccessful, and the final response was 59 per cent, as set out in Table 3.5.

Table 3.5 Percentage response to the follow-up interviews

	Telephone interviews (n = 387)[a]	Personal interviews (n = 58)[a]	Overall percentages (n = 445)[a]
Positive response	57	76	59
Person sought unavailable	26	5	23
No reply	15	2	13
Refused	2	19	4
Total[b]	100	100	100

[a] n = total numbers in each column to which the percentages relate.
[b] Columns do not exactly sum to 100 because of rounding.

The interview response over-represents traders up to £100,000 and under-represents larger firms in comparison with the mail questionnaire response (see Table 3.6), but the differences are largely accounted for by the higher sampling fraction used in the mail questionnaire for firms with a taxable turnover of over £1 million.

Table 3.6 Distribution of interview respondents by size and sector and comparison with NAS response

Taxable turnover £000 p.a.	Primary	Manufacture and utilities	Construction	Transport and communication	Distribution and services[a]	Overall interview response	Overall NAS response
0– 9.9	3.8	1.9	1.5	0.4	9.1	16.7	14.5
10– 19.9	2.7	1.1	1.9	0.8	12.5	18.9	16.7
20– 49.9	2.7	2.7	2.7	0.8	13.6	22.3	19.4
50– 99.9	3.0	1.9	1.1	0.4	11.7	18.2	14.7
100–499.9	1.1	3.4	1.5	0.8	5.7	12.5	16.0
500–999.9	—	1.5	0.4	—	1.1	3.0	4.1
1000 and over	0.4	3.0	1.5	—	2.7	7.6	14.5
Total	13.6	15.5	11.4	3.0	56.4	100.0	100.0
Overall NAS response	15.8	14.2	12.1	4.2	53.8	100.0	

The telephone interviews also included two respondents in the construction sector who did not provide information on taxable turnover.

[a] Includes wholesale & dealers, retail, financial & business services, professional & scientific services, and miscellaneous & public services.

Interviews with Professional VAT Advisers

Additional cross checks on the reliability and accuracy of information provided by registered traders were obtained from discussions with specialist VAT advice bureaux and from accountants in private practice who offer VAT advice to clients. (A copy of the questions on the interview schedule used in the accountants' interviews is included as Appendix D4.) The accountants were selected on a non-random basis with the co-operation of the West of England regional secretaries of the Institute of Chartered Accountants and the Association of Certified Accountants. A short mail questionnaire was also sent to a representative selection of Trade Associations which offered advice to members with VAT problems.

4 The Compliance and Operating Costs of VAT 1977/8

Introduction

How much does it really cost to operate the VAT system? We attempt to give a provisional answer to that question in this chapter. The purpose of the chapter is to present the estimates of total compliance costs in 1977/8 arising from NAS; to examine the components of these costs; to consider their classification (in terms of the types of compliance cost defined in Chapter 2); and to assess the reliability of the estimates. Then, using published data on administrative costs for the same period, we compare compliance and administrative costs of VAT, estimate total operating costs and make some comparisons with the operating costs of income tax.

Aggregate Compliance Costs

Table 4.1 summarises the components of compliance costs in 1977/8, on the basis of data derived from NAS (Q13, 19, and 24). In order to arrive at the figures in the table, the information from the sample of the NAS had to be 'grossed up' to obtain the aggregate for each compliance cost category and the overall totals. The grossing up procedure was as follows. The NAS data were assembled in ten size ranges within each of nine trade sectors* and the mean for each size range within each sector calculated. These means were then multiplied by the number of traders in that size and sector group in the parent population, as supplied by Customs & Excise. The addition of the totals for each size by sector group then gave the total 'measurable' compliance cost.

Taking all traders together the estimated average compliance cost for 1977/8 is £308. However, even if the data were perfect, an overall average is not very meaningful because of the wide variations in compliance costs between traders in different sectors and of different sizes. More significant, the estimate of the total measurable compliance cost of VAT in 1977/8 derived from NAS data was £392 million as Table 4.1 indicates. (A fuller version of the grossing up procedure is given in Appendix F). A similar grossing up procedure was used for each of the components of compliance cost derived from NAS (e.g. fees to accountants). However grossing up from very small numbers is particularly hazardous and the

---

* In some cases in the upper size ranges, because less than 10 responses had been obtained for a particular range, adjacent ranges were combined. The total number of size within sector 'cells' for grossing up was therefore 61.

Table 4.1 Compliance costs 1977/8 (all figures based on NAS data)

Nature of compliance cost	Normal costs (£m)	Special problems (£m)	Normal plus special (£m)
Value of time spent on tax compliance by:			
Proprietors and partners	155	7	162
Directors	59	3	62
Qualified accounting staff	29	9	38
Other staff	103	5	108
Fees to professional advisers	17	3	20
Other costs	negligible	2	2
Total measurable compliance costs	363	29	392
Psychic costs		not measurable	
Social costs		not measurable	

allocation of total measurable compliance cost to its various components in Table 4.1 must be regarded as only a rough approximation.

Before considering the crucial question of the reliability of this total estimate of measurable compliance costs 1977/8 a few comments need to be made on the items in the table and on the types of compliance costs.

Comments on Table 4.1

It is interesting that the estimated costs associated with special problems constitute some 7 per cent of total measurable compliance costs. At the commencement of the tax, or after a major change in legislation, they could be expected to be higher.

The value of the time of proprietors and partners represented the biggest single item in measurable compliance costs, over 40 per cent of the total; if the value of directors' time is added in, the two together amounted to 57 per cent of the total measurable costs.

Conversely, the fees to professional advisers, primarily accountants, were only 5 per cent of the total. In fact some 13 per cent of the respondents to NAS used accountants for VAT work, the proportion rising with size to a peak of 20 per cent for firms with taxable turnover in the range £20,000–£50,000 and falling away to only 3 per cent of firms with a turnover of over £1 million. The two trade sectors with the largest proportion of traders using professional advisers for VAT were retailing and miscellaneous services, both with a relatively high proportion of small firms. The interviews with professional advisers (ADV) confirmed and amplified this finding. Some accountants avoid VAT work altogether. Where a firm of accountants is willing to undertake VAT work, only a small proportion of the registered traders amongst its clients rely on the accountants for regular VAT work; most do it all themselves, except perhaps for an occasional query to their accountant. In other cases the accountant simply checks what clients have done and may complete the first return form. It is not unusual for an accountant to complete the first return for a newly registered client who, having been shown the way, then takes over the VAT work himself. Occasionally a client just 'doesn't want to know', hands over all invoices to the accountant and leaves it all to him.

There are allocation problems about how much of the fee to attribute to the VAT work that accountants do for clients. In rather more than half the relevant cases in the sample the accountant did not charge separately for VAT work, and the fee included in our table is based on the client's estimate of what fraction of the total fee was appropriate. Even where there is a separate billing, because some part of the work may be common to both the VAT and the annual accounting, the fee may be less than if the accountant only did the client's VAT work. The bill for other accounting may also be less.

'Other costs' in the table covers items such as travelling, postage, telephone calls. Where the tax is operating smoothly such costs will be very low; the regular postal charge of sending in the tax returns is an administrative not a compliance cost, for the trader is supplied with pre-paid envelopes. Small and irregular costs are especially likely to be misreported and the grossing up of very small sums is also particularly liable to inaccuracy. The NAS questionnaire did not ask for a figure of other costs except where special problems were likely to increase their importance. In the 'normal costs' column, 'other costs' have therefore been recorded as 'negligible'; but clearly there are some such costs, if only the occasional telephone call; and when multiplied across a trader population of one-and-a-quarter million they may well add up to several million pounds. Another cost within this item is that incurred by traders in obtaining advice from their trade associations. Some 8 to 9 per cent of respondents to the survey obtained help from this source (see Chapter 12). Correspondence with trade associations indicates that VAT advice was a minor activity (though sometimes an important one) and that members almost always paid for it through their subscriptions. Such costs are in principle measurable but are very difficult to calculate and constitute only a small proportion of the overall compliance costs of VAT; hence no figure has been included for them. But it is clear that in not attributing any value to normal 'other costs' we are under-estimating the total of compliance costs.

Two further categories of compliance costs are listed in the table: psychic costs and social costs. As discussed above (p. 23) psychic costs are virtually impossible to measure, but that is no reason for ignoring them. They may figure very prominently in a taxpayer's thinking and affect his behaviour. The psychic costs of VAT are particularly important. One such cost is the anxiety engendered in the minds of those who find it difficult to cope with the requirements of the tax. Anxiety is a common form of psychic cost, but it takes an additional dimension with VAT because of the control visit by VAT officers. Our survey showed that most VAT officers were found to be helpful and courteous, but some honest traders suffer much anxiety about the visit and worry about what might happen to them if the Customs & Excise officer discovered an inadvertent error. Press exaggeration of intimidation by officials* has done nothing to calm this anxiety. Even the employment of an accountant for VAT work does not relieve the trader of all stress, for whereas an Inland Revenue inspector will always deal with the client's accountant, Customs & Excise officers normally require to visit the trader at his place of business; thus the accountant cannot 'protect' his VAT client in the same way as he can his income tax client, by standing between him and the tax authorities. The other most important form of psychic compliance cost is resentment at being required to act as an unpaid tax collector. Interestingly, earlier research (Godwin 1976) suggested that such resentment was often most pronounced, not amongst traders with the highest compliance costs, but rather amongst those who, because much of their output was zero rated, found themselves incurring substantial costs in time and trouble only to hand a paltry sum over to Customs & Excise: they were dismayed that their efforts yielded negligible benefit to the community. The same view appeared in comments on the NAS questionnaires. Strong resentments may lead to anti-social behaviour such as increased evasion.

Social costs which arise from the burden of compliance may take a variety of forms. Thus the compliance costs of VAT may be one factor amongst others which decides a proprietor to cease trading, or not to start trading, or not to expand beyond the exemption limit to avoid the need to register. The existence of multiple rates of VAT may lead a trader to discontinue, or not to start, another line of production or sales in order to keep his VAT work simple. Thus, for example, a fish and chip shop proprietor may confine himself to take-away food (zero rated) and no longer run a café (standard rated). Two NAS respondents specifically mentioned lines of business they had discontinued in order to keep their VAT compliance work simple. It is difficult to know how frequently these social costs occur. When they do, their effect is to reduce services to the public and diminish competition. It is hardly possible to quantify such social costs.

As a matter of convenience in the remainder of the book, unless expressly stated otherwise, 'compliance costs' will be taken to mean 'measurable compliance costs'. But psychic and social compliance costs should not on that account be ignored.

Temporary and Regular, Mandatory and Discretionary Costs

In Chapter 2 we distinguished between *temporary* and *regular* costs, with *commencement* costs being a particular once-and-for-all type of temporary cost; and between *mandatory* and *discretionary* costs. How do these categories tie in with total VAT compliance costs for 1977/8 as estimated in Table 4.1?

We need to distinguish between the individual traders' costs and the aggregate

* In reply to Parliamentary Questions (*Hansard* 25 May 1979, col 1440 and 21 December 1979, col 1130) Mr Peter Rees, Financial Secretary to the Treasury stated that since the introduction of VAT only 30 cases concerning the tax had been investigated by the Parliamentary Commissioner for Administration and in less than one-third of the cases reported on had any degree of mal-administration been found. In the year ending 30 June 1978, out of 400,000 visits only 150 complaints were made about the behaviour of the officers. After examination by the Department only 29 were found to be wholly or partially justified.

costs of the tax. Any individual trader on registration will have commencement costs and will incur temporary costs as part of the learning process. Such temporary costs might be the extra time the trader himself takes to complete records and returns with which he is unaccustomed; or they could be the margin of extra cost he incurs if he pays an accountant to help him through his first return period. In the overall situation, when the tax is introduced there will be commencement and temporary costs (as in Figure 2.1); but once this stage is over, such commencement and temporary costs of individual traders as arise from the normal turnover of traders, are simply part of the regular costs of the system. Thus the commencement and temporary costs which arise from the annual turnover of some 10 per cent of VAT traders should be regarded as part of regular costs. Temporary costs are incurred for the system as a whole when a change in legislation raises the costs of established traders.

The year 1977/8 to which NAS relates had no major changes; the NAS was in fact brought forward to pre-date the new VAT form and other administrative changes (p. 206). The period is therefore characterised by a lack of temporary costs for the system as a whole; all the costs recorded should therefore be regarded as regular costs. Indeed, because the sample was chosen from 'eligible' rather than total traders in order to ensure that respondents could answer questions on the most recent accounting year (p. 29), the newest entrants were omitted; thus the estimate of total compliance costs in Table 4.1 understates the regular costs of the system.

As to the distinction between mandatory and discretionary costs, (p. 14), it would seem appropriate to regard all the VAT costs in 1977/8 as mandatory. Avoidance opportunities under VAT would seem to be much fewer than under income tax or capital gains tax and it is unlikely that any significant proportion of the cost of VAT compliance takes the form of discretionary costs. This judgement is borne out by the very small share of fees to professional advisers in the total compliance costs.

The Reliability of the Estimates

The crucial question is, how reliable are the estimates of total compliance costs derived from NAS? In a number of ways and at a number of stages errors and inaccuracies may creep in. This section examines the main possibilities of error and the cross-checks on accuracy.

Sampling and Grossing Up

One minor source of error, which has already been discussed (p. 29 and p. 204) arose because (for reasons indicated p. 29) the sample was based on 'eligible' rather than total traders. The effect is to understate the component of commencement and temporary costs which form part of the regular costs of the system and therefore, in some small measure, to understate total compliance costs 1977/8.

Clearly the low response rate to NAS was a source of concern for fear it might undermine the representativeness of the data collected. Because of the method by which the survey had to be run (p. 30) no approach to non-respondents (other than reminders) was possible. It is therefore conceivable that respondents differ in important respects from non-respondents. Thus, it might be argued that the respondents included a disproportionately large number of those most discontented with VAT who felt strongly enough to wish to make their views known. Alternatively one could argue the opposite way, that those most discontented with VAT were traders for whom form-filling was anathema and who would therefore be least likely to respond to a long complex-looking questionnaire. One must beware the 'argument of equal ignorance' by which two tendencies working in opposite directions are assumed to cancel out. We do not know. We can say that a range of views about VAT was expressed by respondents but we have no means of establishing whether the attitudes of respondents differed significantly from those of non-respondents.

We have already indicated (p. 29 and Appendix E5) that the size within sector distribution of the respondents to NAS corresponded closely to that of the list of VAT registered traders held by Customs & Excise. As the grossing up from the sample of respondents to the total trader population was effected on the basis of over sixty size/sector cells the scope for large errors was minimised. (The grossing up procedure and the statistical reliability of the estimates is discussed in Appendix F1.) The tendency for the response rate to be higher for larger firms may have introduced some slight upward bias into the means *within* cells, which in turn would push up the total figure.

Checks Internal to NAS
Besides the direct questions on compliance costs in NAS, which form the basis for the estimates in Table 4.1, two other questions were inserted in the questionnaire which it was hoped would both check consistency and provide an additional dimension to the measurement of compliance costs.

Respondents were asked (Q33):

If you could have claimed from Customs & Excise for time and money spent on VAT accounting in the financial year 1977/8, about how much would you have claimed?

It was hoped that the answers to this question would have been consistent with the response to the direct questions on compliance costs, and also might reflect 'other costs' not covered in these direct questions and possibly include a valuation of psychic costs. In the event the 'claim' figures given by respondents were often identical to compliance costs;* occasionally slightly lower; but overall consistently higher across all sizes and sectors. In total they were 19 per cent higher so that, when grossed up on the same basis as the compliance costs, they totalled £465 million. In the follow-up interviews (FOL(P)) the differences between the claim and compliance cost estimates were explored. The one or two interviewees who had put claim somewhat lower than compliance cost justified their replies on the basis of the cash flow benefit they derived from VAT. The majority of those who had put claim higher referred to other costs (like computer charges and 'overheads') not included in their measure of compliance costs; in

* The coefficient of correlation between the two measures was 0.86 overall.

one or two cases the higher figure for claim was 'compensation for inconvenience'. In addition also there was a distinct element of 'rounding up' when putting in a claim to the government.

The other question (Q26) which it was hoped would confirm and supplement the direct data on compliance cost was interpreted in different ways by respondents and failed to produce usable results (see Appendix F4).

The Accuracy of Responses

The reliability of the data in a study of this kind rests heavily on both the accuracy of recollection and the personal integrity of the respondents and there are a number of possible sources of error on this account.

First, there is the possibility of inadvertent error arising from inaccurate recall; thus the amount of time spent on VAT work may be incorrectly stated because of a failure of memory. Such an error may be either an under or over-statement. It would seem unlikely that the normal cost of VAT would be subject to much inadvertent error from faulty recollection because VAT work is an almost continuous process and returns are submitted frequently, at monthly or three-monthly intervals. There is more chance of faulty recollection of the costs of special problems, which are irregular in incidence and may have occurred almost a year before the questionnaire was completed; but such problems only account for 7 per cent of total compliance costs.

Another possible source of error is a tendency, especially on the part of small proprietors, to attribute *all* day to day book-keeping to VAT instead of the margin of additional book-keeping work which VAT imposed. A second possibility, which likewise applies particularly to sole proprietors doing their own VAT work, is a tendency to exaggerate the amount of time VAT work takes, either because of resentment at an uncongenial task or in a deliberate attempt to impress the researchers, and those who will read their report, with the burden of compliance. Whilst this possibility would apply equally to partners and to directors of small businesses who do their own VAT work, it seems unlikely that exaggeration would affect estimates of larger firms where VAT work is done by paid staff. So much of compliance costs are made up of costs from sole proprietors, partners and directors, that this possibility of exaggeration must be taken very seriously. It is also possible that the charges of professional advisers might be exaggerated by their clients, but here the significance is small because of the small part played by this item in compliance costs.

A final possibility is that the *value* placed on the time taken up by compliance work may be inappropriate, because it is deliberately exaggerated or because VAT work is done in time which would not have been used for anything else, e.g. slack periods in a small shop, or in leisure time, which should be given a lower value.

Interview Checks

The follow-up interviews (FOL(P)) provided a limited opportunity to probe the accuracy of the compliance cost statements amongst respondents, but, clearly, any who had given inaccurate information in the questionnaire from faulty memory might repeat the inaccuracy at interview and any who deliberately exaggerated might continue to do so. A better check, but limited to the accuracy of statements of professional fees, was provided by interviews with accountants (ADV). Each accountant interviewed was given the most relevant details of four actual (but, of course, unnamed) firms which employed professional advisers for VAT work, and asked what fee he would have charged in 1977/8 for undertaking all the VAT work in each case. The answers were then compared with the figure given by the respondent. The exercise was not without its difficulties. Accountants often felt obliged to offer alternative values because so much depended on the state of the client's records. Again, it was clear that there were big differences between the fees charged by different firms of accountants; a few had made a point of specialising in VAT work and welcomed VAT clients; some other accountants charged high fees in order, they said, to discourage VAT clients. Whilst the evidence did not lend itself to precise quantitative analysis, the general picture was reassuring. The fees which different accountants said they might charge for any particular case covered a wide range, but there was no recognisable tendency for the fee which respondents said they paid to be consistently or even frequently at the top of the range. In other words the evidence from ADV suggested that there was no tendency for respondents to exaggerate the fees they paid to professional advisers for VAT work.

The Value Accorded to Time

One check on the accuracy of the values accorded to time is to convert them to a common basis and compare them with the wage and salary rates for similar occupations recorded in the *New Earnings Survey*. There are difficulties of comparability and special problems about the appropriate rates for the self-employed and directors. However, the results of these comparisons are reassuring. When allowance is made for the national insurance contributions which should properly be included within the reported values, the two sets of data are consistent and offer no evidence that respondents exaggerated time values in the sense of charging them at rates above the normal for the appropriate occupations. (For details see Appendix F2.)

A rather different problem (considered in Chapter 2, pp. 22–3) arises about the valuation of the time of the self-employed. If the self-employed do their VAT book-keeping during slack or leisure time, should it be charged at the full wage-rate? For transport cost-benefit studies the practice has evolved of valuing leisure travel time at one-third the average wage rate. If *all* the time spent by proprietors, partners and directors of small firms on VAT work was valued at one-third the value they report, the total compliance cost would fall to £258 million. This figure is included for the record because it represents an estimate based on an alternative valuation principle. But, even on its own terms, the figure must be regarded as a considerable under-estimate. Firstly, it is certain that not all VAT work would be done in leisure time; some would be at the cost of other work in the business. Secondly, the value of time given by some respondents in the first place may have been set lower where leisure was the alternative. In addition, there may be an important difference between leisure spent on VAT work and leisure spent travelling. When travelling in leisure time it is often possible to do other things at the same time, like reading (in a train) or enjoying the scenery (in a car or train). Such complementary activities are incompatible with VAT book-keeping, so that it can be argued that cost of leisure spent on VAT work should be valued more highly than the one-third wage rate usual in transport studies.

The Charges of Specialist Firms

In the course of the study the researchers discovered two firms (hereafter referred to as Firm A and Firm B) who specialised in offering a VAT service, with accompanying management accounting information. Client firms despatched all invoices on a monthly basis to Firms A and B who took responsibility for the necessary record keeping, completed the VAT returns and advised and supported the client should he have any special problems.

The clients of both firms were confined to the retail and service sectors. Both firms had a set scale of charges; their clients were generally limited to those with an annual turnover of up to £100,000. For purposes of our comparison the scale of charges made by the firms in 1977/8 have been applied to *all* firms with a taxable turnover* of up to £100,000. Clients of Firms A and B do incur additional 'other costs', principally in the form of postage and to a lesser extent telephone calls, and an allowance has been made for this increase based on the average costs of a small sample of the clients of the two firms. The effects of this procedure on the components of total compliance costs are shown in Table 4.2. The overall effect is to reduce the estimate of total compliance cost to £343 million using Firm A's charges and to £327 million using Firm B's. (Further details are given in Appendix F3.)

These estimates are interesting in two main ways. First, firms specialising in a VAT service, with appropriate equipment, can be expected to undertake VAT work more efficiently than most small firms doing it for themselves. The fact that calculations (on the assumption that all traders with a turnover of less than £100,000 used these services at the scale charges) generate a total compliance cost which is only some 12 to 17 per cent less than that based on reported values gives credence to the accuracy of the reported values. Secondly, it can be argued that an appropriate measure of compliance cost is the lowest cost at which a trader could get the work done satisfactorily – an 'opportunity cost' estimate; the figures derived from our calculations using Firm B might be regarded as such an estimate of compliance costs.

The various alternative estimates of compliance costs as considered above are set out in Table 4.2. Clearly any figure is likely to contain a fairly wide margin of error. Nonetheless the effect of the cross-checks has been to support the general accuracy of the NAS figures and a sum of around £400 million represents the best

---

* Firms A and B used turnover rather than taxable turnover as their basis for charging; but the number of firms whose total turnover fell into a higher range than their taxable turnover was very small and no serious errors should be caused by equating the two.

estimate that can be made from the data available of the value of the measurable compliance costs of VAT incurred by registered traders in 1977/8.

Table 4.2 Alternative estimates of compliance costs, 1977/8

	NAS (£m)	NAS claim (£m)	Valuing proprietors[a] time at ⅓ rate (£m)	Using charges of specialist firms for all traders under £100 000 taxable turnover	
				Firm A (£m)	Firm B (£m)
Values of time costs within business of:					
Proprietors & partners	162	n.al.	54	29	29
Directors	62	n.al.	36	30	30
Qualified accounting staff	38	n.al.	38	29	29
Other staff	108	n.al.	108	76	76
Fees to professional advisers	20	n.al.	20	147	131
Other costs	2	n.al.	2	32	32
Total	392	465	258	343	327

n.al. = not allocable
[a] Proprietors include directors of small firms doing own VAT work.

Administrative and Total Operating Costs

The official cost of administration of VAT in 1977/8 was £85.5 million (Cmnd 7455, 1979). The revenue from VAT in the same year was £4,235 million. The administrative costs were thus 2.00 per cent of the net revenue collected.

At £392 million the compliance costs represented 9.26 per cent of revenue.* Thus costs of operating VAT in 1977/8 were of the order of £480 million with an overall cost in proportion to revenue of around 11¼ per cent. The costs of compliance were some 4½ times the cost of administration.

Little data on the operating costs of other taxes are available, but a study relating to 1969/70 (Sandford 1973) put the total operating costs (administrative plus measurable compliance costs) of personal direct taxes in England and Wales at between 3.8 and 5.8 per cent of tax revenue plus up to 4 per cent more for tax work not billed as such. 'Measurable compliance costs were at least 180 per cent of total administrative costs and, allowing for all tax-generated work not billed as tax work, might be more than six times as large as administrative costs.'

On this comparison the operating costs of VAT in 1977/8, expressed as a percentage of revenue, came out higher than the 9.8 per cent which represents the upper limit of the operating costs of personal direct taxes in 1969/70. On

* The Customs & Excise year does not exactly coincide with the period to which the compliance costs relate. Of necessity respondents to NAS were asked (in a questionnaire sent out during September 1978) to reply in relation to their latest complete financial year – which could end on any date. *On average* the correspondence between the two periods is likely to be fairly close, but with the NAS data tending to relate to a slightly later period.

the other hand the ratio of compliance to administrative costs for VAT lies between the lower and upper limits which emerged from this earlier research for personal direct taxes.

In considering this conclusion some vital caveats must be made. Expressing operating costs as a percentage of tax revenue is a useful measure of 'input' to 'output' but tells us nothing about the efficiency of the tax operation. The ratio can change dramatically (as it has done with VAT, see Chapter 14) simply because tax rates change. This point has particular relevance to VAT in the United Kingdom because of widespread zero rating – a characteristic which, among EEC countries, is restricted to the UK and Ireland (see Appendix A). If the zero rate (except for exports) was a positive rate, then administrative costs would probably fall because far fewer monthly repayments would be required; but, even if they remained the same, higher receipts would reduce the ratios of both compliance costs and administrative costs to tax revenue. Because of the limitations of using tax revenue as a denominator, the ratio of compliance to administrative costs may sometimes prove a more useful measure than that of compliance costs to tax revenue.

A second vital consideration is that our figure of total compliance cost is 'gross' – it takes no account of any benefits of VAT, in particular the cash flow benefit to traders other than repayment traders. We shall be examining benefits in Chapters 8 and 9. We need to remind the reader, however, that what may be a benefit to the trader may be a cost to the Exchequer (p. 17).

As a final point it should be stressed that the figures relate only to measurable compliance costs. Additionally there are psychic and social costs.

5 The Differential Incidence of Compliance and Administrative Costs, 1977/8 – Size and Sector

Introduction
A well-established finding from the limited previous research on the compliance costs of taxation is that such costs tend to bear relatively less hard on the large than on the small unit. The finding is important for its effects on both the efficiency with which resources are used and the distribution of income. It is important to try to establish where the economies of scale in tax compliance work lie and their size; it is no less important to discover how far tax compliance costs are regressive.

In this chapter we seek to answer these questions in relation to VAT from the NAS data. We begin by looking at possible measures of size and their advantages and limitations. We then examine the incidence of compliance costs by size, by trade sector and by size within sector. Then, by inference from published data, we hypothesise about the distribution of administrative costs by size of firm, so that we can make some reasonable conjectures about the distribution of total VAT operating costs in 1977/8.

Measurement of Size
There are a number of possible ways to measure the size of a firm, all of which may be useful for specific purposes. These measures include value added, aggregate turnover, taxable turnover, employment and capital employed. Even if the conceptual problems involved in measuring capital could be overcome, there are no data from this study to enable us to use capital as a measure of size. Some data on the other measures are available from the present study.

Value Added
Value added as a measure of size is particularly appealing in the present context as it is the basis for levying VAT; it is also a measure of the net importance of the business, used in the compilation of national income accounts. However, no information on value added was sought directly in the NAS and no general data exist giving the size distribution of firms on this measure. Data from the NAS questionnaire can be used to derive value added where both the input and output tax rates are positive, and where the respondent also records either (a) the net

tax paid (if the input and output tax rates are the same) or (b) the net and gross tax paid (if the input and output rates are different). These conditions, however, were met in only 188 cases (6.7 per cent of respondents), too few to make possible a meaningful analysis of compliance costs based on size within sector.

Aggregate Turnover
Aggregate turnover is a useful measure of size, but does not allow for the value of inputs into the firm. A firm with a high turnover may in fact have a low value added, and thus total turnover may be misleading when used for comparisons between different sectors of business. Firms whose size will tend to be over-stated by this measure are those with high value inputs, which may occur if they use some very expensive raw material or process, or if they are at a late stage in the production and distribution chain. Conversely the size of service industries, where the output is almost wholly a product of labour, will tend to be understated.

Taxable Turnover
Taxable turnover is the measure of size used in the Customs & Excise reports. It is a less satisfactory measure of size than aggregate turnover. Besides taking no account of the value of inputs, taxable turnover excludes any turnover arising from activities that are exempt from VAT (p. 6). Thus, a knowledge of the trading activities of a business is needed before taxable turnover can be used as a measure of size of the business as a whole.

The NAS questionnaire requested information on taxable turnover, and on aggregate turnover if it fell into a different range. Subsequent analysis showed that overall only 58 (2 per cent) of the 2,709 questionnaires giving information on sectors of business and turnover had an aggregate turnover in a different range from taxable turnover. On a sectoral basis only financial and business services showed a significant number of cases where the difference occurred – 13 out of 122, or 11 per cent. (Twenty per cent of respondents in this sector stated that they were partly exempt, but in a number of cases they remained within one range for both taxable and total turnover. For details see Appendix G1.)

Employment
Employment is widely used as a measure of size (e.g. in the Census of Production), but again has drawbacks. In particular, capital–labour ratios may differ between industries, or even between firms within the same industry. Thus, employment may prove to be a poor basis for classification.

Data on employment are available from the NAS and, unlike taxable turnover, where respondents only indicated the broad band appropriate to their firm, respondents were asked for the exact number of employees. Thus, in principle, employment data can be used as a basis for a more refined classification of size. However, apart from the inherent limitations of the measure, employment proved to be a poor discriminator in this instance for over 70 per cent of all respondents had ten or fewer employees, including the proprietor (see Appendix G). Only the manufacture and utilities, and the wholesale and dealers sectors had significantly more than half respondents with over five employees. (Figures for the differential burden of compliance costs for firms classified by employment are given in Appendix G2; in general a markedly regressive pattern is observable.)

Conclusion
Value-added would be the preferred measure of size, but it is not feasible to use it both because of lack of information from NAS and the lack of general information on this basis. Employment is unsuitable because of the heavy concentration of firms with fewer than five employees.*

We are thus left with the (virtually interchangeable) measures of aggregate turnover and taxable turnover. Following Customs & Excise practice, taxable turnover will be used.

Incidence of Compliance Costs by Size and Sector
In order that the broad picture may be readily appreciated Table 5.1 presents data on average compliance costs, the ratio of compliance cost to size and total compliance costs for certain broad ranges of taxable turnover. What immediately emerges from the table is that compliance costs to the individual firm rise steadily with size;† that the rise is not proportional to size, the burden on large firms being, relatively, much less than that on small, giving a highly regressive effect; and that a very large proportion of the compliance costs are incurred by small firms (e.g. 43 per cent by firms with a turnover of under £50,000).

Table 5.1 Compliance costs in relation to taxable turnover, 1977/8

Range of taxable turnover (£000 p.a.)	No. of traders ('000)	Mean compliance cost (£)	Compliance cost as % of taxable turnover (Mean)ᵃ	Total compliance cost (£m)
0– 49.9	881.1	190	1.17	167.0
50– 99.9	177.7	390	0.54	69.3
100–999.9	185.4	569	0.24	105.5
1000 and over	30.0	1663	0.04	49.9
Total	1274.2	308	0.92	392.0

ᵃ In each case the compliance cost is expressed as a percentage of taxable turnover and the resulting percentages are averaged.

* It is, however, interesting to note that the overall coefficient of correlation between size measured by taxable turnover and size measured by employment is 0.88.
† The coefficient of correlation between compliance cost and size (as measured by taxable turnover) is as high as 0.84.

Table 5.2 Compliance costs for each sector of business, 1977/8

Sector	No. of traders ('000)	Mean compliance cost (£)	Total compliance cost (£m)
Primary	179.9	114	20.6
Manufacture and utilities	120.8	400	48.4
Construction	179.2	290	52.0
Transport and communication	56.4	309	17.4
Retail	280.2	291	81.4
Wholesale and dealers	87.7	430	37.7
Financial and business services	44.0	475	20.9
Professional and scientific services	63.2	380	24.0
Miscellaneous and public services	262.9	341	89.7
Total	1274.2	308	392.0

Table 5.3 Mean compliance costs by sector and taxable turnover, 1977/8 (£)

Taxable turnover (£000 p.a.)	Primary	Manufacture and utilities	Construction	Transport and communication	Retail	Wholesale and dealers	Financial and business services	Professional and scientific services	Miscellaneous and public services	Weighted overall mean[a]
0– 9.9	54	118	107	80	165	74	179	123	121	107
10– 19.9	86	272	196	199	150	211	302	266	203	184
20– 49.9	95	279	278	235	237	353	354	474	314	259
50– 99.9	141	294	592	305[b]	318	317	665	363	607	392
100–999.9	381	517	513	763	535	619	437	1156	584	569
1000 and over	1400[b]	1220	2109	1923	4714	877	3786	1714[b]	1756	1663
Weighted overall mean	114	400	290	309	291	430	475	380	341	308

[a] The weights applied are the total number of registered traders in the parent population in each cell.
[b] Fewer than ten respondents to NAS in cell.

Table 5.4 Compliance costs as a percentage of taxable turnover by sector and taxable turnover, 1977/8 (means)

Taxable turnover (£000 p.a.)	Primary	Manufacture and utilities	Construction	Transport and communication	Retail	Wholesale and dealers	Financial and business services	Professional and scientific services	Miscellaneous and public service	Weighted overall mean[a]
0– 9.9	0.92	1.78	1.65	1.27	2.42	1.22	2.84	1.84	1.78	1.64
10– 19.9	0.58	1.81	1.31	1.32	1.00	1.41	2.01	1.77	1.35	1.23
20– 49.9	0.27	0.80	0.79	0.67	0.68	1.01	1.01	1.35	0.90	0.74
50– 99.9	0.18	0.40	0.87	0.48[b]	0.45	0.47	0.88	0.53	0.76	0.54
100–999.9	0.19	0.18	0.23	0.29	0.28	0.19	0.21	0.65	0.22	0.24
1000 and over	0.01[b]	0.04	0.06	0.03	0.03	0.02	0.06	0.04[b]	0.05	0.04
Weighted overall mean[a]	0.53	0.78	1.11	0.92	0.83	0.65	1.61	1.45	1.06	0.92

[a] The weights applied are the total number of registered traders in the parent population in each cell.
[b] Fewer than ten respondents to NAS in cell.

Table 5.2 shows the average and aggregate costs of compliance for each sector of business. This table shows the relatively low average costs of compliance in the primary sector and the relatively high cost in financial and business services. A further point is the large proportion of compliance costs incurred at the final stage in the production chain – retailing and the various services many of which are supplied to the final consumer. However, the business sectors differ very considerably in the proportions of firms of different sizes they contain and Tables 5.3 and 5.4 offer a more sophisticated classification looking respectively at mean compliance cost and compliance cost as a percentage of taxable turnover within an increased range of size bands for each sector.

With few exceptions the picture revealed is of rising compliance costs with size within each business sector (Table 5.3). The primary sector continues to stand out as that with the lowest compliance costs, with a lower than average cost at every size range. This can probably be explained by the widespread zero rating for farm products (which simplifies calculations even though repayment traders often make monthly returns); by the low number of sales invoices handled by farmers; and by the use of the simple 'modified control scheme' of cash book accounting for VAT, designed for farmers in consultation with the National Farmers' Union. Table 5.3 reveals that the particularly high average compliance cost in financial and business services applies to almost every size range. The discrepancy already discussed (p. 48 and Appendix G) between total turnover and taxable turnover in a significant number of cases in this sector of business, which includes the highest proportion of partly exempt traders, may account for this result. Amongst the very smallest firms retailers (and the other suppliers of services) have relatively high costs; but it is notable that the mean compliance costs for retailers soon fall off below average with increasing size and overall are below the mean for all firms.

Table 5.4, in which compliance cost is expressed as a percentage of taxable turnover, reveals the full extent of the regressive nature of compliance costs (despite a few minor exceptions to the pattern). Overall, as a percentage of taxable turnover, the compliance costs of the smallest firms in 1977/8 were over forty times those of the largest. In some sectors the difference was even more pronounced. In manufacture and utilities it was around forty-five times, in wholesaling something like sixty times and in retail and primary industry a staggering eighty times or more. If one omits the very lowest range as being below the exemption limit and therefore consisting of traders who have registered voluntarily, the ratios are something like thirty-fold overall, still around forty-five-fold in manufacturing, over thirty-fold in retailing and jumping to seventy-fold in wholesaling. To put the point in a more readily understandable form: in 1977/8, if our figures are correct, on average a small manufacturer in the second lowest turnover range incurred compliance costs of £181 for every £10,000 of taxable goods he sold; in selling the same value of goods the compliance costs to the largest manufacturer would have been only £4. The cost of VAT compliance to a retailer in the second lowest turnover range was £100 for every £10,000 of taxable goods sold; the tax compliance cost to the largest retailer of selling £10,000 worth of goods was only £3.

Little reliance should be placed on the precise figures. Because of sampling errors it is possible that the figures could overstate, by a considerable margin, the difference in the relative costs of large and small firms. On the other hand the tests for accuracy against external evidence (fees charged by accountants, the charges of specialist firms, comparison with *New Earnings Survey* data – see Chapter 4) all supported the general accuracy of our data. Moreover, if we had compared the relative compliance costs of the smaller traders with traders in ranges with a higher minimum than £1 million the differences would have been still more pronounced. Thus the compliance costs as a percentage of taxable turnover for the 115 firms in NAS in the range over £5 million was 0.01, over 100 times less than that of the firms in the £10,000–£20,000 range. For the fourteen firms in NAS in the over £50 million range compliance costs averaged less than 0.005 per cent of taxable turnover. There is no gainsaying the conclusion that the compliance costs of VAT are outstandingly regressive.

Economies of Scale in VAT Compliance Work
These figures raise the question, why is the burden of compliance so much less for large than for small firms? Wherein lie the economies of scale which appear to exist in VAT compliance work?

A number of possibilities can be hazarded. Traditionally economies of scale have rested on the scope offered for specialisation and we can expect specialisation to play its part in VAT compliance work. The large firm has staff working full-time on book-keeping and accounting activities; much of the VAT work can be done by relatively unskilled staff who can refer to a qualified accountant within the business as required. In the very small firm, the proprietor may do VAT work along with everything else, and he often lacks the relevant skills derived from training and practice. With rather larger, but still small firms, specialisation in staff will be less than with the largest firms.

Further, it is likely that the number of invoices to be dealt with will not rise in proportion to size. Large firms are likely to buy in bulk and often to sell in larger quantities than small firms.

There will also be an element of fixed costs in setting up a system to deal with VAT which will be the same for any particular kind of system. Moreover, the larger the firm the greater the likelihood that it will go in for a sophisticated non-manual accounting system which can deal with most VAT work with very little additional cost.

Some of these possibilities are explored more fully in Chapter 6.

Incidence of Administrative Costs by Size and Sector

No official information is available about the distribution of administrative costs over the different sizes and categories of business,* but using data from NAS

Table 5.5 Mean length of VAT officer visit derived from NAS (hours)

Taxable turnover (£000 p.a.)	Primary	Manufacture and utilities	Construction	Transport and communication	Retail	Wholesale and dealers	Financial and business services	Professional and scientific services	Miscellaneous and public services	Weighted overall mean[a]
0– 9.9	1.85	1.86	2.77	2.42	3.19	2.13	2.76	2.08	2.21	2.35
10– 19.9	2.49	2.76	1.37	2.45	3.20	3.15	2.42	2.80	2.91	2.60
20– 49.9	2.17	2.87	2.98	3.22	3.13	2.91	3.29	3.30	3.18	2.97
50– 99.9	2.19	3.16	3.74	2.14[b]	3.84	3.29	3.23	3.58	4.41	3.58
100–999.9	3.10	5.39	6.38	4.41	6.34	6.58	4.61	4.16	5.43	5.29
1000 and over	5.08[b]	11.36	8.68	12.05	8.83	9.94	7.07	9.86[b]	11.54	10.40
Weighted overall mean[a]	2.22	4.19	2.99	3.14	3.54	4.85	3.32	2.90	3.48	3.36

[a] The weights applied are the total number of registered traders in the parent population in each cell.
[b] Fewer than ten respondents to NAS in cell.

* In a Parliamentary reply, Mr Peter Rees indicated: 'No reliable information is available about the administration costs related to different categories of businesses but the cost of collecting VAT from a small firm is believed to be less than the average for all businesses.' *Hansard* 14 January 1980.

and published data on VAT staffing and visits it is possible to make some conjectures about that distribution.

The NAS asked respondents how long their most recent VAT officer visit had lasted and also when it had taken place (in broad terms). Table 5.5 shows the mean length of VAT officer visits by size and sector. On average a visit lasted 3.4 hours, but there was a very clear tendency for the length of time taken to increase with size, the increase being particularly marked for firms above £100,000. Firms engaged in primary activities had a length of visit consistently below the average for the size group; the smallest retailers tended to have relatively long visits.

Table 5.6 Most recent VAT officer visit in relation to size of firm (figures represent percentages of those in each size band)

How long ago (months)	Taxable turnover (£000 p.a.)				
	0–49.9	50–99.9	100–999.9	1000 and over	Overall
Less than 3	12	18	19	35	18
3–6	15	16	20	27	18
6–12	24	23	24	28	25
More than 12	49	42	37	10	40
Total	100	100	100	100	100
	(1276)	(382)	(529)	(388)	(2575)

Note: totals may not exactly balance because of rounding. Figures in brackets are number of respondents in the range.

Table 5.6, from NAS data, bears out the Customs & Excise statement that 'larger traders receive visits more frequently' (Cmnd 7415, 1978), but the data form an inadequate basis to enable us to produce a pattern of the frequency of visits by size or sector. Published data on the frequency of visits show that traders with a turnover of £1 million or more are visited annually; those whose turnover lies between £250,000 and £1 million every other year; those with a turnover between £25,000 and £250,000 every three years; and those with a turnover smaller than £25,000 every four years (Trimby 1980).

Data on VAT staffing are contained in the *Review of Value Added Tax* (Cmnd 7415, 1978) which indicated the various categories of staff, as set out in Table 5.7.

The general overhead and support activities (items 5, 6 and part of 3) which account for well over one-third of staffing can be appropriately allocated on a per unit basis. Staff in item 4, registration and de-registration, would be particularly concerned with smaller firms. Control visits (item 1), as we have seen, concentrate more on the larger firms and the same may be true of parts of the miscellaneous item 3. As a very rough and ready method it might be reasonable to allocate half the administrative costs on a per unit basis and the other half weighted towards larger firms in the proportions determined by the length of

Table 5.7 VAT staffing

	Equivalent man-years
1. Control visits and associated action	4600
2. Enforcement	850
3. Prosecution, VAT tribunals, imports, exports, warehouses, general support	1150
4. Registration and de-registration	1300
5. HQ – collection, management, computer	2100
6. VAT share in C&E general support services	2250
	12 250

Table 5.8 Comparison of compliance and administrative costs, 1977/8

	Administrative cost (AC) (£m)	Compliance cost (CC) (£m)	Ratio $\frac{CC}{AC}$
(a) By sector			
Primary	9.3	20.6	2.22
Manufacture and utilities	11.1	48.4	4.36
Construction	11.0	52.0	4.73
Transport and communication	3.7	17.4	4.70
Retail	18.2	81.4	4.47
Wholesale and dealers	8.4	37.7	4.49
Financial and business services	3.0	20.9	7.00
Professional and scientific services	3.7	24.0	6.49
Miscellaneous and public services	17.4	89.7	5.16
Total	85.5[a]	392	4.58
(b) By range of taxable turnover (£000 p.a.)			
0– 9.9	13.3	29.0	2.18
10– 19.9	13.7	49.7	3.63
20– 49.9	20.5	88.5	4.32
50– 99.9	11.6	69.3	5.97
100–999.9	17.0	105.6	6.21
1000 and over	9.4	49.9	5.34
Total	85.5[a]	392	4.58

[a] The column does not sum to £85.5 million because of rounding.

VAT officer visits as derived from NAS and the frequency of visits. On this basis we can calculate operating costs for each sector and size range, compare compliance and administrative costs and relate tax yield to operating costs for each size and sector. The results are set out in Tables 5.8 and 5.9. The rough and ready nature of the allocation must be stressed, however, particularly in relation to the allocation by sector (which is done simply on the basis of the size of firms within the sector).

Perhaps the most interesting feature of Table 5.8 is that brought out by the ratio of compliance to administrative costs. The ratio rises steadily with size up to the largest size range, where the increased frequency of VAT officer visits reduces the ratio. In other words although compliance costs are heavily concentrated in the lower size ranges, if our apportionment is even approximately correct, administrative costs are even more heavily concentrated there. Thus, over 40 per cent of compliance costs are incurred in relation to firms of under £50,000 turnover, but over 55 per cent of administrative costs are incurred by firms of that size.

Table 5.9 is even more interesting. The analysis by sector suggests that almost £100 million of operating costs may be incurred in relation to two sectors, primary and construction, from which no net revenue is obtained. The analysis by size reveals that the resources used to collect VAT in each of the two lowest size ranges were in excess of the tax collected. Indeed, the net revenue (£330 million) was barely more than the resources required to collect it (£295 million) for all firms with a taxable turnover up to £100,000. The two lowest groups together comprised over 40 per cent of registered traders; traders with a turnover up to £100,000 comprised over 80 per cent of registered traders.

The Significance of the Findings

The most significant finding is that both compliance costs and administrative costs in 1977/8 were heavily concentrated on the lowest size ranges, which contained the bulk of registered traders and yielded very little revenue. Even if the basis on which administrative costs have been apportioned was shown to be wrong, and even if compliance costs have been over-estimated, the general conclusion, of substantial operating costs heavily concentrated on the smaller firms, would still stand.

Again, however, certain caveats must be added. If VAT rates had been higher (and they have subsequently been raised) or if zero rating (except for exports) were replaced by a reduced rate of VAT, the ratio of tax to operating costs would change markedly.

Secondly, it should not be assumed that if the smallest firms were suddenly taken out of liability the operating costs allocated against them would wholly disappear. This would be true of the compliance cost component, but not necessarily of the administrative cost component. Administrative costs would certainly fall, but certain overhead costs might need to be incurred more or less regardless of the size of the tax collecting operation. In other words, our allocation

Table 5.9 Comparison of operating costs with tax revenue

	No. of registered traders ('000s)	Net tax[a] paid (£m)	Tax operating costs (£m)	Tax operating costs as % of net tax collected (where positive)
(a) By sector				
Primary	179.9	−217	30	n.a.
Manufacture and utilities	120.8	2268	60	2.6
Construction	179.2	−252	63	n.a.
Transport and communication	56.4	206	21	10.2
Retail	280.2	338	100	29.6
Wholesale and dealers	87.7	976	46	4.7
Financial and business services	44.0	228	24	10.5
Professional and scientific services	63.2	194	28	14.4
Miscellaneous and public services	262.9	507	107	21.1
Total	1274.2	4235[b]	478	11.3
(b) By range of taxable turnover (£000 p.a.)				
0– 9.9	270.7	15	42	280.0
10– 19.9	269.5	55	63	114.5
20– 49.9	340.9	120	109	90.8
50– 99.9	177.7	140	81	57.9
100–999.9	185.4	600	123	20.5
1000 and over	30.0	3305	59	1.8
Total	1274.2	4235[b]	478	11.3

[a] Source: HM Customs & Excise, *69th Annual Report*.
[b] Includes £48 million allocated by size but not by sector.

of administrative costs across the size bands was on an average and not a marginal basis.

Finally, the point must be reiterated that our figures of compliance costs are gross; they take no account of the benefits of VAT to traders. We shall examine this topic in Chapters 7 and 8 after we have looked more closely at some of the more detailed influences on compliance costs.

6 The Differential Incidence of Compliance Costs – Accounting Systems, Multiple Rates and Other Influences

Introduction

In this chapter we seek to probe more deeply into what factors influence the size of compliance costs. We look, in particular, at features which may account for the huge economies of scale in VAT compliance work described in the previous chapter; and at structural features of VAT which may have a significant effect on compliance costs, notably the presence of different VAT categories.

Factors Associated with Size

Accounting Systems

Traders were asked in NAS (Q12) whether accounting records were kept in handwritten ledgers, a Kalamazoo type of system, a machine accounting system, or a fully computerised system.

The most common type of accounting record-keeping was by handwritten ledgers – indeed 95 per cent of respondents to the questions with a taxable turnover of less than £100,000 used this method, and overall more than three-quarters of respondents used a handwritten system.

Table 6.1 shows the percentage of respondents using various types of record-keeping. As the range of taxable turnover increases more systems are used, but only in the taxable turnover range over £1 million do handwritten systems stop being the most common type. Computer-based systems are used by 70 per cent of firms with a taxable turnover of more than £10 million.

Table 6.2 gives the mean compliance costs associated with each type of record-keeping for respondents in each range of taxable turnover expressed as a ratio to mean compliance for that size range. It is clear that as the size of business increases, so the more sophisticated systems are more widely used, but there is no obvious pattern associating type of system with compliance cost. The apparently high cost of computer-based systems is misleading because they are used by the very large firms. Expressing compliance costs as a percentage of taxable turnover showed that in general, users of computers had a burden of compliance costs very similar to that of the relatively few users of other systems amongst the large firms.

Table 6.1 Percentage of NAS respondents using various types of accounting system analysed by size

Taxable turnover (£000 p.a.)		Hand system	Kalamazoo	Machine	Computer	Hand + kalamazoo	Hand + machine	Computer + other	Total
0–	9.9	97	*	*	*	—	—	*	100 (336)
10–	19.9	98	*	—	*	*	—	—	100 (376)
20–	49.9	95	3	*	—	*	—	*	100 (456)
50–	99.9	91	7	*	*	*	—	—	100 (349)
100–	499.9	70	17	6	3	*	*	*	100 (389)
500–	999.9	38	20	26	10	*	*	*	100 (101)
1000–9999.9		22	14	34	21	—	*	7	100 (304)
10 000 and over		*	*	21	63	—	*	4	100 (67)
	Total	77 (1824)	8 (180)	7 (178)	5 (130)	1 (13)	1 (17)	2 (36)	100 (2378)

* Fewer than ten respondents in cell.
— No respondents in cell.
Figures in brackets are number of respondents.

Average Size of Sale and Number of Invoices

One possible determinant of differential compliance costs within a given range of taxable turnover is the average size of sale; the larger the average sale, the fewer invoices to be processed and thus the lower the compliance costs. Information obtained from NAS gave general support to this hypothesis, but the evidence was not clear cut. The range of sizes of sale covered by each category in NAS (Q_9) was very wide, and there were too few respondents to allow a full analysis by size and sector.

An alternative approach is to look directly at the difference in compliance costs for firms issuing differing numbers of sales invoices within the same range of taxable turnover and sector of business.

Table 6.3 shows that, excluding the lowest and highest taxable turnover ranges, traders who do not issue sales invoices have compliance costs about 30 per cent below the mean for the taxable turnover range, and there is some evidence to

Table 6.2 Comparison of compliance costs for NAS respondents using different accounting systems

Taxable turnover (£000 p.a.)	Mean compliance cost (£)	Hand	Kalamazoo	Machine	Computer	Hand + machine	Computer + other
	£			Ratios to mean compliance cost			
0- 9.9	107	0.96	*	*	*	—	*
10- 19.9	184	1.00	*	*	*	—	—
20- 49.9	259	0.98	1.17	*	—	—	*
50- 99.9	392	0.99	0.59	*	*	—	—
100-499.9	555	0.89	1.38	1.20	0.52	*	—
500-999.9	612	1.07	0.67	1.37	1.06	*	*
1000 and over	1663	0.71	0.62	0.69	2.06	1.39	0.54

The column of mean compliance costs is the weighted average for all traders and not just NAS respondents. There is no published data from which the weighted mean compliance cost can be calculated for higher taxable turnover ranges.

A ratio of less than one implies lower than average compliance costs. A few firms combined hand and Kalamazoo methods but in all size ranges there were fewer than ten respondents in cell.

 * Fewer than ten respondents in cell.
—No respondents in cell.

Table 6.3 Comparison of compliance costs for NAS respondents issuing different numbers of sales invoices

Range of taxable turnover (£000 p.a.)	Mean compliance cost (£)	Number of sales invoices					
		Not issued	1-500	501- 1000	1001- 10000	10001- 100000	Over 100000
		Ratios to mean compliance cost					
0- 9.9	107	1.04	0.98	*	*	*	—
10- 19.9	184	0.73	1.14	1.35	1.24	—	—
20- 49.9	259	0.68	1.03	1.13	1.75	*	—
50- 99.9	392	0.70	1.05	1.06	1.04	*	—
100-499.9	555	0.68	0.81	0.86	1.30	0.98	—
500-999.9	612	0.80	1.03	0.85	1.12	0.99	*
1000 and over	1663	4.01[a]	0.82	0.83	0.70	0.93	2.97[a]

—No respondents in cell.
 * Fewer than ten respondents in cell.
 [a] Influenced by a few very large firms.

suggest that compliance costs increase with the number of sales invoices. Little comparison was possible in individual sectors, but the pattern was repeated in miscellaneous and public services, and also in retail (although here the difference was less pronounced because such a high proportion do not issue sales invoices).

Compliance costs were also found to rise with the number of purchases invoices processed in each range of taxable turnover (Table 6.4). The only individual sector with sufficient cases for individual comparisons was retail, which followed the overall trend closely.

Table 6.4 Comparison of compliance costs for NAS respondents processing different numbers of purchases invoices

| Range of taxable turnover (£000 p.a.) | Mean compliance cost (£) | Number of purchase invoices | | | | |
| | | 1–500 | 501– 1000 | 1001– 10 000 | 10 001– 100 000 | Over 100 000 |
		Ratios to mean compliance cost				
0– 9.9	107	0.94	1.37	1.83	—	—
10– 19.9	184	1.04	1.05	0.93	—	—
20– 49.9	259	0.80	1.00	1.58	*	—
50– 99.9	392	0.78	0.90	1.73	*	—
100–499.9	555	0.87	0.87	1.14	1.00	—
500–999.9	612	0.63	0.68	1.18	*	*
1000 and over	1663	0.75	0.46	0.72	1.22	8.30[a]

— No respondents in cell.
* Fewer than ten respondents in cell.
[a] Influenced by a few very large firms.

Factors Determined by the Structure of VAT

Net Payment or Repayment Traders

A comparison of the compliance costs of net payment and repayment traders in the same sector and taxable turnover bands (Table 6.5) shows that repayment traders tend to have lower compliance costs than payment traders despite the fact that they normally submit three times as many VAT returns to Customs & Excise. Indeed, the average compliance cost for all repayment traders among NAS respondents was 35 per cent lower than that of payment traders. Clearly there are exceptions, particularly among the traders with a very low taxable turnover, or in the transport and communication, and financial and business services sectors.

The very low ratio of compliance costs for repayment traders in the primary sector can be explained by the fact that there is a special accounting arrangement in operation for farmers, who also tend to have few sales invoices. Where outputs are zero rated or exempt, book-keeping is simplified and this may well account for the low ratios in most sectors.

Table 6.5 Comparison of compliance costs of net payment and repayment
traders amongst NAS respondents[a]

Taxable turnover (£ooo p.a.)	Primary	Manufacture and utilities	Construction	Transport and communication	Retail	Wholesale and dealers	Financial and business services	Professional and scientific services	Miscellaneous and
0– 9.9	0.65	0.31	1.17	*	1.92	*	2.09	1.89	1.
10– 99.9	0.36	0.54	1.31	1.76	0.81	0.53	*	0.69	0.
100–999.9	0.37	0.98	0.89	2.16	0.46	0.39	1.14	*	0.
1000 and over	*	0.82	0.27	2.22	0.21	1.11	0.48	*	1.

[a] The figures are obtained by dividing the mean compliance cost of net repayment traders by that (
payment traders in the same size and sector. A figure of less than one shows that, on average, pay
traders have higher costs than repayment traders, and vice-versa.
* Fewer than five respondents in either the numerator or denominator.

Mix of VAT Categories

At the time of the NAS there were, in effect, five categories of VAT: standard
rate, higher rate, zero rate for exports, zero rate other than exports, and
exemption. The more categories of VAT operated by a business, the higher the
expected compliance costs. Table 6.6 compares mean compliance costs of traders
operating various numbers of VAT categories, but provides only limited support
for the hypothesis.

There are complications in the comparisons. Only the larger firms operate
the full range of rates: over half the 350 firms operating the 'export' category
have a taxable turnover greater than £1 million. Most of the traders operating
two rates use standard and zero rates and this particular combination appears
from the figures to cause relatively few problems. This may be partly because
no calculations are required with the zero rate; but the figures are to some extent
misleading in the absence of sufficient numbers to make possible a breakdown
by sector as well as size. We know (Chapter 7) that this combination causes
problems in the construction industry. Further, eight of the nine retail schemes
were devised as a means of separating standard rated from zero rated outputs.
Thus, to some extent, the relatively low compliance costs associated with the
combination of rates has been obtained at the cost of more inaccuracy and
possibly higher tax payments (see below p. 65). There were 980 respondents
to NAS using both standard and zero rates (but no others) who had an average
compliance cost of £762, compared with £1,191 (50 per cent higher) for the

323 respondents operating standard and higher rates. Traders operating only the zero rate (mainly farmers) had a mean compliance cost of only £219; but exporters and traders with exempt outputs tended to have higher compliance costs – £1,136 and £1,150 respectively (though, as earlier mentioned, the exporters tended to be relatively large firms).

Table 6.6 Compliance costs in relation to number of VAT categories

Range of taxable turnover (£000 p.a.)	Mean compliance cost (£)	Number of categories				
		1	2	3	4	5
		Ratios to mean compliance cost				
0– 9.9	107	0.96	0.86	0.95	*	*
10– 19.9	184	1.03	0.88	0.97	1.26	*
20– 49.9	259	0.81	0.83	1.57	0.94	*
50– 99.9	392	0.77	0.96	0.87	1.41	*
100–499.9	555	0.89	0.98	1.05	0.98	1.52
500–999.9	612	0.46	1.00	0.68	1.95	0.73
1000 and over	1663	0.53	0.69	1.62	1.23	1.31

* Fewer than ten respondents in cell.

Whilst, from our figures the *number* of categories operated does not appear as a very significant influence on compliance costs, the *mix* of VAT categories does. In particular the operation of the higher rate appears to be very important as it is the only rate apart from standard rate to require calculations. Table 6.7 compares compliance costs of respondents *with* higher rated outputs with those without. The differences are highly significant.

Operating the higher rate also imposed additional administrative costs on Customs & Excise. In evidence to the Public Accounts Committee Sir Ronald Radford (then Chairman of the Board of Customs & Excise) estimated that the higher rate category cost an additional two hundred and fifty extra staff in 1975/6 (Public Accounts Committee 1975/6). In reply to a Parliamentary Question about what savings were made in Customs & Excise staff as a result of the unification of standard and higher rates, Mr P. Rees, Minister of State, said, 'It is estimated that the current staff effort directly involved in the administration and collection of VAT is some four hundred man years below the level in 1978–79. But it is not practicable to isolate and quantify realistically the savings attributable to the adoption last year of a single positive rate of 15 per cent.' (*Hansard* 24 June 1980, col 141).

Thus the operation of two positive rates of VAT was a significant determinant of differential compliance costs, and also added significantly to administrative costs.

Table 6.7 Comparison of compliance costs of traders with and without higher rate outputs

Taxable turnover (£000 p.a.)	Mean compliance costs[a]		Percentage difference $\dfrac{(1)-(2)}{(2)} \times 100\%$
	(1) With higher rated outputs	(2) Without higher rated outputs	
0– 9.9	173 (14)	100 (306)	73
10– 19.9	271 (23)	179 (334)	51
20– 49.9	484 (33)	242 (396)	100
50– 99.9	463 (39)	368 (295)	21
100–999.9	798 (84)	525 (382)	52
1000 and over	1606 (69)	1305 (275)	19

[a] Number of respondents in brackets.

Retail Schemes*

In order to help retailers to calculate their output tax, a number of retail schemes were devised (see Appendix H). Scheme A is a simple scheme for use where all outputs are standard rated, and scheme F involves separating differently rated

Table 6.8 Mean compliance costs of users of retail schemes[a]

Taxable turnover (£000s p.a.)	Users of scheme A or F	Users of scheme C or D	Users of scheme B, E, or G	Users of scheme H or J	Respondents making retail sales but using no scheme
0– 9.9	63 (9)	140 (8)	151 (4)	— (0)	119 (57)
10– 99.9	249 (112)	196 (71)	248 (32)	304 (7)	280 (288)
100–999.9	755 (42)	119 (1)	565 (14)	768 (5)	496 (106)
1000 and over	1994 (11)	136 (2)	975 (1)	2314 (4)	2065 (66)
Overall	472 (174)	188 (82)	342 (51)	952 (16)	535 (517)[a]

[a] Number of respondents in brackets.
[b] 11 respondents used more than one retail scheme, including some very large firms.

   * It had been hoped that the scheme for secondhand works of art, antiques and scientific collections might have been explored because interviews with accountants (ADV) suggested that this was one which gave considerable trouble; however, the NAS provided only 29 respondents spread across the size ranges, so no analysis was worthwhile. (It should be noted, however, that the secondhand schemes, unlike the retail schemes, were introduced at the request of the trade to enable them to pay less tax.)

outputs at the point of sale. All other schemes involve some form of apportionment where an accurate separation at point of sale is infeasible.

It was therefore to be expected that those using schemes A and F would exhibit the most similarity to those using no scheme (see Table 6.8). In general, schemes C and D (which are designed to be the simplest but are least accurate – and therefore more likely to result in higher tax payments) involve the lowest compliance costs, and schemes H and J (which are designed to be the most accurate and are thus the most complex) involve the highest compliance costs. However, further analysis was not possible because there were insufficient cases in so many cells.

Other Factors

Other general factors with a possible influence on compliance costs were the length of time the business had been registered for VAT (p. 26), the category of staff who completed the VAT returns, and the formal education and book-keeping training of sole proprietors, partners and directors of small firms who completed their own VAT returns.

The need to use 'eligible' traders in the sample (p. 29) reduced the numbers of recently registered traders. In fact about 78 per cent of respondents to NAS had been registered at the outset of the tax (1972/3), and no detailed analysis to try to estimate the 'learning effect' was worthwhile. But there was a hint that earlier registrations tended to have lower compliance costs than more recent registrations.

Table 6.9 Comparison of compliance costs for NAS respondents where different categories of staff complete the VAT returns

Taxable turnover (£000 p.a.)	Mean compliance cost (£)	Proprietor or partner	Director	Company secretary	Accountant in the business	Outside accountant	Book-keeping staff	Other staff
				Ratios to mean compliance cost				
0– 9.9	107	1.02	1.06	*	*	0.99	0.97	0.75
10– 19.9	184	1.07	1.16	*	*	1.10	0.51	0.73
20– 49.9	259	0.88	1.64	0.81	*	1.19	0.80	0.63
50– 99.9	392	1.18	0.91	1.40	*	0.89	0.71	0.32
00–499.9	555	0.94	1.13	0.90	0.74	1.04	1.07	0.50
00–999.9	612	*	0.99	1.10	0.90	*	0.90	*
000 and over	1663	1.75	1.03	0.45	1.51	*	0.98	1.15

* Fewer than ten respondents in cell.

A reasonably consistent pattern of compliance costs emerges when looking at the category of staff completing VAT returns (Table 6.9). In general the lowest level of compliance costs occurred when returns were filled in by 'Other' staff or 'Book-keeping' staff; in all but two ranges of taxable turnover the reported compliance costs were below the overall population mean for the range. When returns were filled in by the proprietor, partner or a director, compliance costs tended to be relatively high.

Another finding was that where outside accountants were employed compliance costs tended to be above average. There was some evidence that formal book-keeping training was associated with relatively low compliance costs in the smaller firms (£10,000–£100,000 p.a. taxable turnover).

Conclusions

The most important of the factors determining the differential incidence of compliance costs discussed in this chapter are those associated with the structure of the tax – namely the mix of VAT rates, and whether a trader made net payments or received net repayments. Other influential factors are the number of invoices processed and the status of staff who filled in the VAT returns.

The other factors discussed may have had some effect, but there were too few respondents for a full analysis.

7 Difficulties and Problems

Introduction
The size of compliance costs depends in no small measure on the recurring difficulties which traders have in coping with VAT and on the special problems which arise from time to time. In this chapter we analyse those difficulties and problems as indicated by respondents to NAS and interviewees (FOL(P) and (T)). We also go outside NAS data to take a brief look at the VAT tribunals which are both a symptom of the problems and a means for their solution.

Recurring Difficulties
Respondents to NAS were asked, 'Do you have any difficulties with VAT which keep cropping up?' Eleven possible difficulties (e.g. 'self-billing') were set out, and there was space for respondents to describe any other difficulties encountered (Q23).

Slightly more than 20 per cent of all respondents reported recurring difficulties with VAT work, and this proportion remained fairly constant throughout all size ranges, with a slight tendency for the proportion to decline as size increased. However, there were highly significant differences by sector, with as few as 15 per cent reporting difficulties in the primary and the manufacture and utilities sectors, and as many as 33 per cent in construction (see Table 7.1).

These sectoral differences may be largely explained by the different treatment for VAT purposes of each sector. For example, there was at the time of the survey extensive application of the complicated partial exemption provisions in the financial and business services sector, whereas the primary sector was heavily weighted by food production which is zero-rated; accounting was therefore much simpler.

'Liability borderlines' were frequently cited as a difficulty in the construction sector, where construction and alterations are zero-rated, but repairs and maintenance are standard rated. 'Partial exemption' is mentioned frequently, not only in financial and business services, but also in the construction, retail, and the miscellaneous and public services sectors. It is possible that respondents in these three latter sectors could have had some exempt income from a source such as rent, but the researchers gained a strong impression that many respondents confused the technical terms 'partial exemption' and 'zero-rating'.

The most common difficulty reported in all sectors was 'understanding VAT instructions' (13 per cent of all respondents mentioned this difficulty). 'The number of arithmetical calculations' was the next most frequently reported difficulty. These difficulties were particularly prevalent in the retail, miscel-

Table 7.1 Common difficulties by size and sector (NAS) (percentage of respondents in each cell reporting common difficulties)

Taxable turnover (£000 p.a.)	Primary	Manufacture and utilities	Construction	Transport and communication	Retail	Wholesale and dealers	Financial and business services	Professional and scientific services	Miscellaneous and public services	Overall	Number of respondents with difficulties
0— 9.9	14	17	40	19	31	20	38	19	22	24	93
10— 19.9	16	20	32	25	22	15	37	26	26	24	109
20— 49.9	15	19	29	28	27	24	22	21	27	24	126
50— 99.9	13	12	30	14	32	15	15	19	28	24	94
100—999.9	16	13	25	18	20	16	12	31	19	18	98
1000 and over	14	14	41	33	27	19	44	57	17	22	88
Overall	15	15	33	24	27	18	28	24	24	22	608
Number of respondents with difficulties	63	57	107	27	138	43	35	39	99	608	

laneous and public services, primary and construction sectors. The use of special schemes where traders are selling goods and services to the public which are taxed at more than one VAT rate may well explain the prevalence of these difficulties in retail and miscellaneous and public services, since most of the schemes involve understanding the different methods of apportionment to arrive at the VAT liability. In the construction sector it is again probable that rating different jobs correctly gives rise to these difficulties. In the primary sector, these are the most common difficulties, which is perhaps surprising as the bulk of primary output is at the zero rate, and it is known (Chapter 5) that compliance costs overall are lowest in this sector. The comprehension and calculation of deductible input tax may sometimes give rise to difficulties. But, although predominant in that sector, these difficulties occur less frequently than in retail, construction or miscellaneous and public services (Table 7.2).

Although respondents were classified by sector according to the main business pursued, there were some overlaps, e.g. wholesalers operating retail outlets, and this situation often gave rise to difficulties, as different methods of accounting for VAT might be necessary for each separate aspect.

No general pattern was apparent in the replies to the open-ended question on other difficulties; replies ranged from 'apportioning private use of company car' to 'difficulty in finding the money at the end of the return period'.

Table 7.2 Percentage of NAS respondents reporting common difficulties

Cause of difficulty	Primary	Manufacture and utilities	Construction	Transport and communication	Retail	Wholesale and dealers	Financial and business services	Professional and scientific services	Miscellaneous and public services	Overall	Number of cases
Understanding VAT instructions	10	8	19	12	18	10	13	12	16	13	377
Number of calculations	6	4	11	10	14	7	10	6	13	9	263
Number of invoices	4	4	9	9	10	6	4	4	7	7	182
Liability borderlines	2	3	18	5	3	5	6	7	6	6	161
Number of VAT rates	4	4	9	6	7	6	4	2	6	6	154
VAT rate changes	4	3	5	3	4	3	3	3	3	3	88
Partial exemption	2	*	4	2	2	*	10	4	3	3	70
Self-billing	1	*	4	3	2	3	6	2	3	2	65
Import paperwork	*	4	*	1	1	5	3	*	1	2	46
Export paperwork	*	3	*	3	1	2	2	2	1	1	40
Secondhand schemes	1	0	1	2	1	0	2	*	3	1	30

* = less than one half of one per cent.
Note that some respondents cited more than one difficulty.

It is interesting to note that the NAS mean compliance cost for traders reporting at least one difficulty was £1,030 compared with only £409 for respondents without difficulties, less than half as big.

Changes since 1978
There have been several changes in VAT regulations since the NAS questionnaire, which should have reduced the number of common difficulties. Liberalisation of the rules governing partial exemption has reduced the number of traders who have to make complicated calculations from about twenty thousand to about three thousand. This alteration will have made a significant improvement, particularly in the financial services sector.

The simplified VAT return form has made completion of this document easier, although many of the FOL(T) respondents asserted that the improvement was only marginal.

Another important change has been the abolition of the higher rate of VAT which will certainly have eased liability borderline difficulties, especially among traders in electrical goods. To some extent this may have eased construction industry borderline problems where electrical work was being done, but the fundamental difficulty of the distinction between zero-rated construction and alterations, and standard rated repairs and maintenance remains.

Special Problems with VAT

In addition to the common difficulties, 141 traders (5 per cent of respondents) reported that they had encountered one or more special problems with VAT, involving particular extra costs. The percentages of respondents reporting such special problems are set out in Table 7.3, from which it may be seen that the largest firms report the highest percentage. Sectoral differences are less marked, with the manufacture and utilities sector reporting the highest percentage of problems. The stated costs of special problems are set out in Appendix I. The

Table 7.3 Percentage of respondents reporting special problems (number of cases in brackets)

Taxable turnover (£000 p.a.)	Primary	Manufacture and utilities	Construction	Transport and communication	Retail	Wholesale and dealers	Financial and business services	Professional and scientific services	Miscellaneous and public services	Overall
0- 9.9	3 (4)	0	13 (3)	1 (1)	6 (1)	0	8 (2)	3 (1)	4 (2)	4 (14)
10- 99.9	2 (4)	6 (6)	7 (11)	2 (1)	3 (11)	4 (2)	4 (2)	0	6 (14)	4 (51)
100-999.9	3 (2)	5 (6)	8 (5)	14 (3)	4 (3)	7 (5)	4 (1)	15 (4)	7 (5)	6 (34)
1000 plus	0	14 (19)	5 (2)	10 (3)	10 (6)	6 (6)	22 (4)	43 (3)	7 (3)	11 (42)
Overall	2 (10)	8 (31)	6 (21)	6 (7)	3 (18)	5 (13)	7 (9)	5 (8)	6 (24)	5 (141)

special problem areas were described by the traders as in Table 7.4.

Import documentation was singled out for criticism, especially when no VAT liability was involved. One interviewee said that 'import procedures are annoying – computerised forms from the airport come in late or not at all.' Other comments included: 'I can't see what use they make of the import figures as it appears on both sides of the account,' and 'We are importing things, overpaying on goods in bond, and getting it back at once. Rather pointless and irrelevant – I skip it now and don't tell them about it.'

One interviewee felt that the information provided about imports was inadequate and badly worded.

Table 7.4 Types of special problem

Import and export	21
VAT office error or delay	17
Input invoices (especially petrol)	14
Construction industry borderline problems	14
Exempt items	10
Late deliveries, discounts, invoices or payments	8
Gaming and vending machines	6
Multiple businesses	5
Credit notes etc.	4
Self-billing	4
Change of business status	4
VAT computer problem	4
VAT officer behaviour unhelpful	4
Other	25

Import and export of services also gave rise to a number of problems, e.g. 'professional services provided to a firm in the Isle of Man'; 'VAT chargeable to overseas companies for management services performed in the UK'; 'Treatment of overseas services and disbursements'; 'Consultancy services rendered offshore on a vessel'; and 'zero rating of services to non-EEC residents'.

Agency and partnership agreements with overseas businesses caused some problems, such as 'classification of sales to the UK agent of an overseas customer'; 'VAT status of payments made by company A in Malaysia to company B in the UK to partly defray joint overheads'. Another respondent had difficulty in 'determining whether invoices raised to foreign government offices and other foreign bodies in the UK are liable to VAT'.

It is apparent that for a tax which aims to facilitate international trade, VAT can cause considerable problems for importers and exporters. For example, one trader, who had invited a VAT officer to tour his business, complained that: 'During the tour the VAT inspector asked a number of questions specifically biased to VAT of the staff who knew nothing about the tax. This upset some members of the staff and annoyed others.'

Often, administrative problems seemed to centre on businesses changing status or function; for example, one trader wrote: 'We moved from a large, sole proprietor garage, where the car sales were under a limited company, to this very small garage. It took many, many telephone calls to get the Customs & Excise to understand we were moving and would trade solely under the limited company name.'

Delays sometimes occurred when a trader who normally paid VAT made a refund claim: 'On occasions when VAT repayments are due to us, there are delays and difficulties for which various explanations have been given, usually blaming the computer.' 'The computer queried high repayments due to purchase of new machine, and returned the money to the wrong partner.'

Obtaining valid input invoices was a problem in certain circumstances, such as for sales representatives' lunches, taxi fares and petrol expenses. In one large group, four companies were asked for an additional £30,000 VAT because of unsubstantiated expense claims. The group accountant said that it is not really practicable to get invoices for everything. He suggested that some VAT offices check much more stringently on these claims than others.

Petrol supplied to employees partly for private use gave rise to several problems, as did the separate calculation of the pre-tax price of petrol which was higher rated at the time of the survey. This latter problem should have been eliminated by the consolidation of positive VAT rates.

Liability borderlines in the construction industry not only figured amongst the common difficulties (see above) but were at the root of many special problems. One respondent commented: 'The borderline cases in the construction industry are not related to the whole building but to parts of the work done. The contractor has to guess because the client and his architect or quantity surveyor are not interested in spending time on this problem.'

A number of respondents had had difficulties with obtaining payments from their customers, or valid VAT invoices from their suppliers. One interviewee said: 'We shouldn't have to pay VAT before receiving payment. We give seventy-five days' credit in this firm; either they should wait for the money or they should compel people to pay in time.'

Finally, there were several individual problems which did not fit into recognisable categories, for example: 'I filled in the wrong figures on the wrong form (wrong month) and had no idea what I had done wrong. It took several phone calls and letters and re-filling in another form which had to be dated *wrongly* to suit the computer!'

VAT Tribunals

An analysis of *all* the disputes which began to be heard by VAT Tribunals* during the financial year 1977/8 shows that the majority occurred in the miscellaneous and public services sector; 42 per cent of the 206 Tribunal cases were in this sector, compared to 21 per cent of the population of registered traders. The sectoral analysis is given in Table 7.5. The subjects of the appeals are set out in Table 7.6. (These analyses were on a slightly different basis from the Customs & Excise breakdown published in their annual report.)

Appeals against assessment were most common among cash traders where assumed levels of mark-up were in dispute; 48 of the 86 appeals were either from retailers or from landlords of public houses. Appeals concerning liability included disputes over export of services (3), gifts to employees and associates (3), catering (4), rents (4), educational services (2), and construction (3). Registration disputes included two group registration problems, two appeals for voluntary registration and two appeals by religious organisations against being registered as businesses. Secondhand scheme appeals centred on whether the records kept by traders

---

* In considering the analysis of tribunal cases the reader should remember that many cases waiting for appeal are settled before they reach the tribunals.

Table 7.5 Sectoral analysis of tribunal cases, 1977/8

Sector	Percentage of cases	Percentage of total population in the sector
Primary	1	14
Manufacture and utilities	2	9
Construction	6	14
Transport and communication	5	4
Retail	17	22
Wholesale and dealers	6	7
Financial and business, professional and scientific services	9	8
Miscellaneous and public services	42	21
Unidentified or not registered	10	n.a.

Table 7.6 Analysis of tribunal cases by subject, 1977/8

Subject	Number
Assessment	86
Liability	33
Registration	14
Secondhand records	13
Input tax	12
Retail scheme operation	7
Appeals by unregistered purchasers about VAT charged by suppliers	7
Appeals by do-it-yourself builders about refunds	6
Proof of export	5
Partial exemption	4
Definition of 'in course of business'	4
Deregistration	3
Other	12

were adequate. Input tax disputes included problems with the validity of input tax invoices, goods supplied to an agent rather than direct to the trader and non-deductible input tax. Other appeals in general appeared to reflect the recurring difficulties and special problems encountered by NAS respondents, such as partial exemption and proof of export.

78 per cent of cases were completed within one day, and a further 14 per cent within two days. The longest case, nine days, involved an argument over whether a Church training programme was an exempt educational activity or not.

One criticism of the appeal procedure emerged during the FOL(P) and ADV interviews: it is necessary to pay the sum assessed to the Customs & Excise during an appeal against the assessment unless waived on grounds of hardship. Interviewees suggested that the procedure should be harmonised with that adopted by the Inland Revenue, whereby the assessment is only payable on the failure of the appeal, but may, in that case, carry additionally the interest on the sum since the due date.

An analysis of Tribunal cases reported in the *VAT Encyclopaedia* (Wheatcroft and Avery Jones 1973) which only selects cases of legal interest, yields a higher proportion of construction industry cases than the analysis above (13 per cent compared with 6 per cent).

Conclusion

Perhaps the main conclusion to emerge from this chapter is the importance of liability borderline problems in the construction industry. The industry was top of the list with common difficulties (Table 7.1). Special problems in the industry, which also centred on liability borderlines, were relatively frequent and costly.

8 Traders' Cash Flow Benefits from VAT

Introduction

So far in our consideration of the compliance costs of VAT we have looked only at gross compliance costs; we have taken no account of any benefits to traders which may result from complying with VAT regulations. Such benefits may be regarded as an offset to the compliance costs traders incur, although the benefits bear no direct relationship to the size of compliance costs.

Such benefits fall into two main categories. First, there are cash flow benefits from tax collected but not yet handed over to Customs & Excise. Second, there may be managerial-type benefits arising from the improved record-keeping which compliance with VAT may entail. We examine the first of these benefits in this chapter and the second in Chapter 9.

Aggregate Cash Benefit from VAT

Payment traders benefit from holding net VAT until such time as it is paid to Customs & Excise. The value of this benefit can be considered as equal either to the interest they could gain by lending the money or alternatively (to traders in overdraft) the cost of borrowing the equivalent amount from a bank or other financial institution. Repayment traders, on the other hand, face a loss or disbenefit on money they have paid out but not yet recovered from Customs & Excise.

A particular trader's cash flow benefit (or disbenefit) from VAT has two elements: money held by the trader, owed to (or from) Customs & Excise and representing the difference between tax collected on output and tax paid on input; and the VAT component of any net credit arising from normal commercial transactions. It is convenient, initially, to consider these two elements separately.

Let us first examine the benefit to payment traders from holding VAT payable to Customs & Excise. The regulations state that VAT is payable within one month after the end of the quarter in which it becomes due. If all traders paid on the last day of the month the average credit would amount to one-half of the net tax due to be paid over to Customs & Excise during the quarter plus a quarter's tax due to Customs & Excise held for one month in four. (The equivalent of one month's tax held throughout the year.) Thus if T is the annual tax take then the average credit $= \frac{1}{8}T + \frac{1}{12}T = \frac{5}{24}T$.

If we assume a linear cash flow and constant stocks then each quarter would break down as follows:

Month 1: Average VAT collected $= \frac{1}{24}T + \frac{1}{4}T$ (All the previous quarter's VAT)

$$= \frac{7}{24}T$$

Month 2: Average VAT collected $= \frac{1}{24}T + \frac{1}{12}T$ (VAT held from previous month)

$$= \frac{1}{8}T$$

Month 3: Average VAT collected $= \frac{1}{24}T + \frac{1}{6}T$ (VAT held from previous two months)

$$= \frac{5}{24}T$$

The months average out to give $\frac{5}{24}T$ held throughout the year.

Repayment traders are, in effect, lending money to Customs & Excise and generally have a return period of one month. If repayment is assumed to take one month, if R = annual repayment, then the loss of credit each month (or the 'loan' to Customs & Excise) is:

$$\frac{1}{24}R + \frac{1}{12}R = \frac{1}{8}R$$

Thus, taking payment and repayment traders together, Customs & Excise are making a considerable net 'loan' to the economy as a whole, especially to the business community.

Data on tax paid and repaid can be obtained from NAS and, in aggregate, from Customs & Excise annual reports. The financial year 1977/8 most closely corresponds to the period of the NAS and the figures will be given for that year, but it should be recalled that the last complete financial year to which traders' responses referred will have brought many of them beyond April 1978.

In order to calculate the value of the benefit (or disbenefit) to traders a suitable rate of interest has to be applied to the 'loans'. For a trader running an overdraft, the appropriate rate would be the overdraft rate he has to pay; if he is a payment trader this is what he saves by the 'loan' from Customs & Excise; if he is a repayment trader this is the cost of the additional borrowing he has to incur. However, this rate itself may vary according to the credit standing of the trader.

Thus the loan to a payment trader in bad credit standing is worth more than to one in good credit standing.

If a trader is not running an overdraft, then the appropriate rate of interest to apply to calculate benefit or detriment would be the highest rate at which he could lend funds on a short-term basis. This is quite likely to be higher for a large firm than a small, both because a large firm is likely to have available the best financial advice and also because the larger the payment trader the larger the absolute amount available to be lent at interest, so the more worthwhile it will be to incur the costs of investment which may be necessary to get the best return on short-term loans.

Another point to bear in mind is that the flow of credit from this source is irregular and does not come according to a time pattern of the trader's own choosing. In some cases this will reduce its value to him.

Whilst these points should not be ignored, in making overall calculations of benefit and detriment we have to make some simplifying assumptions and the rate of interest used in the calculations is minimum lending rate (MLR) which will normally be intermediate between the rates a trader will pay on loans to him or will receive on loans he makes. On this basis, as can be seen from Table 8.1, and with the assumptions we have made about the timing of payments and repayments, the net benefit to the economy in 1977/8 was £73 million made up of £92 million benefit to payment traders minus £19 million disbenefit to repayment traders.

Table 8.1 Aggregate net cash flow benefits[a] from VAT, 1977/8

Aggregate payments (£m)	Amount held (£m)	MLR %	Value of benefit (£m)
$6310 \times \frac{5}{24}$	1315		92
$-2125 \times \frac{1}{8}$	-266	7.0	-19
4185	1049		73

[a] Repayments and detriments indicated by minus signs.

At this point we need to examine more carefully the assumptions about the timing of VAT payments and repayments and the sensitivity of the results to alternative assumptions. We assumed that payments were all made on the last day of the month following the end of the quarter. In fact a few payments will be made before that date and some will be late. In answer to a Parliamentary Question (*Hansard*, W.A., 4 June 1980, cols 735–6) Mr Peter Rees stated that 82.6 per cent of returns were received *after* the due date; but he gave no indication of the proportion of *tax* outstanding or how much was paid before the 'last' day.

More detailed information for earlier dates has been given by the Chancellor of the Exchequer, Sir Geoffrey Howe, in an answer to a question from Mr Joel Barnett (*Hansard*, W.A., 28 February 1980, cols 701–2). Sir Geoffrey indicated that VAT outstanding on unpaid returns and assessments at 31 October 1979 was about £1,750 million of which about £800 million became due only on 31 October. The remaining £950 million represented about 20 days' payments at the average rate during the fourth quarter of 1979 and the full £1,750 million about 36 days.

The tax outstanding a year earlier, at 31 October 1978, was about £580 million of which £335 million became due on 31 October. At the then current VAT rates of 8 and 12.5 per cent the remaining £245 million represented 10 days' payments and the full £580 million 23 days. Sir Geoffrey added that there were indications of a reduction in the average number of days that VAT payments were in arrears.

In his 1980 budget speech (*Hansard* vol 989, col 1469) the Chancellor said that 'There have been signs that some large companies have been delaying their VAT payments to the Exchequer.' He therefore proposed to raise the maximum penalty for late payment from the former £10 per day to one half of one per cent of the tax due (an annual rate of 182.5 per cent!). The Commissioners of Customs & Excise have the power to mitigate this penalty. Such a severe penalty must constitute a strong deterrent to late payments in the future.

As for repayments, in normal circumstances (e.g. where there is no change of address or of trading situation) the Customs & Excise take about two weeks to make a repayment after receiving the claim. Our assumption of one month for refunds to be received therefore implied an average period of two weeks for repayment traders to prepare and submit their claims. Evidence from Customs & Excise indicates that most repayment traders take considerably longer than that to submit so that our assumption understates the size of the 'loan' to Customs & Excise from repayment traders.

Table 8.2 'Loans' from and to Customs & Excise with different payment and repayment periods, 1977/8

Time taken in weeks for		Proportion of annual tax held		Amount held (£m)		Net loan (£m)	
Pay-ments	Repay-ments	Pay-ments	Repay-ments	Pay-ments	Repay-ments	Amount	Value at 7% interest
2	2	0.162	0.079	1022	168	854	60
6	6	0.244	0.156	1540	332	1205	84
2	6	0.162	0.156	1022	332	690	48
6	2	0.244	0.079	1540	168	1372	96
4	4	0.208	0.125	1315	266	1049	73

Table 8.2 analyses the value of the 'loans' from (and to) Customs & Excise on alternative assumptions about the time taken to make payments and repayments. It is clear the value of the net loan from Customs & Excise is quite sensitive to alternative assumptions about payment periods.

Any decision on what periods to assume for our more detailed analysis must contain an element of arbitrariness. We do not know the extent of late payments for the financial year 1977/8 nor do we know how much tax was paid before the deadline date. It is arguable whether or not *all* tax outstanding should be taken into account – some will represent irrecoverable tax from traders going bankrupt or 'disappearing' such as applies with all taxes irrespective of credit periods. The ministerial statements make it clear that the proportion of late payments has fluctuated fairly widely over time; in the future, because of stiffer penalties, late payments are likely to be substantially reduced. In so far as late payers are 'fined', this constitutes an offset to their loan advantage and a compensating gain to Customs & Excise. As for repayments, there is the additional consideration of how justifiable it is to speak of a 'loan' from the trader to Customs & Excise if the trader delays unduly the submission of his claim. He must clearly be allowed some time to prepare his claim, but delay beyond that date, whilst it effectively increases the credit from trader to Customs & Excise, cannot reasonably be regarded as an addition to mandatory compliance costs.

In the tables which follow, we shall continue to assume that payments and repayments each take a month to make, i.e. that payment traders pay on the last day of the month following the end of the quarter and that repayment traders submit claims two weeks after the end of the month, and Customs & Excise take two weeks to pay. It is recognised that this procedure is somewhat arbitrary, and, if anything, is likely to understate both the 'loan' from Customs & Excise to traders and the 'loan' from traders to Customs & Excise.

The Effect of the Commercial Credit Period

In the normal course of his business a trader will be allowed credit on his purchases and will allow credit on his sales. The amount of time given to him before he has to pay his bills results in a loan to the trader of the value of the goods for the time taken to pay. Similarly, if he sells goods for which he is not paid for some time, then he is making a loan to his customer.

The presence of VAT on top of the value of goods bought and sold means that this normal business practice provides extra loans from suppliers and that the trader makes higher loans to customers. The effect can best be shown by means of examples.

A trader who orders and receives goods to the value of £10,000 plus (at 8 per cent) £800 VAT but does not pay for them for 30 days is receiving a loan of £10,800 for that time. From that part of the debt which relates to VAT there is a benefit to the trader of 30 days' worth of interest on £800. At an annual rate of interest of 7.0 per cent the benefit would be $\frac{30}{365} \times 0.07 \times £800 = £4.60$.

With sales, the opposite occurs. Suppose a trader sells goods valued at £15,000 plus £1,200 VAT. If he is paid immediately there is no disbenefit. But if, as is more likely, he has to wait (say) 30 days for payment, then he is making an interest-free loan of £16,200. He would, of course, still be making the loan of £15,000 even if there were no VAT, but the extra 8 per cent is not insignificant.

The cost to him of this loan, as against making a cash sale, is calculated in a similar fashion to the benefit example above, viz. $\frac{30}{365} \times 0.07 \times £1,200 = £6.90$.

In the normal course of events the value of a trader's sales is more than that of his purchases, so input tax will be less than output tax; thus, even if the credit period for sales is the same as that for purchases, there will always be a slight credit loss.

The situation for the repayment trader is slightly different, and some interesting possibilities emerge. Suppose a trader, say a farmer, buys £1,000 of goods which are rated at 8 per cent and that all his output is zero rated; then input tax is deductible. If the farmer pays his bill immediately then he is making a loan of the VAT payment until he recovers it from Customs & Excise. If he does not pay his bill until after he has received the VAT repayment* then he has a loan of the VAT for the time between receiving the repayment and paying the bill. As indicated, Customs & Excise generally make repayments within 14 days of receiving a return. Thus, if the farmer bought the goods at the end of a month, and sent in his return immediately, but did not pay for the goods for a month, he would enjoy a loan of £80 for about two weeks. The possible benefits of this kind to a repayment trader may be a valuable offset to the cost of 'lending' money to Customs & Excise.

Thus, both payment and repayment traders have these types of benefit and disbenefit depending on their credit periods and how quickly they submit their returns.

Payments to Customs & Excise Combined with Effect of Commercial Credit Periods
The interaction of the commercial credit period and payments to (or from) Customs & Excise can be illustrated by examples. Table 8.3 shows a 17 week cycle of trading accounts for a payment trader who starts trading in week 1 of the cycle. The weekly input is assumed to be £700 of goods and weekly output £1,000. Inputs and outputs are all standard rated (8 per cent). Tax payments are made in the fourth week after the end of the quarter. Table 8.3 indicates three situations. The full statement relates to a trader receiving net commercial credit: he pays his bills after 2 weeks and the customers pay after one week. The two final columns show the situations where (1) there are no credit transactions – all sales and purchases are for cash; and (2) the trader is in an unfavourable credit situation with customers paying after two weeks and the trader after one week. The different effects on cash flow are clearly shown in the tables. In the no credit situation the trader has, on average, a 'loan' from Customs & Excise of £260 equal to a benefit of £18 per annum at 7.0 per cent interest. In the situation of favourable commercial credit the net 'loan' is £292 and the benefit £20 per annum. In the situation of unfavourable commercial credit the net 'loan' is reduced to £153 and the benefit to £11 per annum.

---

* This is quite legal: just as a trader is liable for tax on the sale of a good which has been invoiced but not paid for, a repayment trader can claim before having paid for a good he has received.

Table 8.3 Effect of VAT on cash flow of traders in different commercial credit situations

Period	Inputs			Outputs			Output tax – input tax	Total VAT held by traders in different credit situations[a]		
Situation at end of week number	Total value of inputs, excluding tax (£)	VAT paid on inputs (£)	Total cash paid out, excluding tax (£)	Total value of outputs, excluding tax (£)	Total cash received excluding tax (£)	VAT paid by customers (£)	Net VAT payable to C & E (£)	Situation (1) (£)	Situation (2) (£)	Situation (3) (£)
1	700	0	0	1000	0	0	24	0	24	0
2	1400	0	0	2000	1000	80	48	80	48	−56
3	2100	56	700	3000	2000	160	72	104	72	−32
4	2800	112	1400	4000	3000	240	96	128	96	−8
...										
11	7700	504	6300	11 000	10 000	800	264	296	264	160
12	8400	560	7000	12 000	11 000	880	288	320	288	184
...										
16	11 200	784	9800	16 000	15 000	1200	384	416	384	280
17[b]	11 900	840	10 500	17 000	16 000	1280	120	152	120	16

[a] (1) Trader pays suppliers after 2 weeks; customers pay trader after 1 week.
(2) No credit transactions. All goods paid for in cash as received.
(3) Trader pays suppliers after 1 week; customer pays trader after 2 weeks.
All columns except the last two relate directly to trader in credit situation (1).
[b] In all cases net tax due to Customs & Excise for the quarter is £288 paid in week 17. (VAT at 8 per cent on all inputs and outputs.)

The same procedure can be used to show more complicated patterns of sales and purchases and of credit periods. Similarly the procedure can be adopted to show the position of a repayment trader over a nine-week cycle.

Effect of Inflation

Whenever credit is being given, whether between Customs & Excise and trader, or as between traders, the value of the benefit is affected by the rate of inflation. The higher the rate of inflation the more the real value of interest free loans (p. 19). Thus, inflation adds an additional arbitrary element in the distribution of benefits and disbenefits. If the inflation rate has been fully anticipated it will be reflected in the current rate of interest used in assessing the value of the 'loans'. If it has not been fully anticipated the real value of the 'loans' will be understated. Whilst these points should be borne in mind no attempt has been made in the following analysis to complicate the picture further by calculations of the effect of unanticipated inflation.

Estimation of Credit Periods from NAS

The NAS questionnaire asked traders to give their total tax due, total tax deductible and their net payment, which would be negative in the case of a repayment trader (Q5). They were also asked for the proportions of purchases and sales invoices settled over a series of time periods (Q11):

Excluding bad debts, approximately what percentage of purchases and sales invoices are settled within each of the following periods after invoicing?

Invoices settled:	Percentage of Purchases Invoices		Percentage of Sales Invoices
Within 1 week		. . .	
Between 1 week and 1 month		. . .	
During the second month		. . .	
During the third month		. . .	
During the fourth month		. . .	
More than four months after invoicing		. . .	

From the proportions given it was possible to calculate an average credit period for sales and purchases, subject to the following assumptions: that traders were neither building up nor running down stocks and that the number of invoices was proportional to their value.

In normal times the first assumption is not likely to cause difficulty; if the number of cases is large the number of traders who are building up stocks is likely to be matched by those running them down. The second assumption, however, is more critical; it is possible that traders tend to leave their largest bills for as long as possible. If this is true for the majority of traders, then the weighting on the averaging procedure for the credit period would be incorrect. The question asked for number of invoices rather than value because it was thought this would make for easier estimation by the trader than assessing proportionate values. Analysis of the personal interview responses (FOL (P)), shows that two-thirds of those interviewed answered either by value or both. This response suggested that the assumption that the number of invoices could serve as proxy for their value was not unreasonable.

The average credit periods for sales and purchases were calculated by weighting the proportions given by the midpoint of the time period in which they occurred (Q11). Thus, if a trader had 50 per cent of his sales invoices settled within one week and the rest in more than a week but less than one month, his sales credit period would be:

$$0.5 \times 4 + 0.5 \times 19 = 11.5 \text{ days}$$

Where goods were paid for in cash (as with most retailing) the sales credit period was zero. Table 8.4 sets out the *net* times taken to pay (or be paid) based on NAS data but weighted to be more representative of the total trader population. The estimated average times taken to settle purchase invoices and to receive payments respectively classified by size and sector are given in Appendix J.

The estimated overall credit periods were 27 days for traders to pay suppliers and 24 days for them to be paid by their customers.

In Table 8.4 the positive figures indicate that, on average, traders in a particular group take longer to pay their bills than their customers take; conversely where the figures are negative. It is clear that the distribution of credit periods is by no means even and varies considerably between businesses of different sizes and sectors. Most noticeable (and expected) are the large positive figures in the retail sector resulting from the short average credit periods on sales. Similarly with the miscellaneous and public services sector, which contains many businesses receiving cash payments, such as hairdressers and social clubs. The primary sector consists predominantly of farmers, and it would appear that they are paid relatively quickly either by Marketing Board or at market.

Firms which grant more credit than they receive are those in the professional and scientific services sector, where the time taken to be paid is abnormally long (Appendix Table J2) and, to a less extent, manufacture and utilities, financial and business services, and transport and communication. In general the larger the firm the longer the credit period both for sales and purchases (Appendix J).

Table 8.4 Commercial credit periods, 1977/8: time taken to pay
minus time taken to be paid in days

Taxable turnover (£000 p.a.)	Primary	Manufacture and utilities	Construction	Transport and communication	Retail	Wholesale and dealers	Financial and business services	Professional and scientific services	Miscellaneous and public services	Overall
0– 9.9	+6	−14	−8	+1	+7	−13	−6	−9	1	−2
10– 19.9	+12	0	0	−11	+12	−2	−3	−9	+11	+5
20– 49.9	+11	−11	−8	−18	+14	0	−6	−19	+10	+5
50– 99.9	+11	−6	−9	−8^a	+16	3	−22	−25	+14	+6
100–999.9	+5	−9	−2	−7	+10	−8	−10	−17	+8	−1
1000 and over	−4^a	−2	+7	−3	+12	−6	−4	−18	+4	−1
Overall	+9	−8	−5	−8	+13	−5	−7	−14	+9	+3

^{a} Fewer than 10 respondents in cell.
Notes. Positive numbers imply favourable commercial credit periods; negative imply unfavourable.
There may be differences between the figures in this table and those obtained by subtracting the figure
in Appendix Table J2 from those in Table J1; the differences arise because of approximation to whole
numbers in the Appendix tables.

Differential Incidence of Cash Benefits

Whilst, as we have already outlined, the existence of benefit (disbenefit) depends
on credit periods for sales and purchases and how late or soon payments (claims)
are made to Customs & Excise, given the total tax revenue and the rate of
interest the most crucial factors are the sector and size of the business. Sector
largely determines whether a trader is in the payment or repayment category;
size of firm determines the absolute size of benefit or disbenefit.

Table 8.5 shows the size of the 'loan' from (or to) Customs & Excise for the
population of registered traders 1977/8, by size and sector (grossed up from the
sample data), on the assumptions that payments to Customs & Excise are made
on the last day of the month following the end of the quarterly period and
repayments are received at the end of the month following the month to which
they relate. No account is taken in this table of the effect of commercial credit
periods.

It will be noted that the size of the overall 'loan' in Table 8.5, £1,351 million,
is considerably higher than the figure of £1,049 million calculated from the
aggregate data in the Customs & Excise Annual Report for 1977/8 (see above
p. 77). The difference is partly because the responses to NAS from registered
traders tend, on average, to relate to a later period than the financial year of
Customs & Excise (p. 45) and the equivalent 'loan' figure for 1978/9, at £1,190
million, was higher than for 1977/8. The remaining difference must probably
be attributed to errors in sampling and grossing up; the estimate is particularly
sensitive to the omission or inclusion of some of the largest firms.

Table 8.5 Loans to traders from Customs & Excise, 1977/8 (£million)

Taxable turnover (£000 p.a.)	Primary	Manufacture and utilities	Construction	Transport and communication	Retail	Wholesale and dealers	Financial and business services	Professional and scientific services	Miscellaneous and public services	Overall
0– 9.9	−1.8	0.8	0.1	0.5	0.8	0.7	0.3	1.8	2.6	5.8
10– 19.9	−2.5	1.5	0.5	1.4	2.8	0.4	1.8	2.8	8.3	17.0
20– 49.9	−5.0	7.3	−1.8	1.6	8.7	1.6	4.2	4.4	15.1	36.1
50– 99.9	−4.0	11.3	1.2	2.0[a]	3.2	4.8	4.6	6.4	15.9	45.4
100–999.9	−1.6	79.8	6.2	9.5	27.1	22.2	16.3	21.8	−18.8	162.5
1000 and over	−52.9[a]	913.0	−28.1	−4.2	179.1	71.8	9.3	9.6	−13.3	1084.3
Overall	−67.9	1013.6	−21.9	10.7	221.7	101.4	36.5	46.8	9.8	1351.1

[a] Based on respondents with fewer than 10 cases.

The distribution of the 'loan' from (or to) Customs & Excise follows a fairly predictable pattern. The main peculiarity is the negative figure amongst the large traders in the miscellaneous and public services sector which result from the presence of some zero-rated local government authorities.

When the effect of commercial credit periods is added (Table 8.6) the size of the 'loan' increases for some traders and decreases for others. The negative 'loans' to the primary sector are much reduced as are the positive 'loans' to manufacture and utilities. There is a very big increase in the benefit to retail and to miscellaneous and public services, both of which benefit from cash sales. In the largest size band in miscellaneous and public services a substantial minus has been turned into a very large plus.

It will be noted that there is a big difference between the aggregate 'loan' from Customs & Excise in Table 8.5 and the aggregate figure in Table 8.6. Whilst some of this difference may be attributable to errors of sampling and grossing up, it is a divergence which we would expect and which arises from the effect of credit sales to the general public and non-registered traders.

It would be misleading to say that retail credit customers received a VAT benefit from delayed payment of bills – without VAT they could still delay and have less to pay – but credit sales to all non-registered traders including the general public do mean that the benefit to the registered trading community as a whole is reduced. If our figures are correct nearly one-quarter of the 'loan' from Customs & Excise is passed on to the final consumer or non-registered trader.

Table 8.6 Loans to traders from Customs & Excise after allowing
for commercial credit periods, 1977/8 (£million)

Taxable turnover (£000 p.a.)	Primary	Manufacture and utilities	Construction	Transport and communication	Retail	Wholesale and dealers	Financial and business services	Professional and scientific services	Miscellaneous and public services	
0– 9.9	− 1.5	0.4	0.1	0.1ᵃ	1.4	0.3ᵃ	0.6	0.9	2.0	
10– 19.9	− 1.5	0.4	− 0.1	− 0.1	4.3	− 0.4ᵃ	1.0	1.5	8.3	1
20– 49.9	− 3.1	1.7	− 1.6	0.3	13.6	0.3	2.2	1.8	15.1	3
50– 99.9	− 2.0	1.5	− 1.8	0.4ᵃ	11.5	1.7	1.2ᵃ	1.5	20.6	3.
100–999.9	0.4	20.4	1.8	2.4	16.6	− 5.1	1.9	7.7	− 5.7	4
1000 and over	− 0.3ᵃ	444.4	− 10.2	− 0.5	386.8	3.4	0.3	11.4ᵃ	74.7	91
Overall	− 8.0	468.8	− 11.9	2.6	434.2	0.2	7.2	24.8	114.7	103

ᵃ Based on cells with fewer than 10 respondents.

The value of the benefit or disbenefit arising from VAT payment/repayment conditions can be calculated by applying a rate of interest to the figures in Tables 8.5 and 8.6. As discussed above (p. 77) we use MLR, and the average MLR for the Government's financial year 1977/8 has been chosen; but this is likely to understate the effect to some extent because MLR was tending to rise and the VAT year of many of the traders responding to NAS will have ended after April 1978. Table 8.7 shows the value of the loan from Customs & Excise before allowing for the effect of commercial credit periods. The figures have been scaled down to bring them in line with the value of the loan as derived from aggregate data from the Customs & Excise Annual Report (see above p. 77). Table 8.8 gives the picture after allowing for commercial credit.

Supplementary data is given in Appendix J. Table J3 shows the average value of the loans to traders from Customs & Excise and Table J4 the average value of loans to traders after allowing for commercial credit periods. The figures in these tables have been scaled down as Tables 8.7 and 8.8. Average values of loans for size groups within sectors are only of limited meaning where a group may consist of both payment and repayment traders. Hence Tables J5 and J6 give the mean size of loans to payment and repayment traders respectively (NAS data).

Table 8.7 Value of loan to traders from Customs & Excise, 1977/8 (scaled data[a], £million)

Taxable turnover (£000 p.a.)	Primary	Manufacture and utilities	Construction	Transport and communication	Retail	Wholesale and dealers	Financial and business services	Professional and scientific services	Miscellaneous and public services	Overall[b]
0– 9.9	−0.1	0[d]	0	0	0	0	0	0.1	0.1	0.3
10– 19.9	−0.1	0.1	0	0.1	0.2	0	0.1	0.2	0.4	0.9
20– 49.9	−0.3	0.4	0.1	0.1	0.5	0.1	0.2	0.2	0.8	2.0
50– 99.9	−0.2	0.6	0.1	0.1[c]	0.2	0.3	0.3	0.4	0.9	2.5
100–999.9	−0.1	4.3	0.3	0.5	1.5	1.2	0.9	1.2	−1.0	8.8
1000 and over	−2.9[c]	49.6	−1.5	−0.2	9.7	3.9	0.5	0.5	−0.7	58.9
Overall[b]	−3.7	55.1	−1.2	0.6	12.0	5.5	2.0	2.5	0.5	73.4

[a] Figures derived by applying a rate of interest of 7.0 per cent (average MLR 1977/8) to the figures in Table 8.5 and scaling down to bring into line with aggregate value of loan as derived from aggregate published data.
[b] Totals do not always exactly sum because of rounding.
[c] Based on cells with fewer than ten cases.
[d] Zeros imply a positive or negative number less than 0.05.

Table 8.8 Value of loan to traders from Customs & Excise after allowing for effect of commercial credit periods (scaled down[a], £million)

Taxable turnover (£000 p.a.)	Primary	Manufacture and utilities	Construction	Transport and communication	Retail	Wholesale and dealers	Financial and business services	Professional and scientific services	Miscellaneous and public services	Overall[b]
0– 9.9	−0.1	0[d]	0	0[c]	0.1	0[c]	0	0.1	0.1	0.2
10– 19.9	−0.1	0	0	0	0.2	0	0.1	0.1	0.4	0.7
20– 49.9	−0.2	0.1	−0.1	0	0.7	0	0.1	0.1	0.8	1.7
50– 99.9	−0.1	0.1	−0.1	0[c]	0.6	0.1	0.1[c]	0.1	1.1	1.9
100–999.9	0	1.1	0.1	0.1	0.9	−0.3	0.1	0.4	−0.3	2.2
1000 and over	0[c]	24.2	−0.5	0	21.0	0.2	0	0.6[c]	4.0	49.4
Overall[b]	−0.4	25.5	−0.6	0.1	23.6	0	0.4	1.3	6.2	56.1

[a] Figures derived by applying a rate of interest of 7.0 per cent (average MLR 1977/8) to the figures in Table 8.6 and scaling down to bring into line with aggregate value of loan as derived from aggregate published data.
[b] Totals do not always exactly sum because of rounding.
[c] Based on cells with fewer than ten respondents.
[d] Zeros imply a positive or negative number of less than 0.05.

Perceptions of Cash Benefits

One question in NAS (Q29) listed a series of statements on possible benefits from VAT, with which respondents were asked to agree or disagree; where they considered that there was a benefit, they were asked to put a value on it, if possible. One such statement was: *Useful extra cash is collected during the VAT period.* Overall 21 per cent of respondents agreed with the statement and an analysis by size and sector is given in Table 8.9

Table 8.9 Percentage of NAS respondents who agree that useful extra cash is collected during the VAT period

Taxable turnover (£000 p.a.)	Primary	Manufacture and utilities	Construction	Transport and communication	Retail	Wholesale and dealers	Financial and business services	Professional and scientific services	Miscellaneous and public services	Overall
0– 9.9	28	24	22	8	17	20	33	35	18	24
10– 19.9	15	16	22	12	13	0	32	18	13	16
20– 49.9	14	12	23	17	16	25	26	22	21	18
50– 99.9	14	8	23	14	18	10	15	38	16	17
100–999.9	19	22	19	32	24	25	23	23	28	23
1000 and over	0	33	11	24	36	25	6	14	33	26
Overall	19	24	20	19	19	22	24	27	21	21

The NAS yielded 1,343 (48 per cent) who were clear net payment traders as against 1,047 (37 per cent) clearly net repayment traders. It would have been expected therefore that a considerably higher percentage would have perceived a cash benefit. It was indeed observable that cash benefits were perceived by repayment traders.

It has already been demonstrated (p. 80) that, in fact, by appropriate timing of payments for purchases and of claims to Customs & Excise repayment traders may indeed obtain a cash benefit. Also payment traders may lose their benefit through the operation of commercial credit periods. The more relevant figures may be, therefore, the numbers of traders in the sample who, after allowing for both VAT and commercial credit periods, emerge as net cash beneficiaries or the reverse. For the NAS these figures were 1,108 and 731 respectively.* Thus, at least 40 per cent of the sample received a cash benefit (on the basis of the assumptions that payment traders paid on the last day of the month following the end of the VAT quarter and repayment traders received repayment one

* These figures are less than the total sample mainly because of a relatively poor response to questions on commercial credit.

month after the end of the relevant month). Especially as we know that payments tend to be late (p. 77) if traders fully comprehended the situation at least 40 per cent should have been claiming a cash benefit.

Even allowing for the important fact (see Table J6) that the amount of loan (and correspondingly its value) is often very small, there are clearly many traders who do not appreciate the cash benefit of VAT. Some are what one accountant (ADV) called 'sales and purchase traders' – who think only of what they get for the product they sell and what they pay for their inputs. Others, perhaps, tend to put the tax on one side (perhaps in a current account) against the date of payment without making the money work for them. It is particularly surprising that, although the benefit was appreciated more by large firms than by small, the proportion of larger firms stating that they perceived the benefit appears to be much lower than those who receive it. Perhaps some were reluctant to acknowledge it. A relevant consideration here could be that the questionnaire was completed by a member of staff who failed to understand the point, although financial directors would have it very much in mind. In general the cash benefit was appreciated more by higher trained staff, in particular 28 per cent of qualified accountants, as opposed to 20 per cent of other staff or 19 per cent of sole proprietors or partners.

Conclusion
The effects of the cash benefit, as we have seen, have a significant effect in offsetting compliance costs for many firms, though disbenefits increase it for others. We examine this effect in detail in Chapter 10 after we have looked at the managerial benefits arising from VAT.

9 The Managerial Benefits of VAT

Introduction

Besides the cash flow benefit discussed in the previous chapter, certain managerial-type benefits may be expected from operating VAT, stemming basically from better record-keeping, which may constitute some offset to the compliance costs of the tax. One group of experts (Conservative Central Office 1977) wrote: 'The standard of the nation's book-keeping has undoubtedly improved in consequence of the tax'; whilst the Consultative Committee of Accountancy Bodies (1977) recorded a similar verdict: 'The demand for quarterly figures for VAT purposes has improved the quality of records maintained by many small businesses.'

Our task in this chapter is to see how far this claim was borne out by the responses to the NAS questionnaire and the views of accountants and other professional advisers (ADV) and what benefits this improved record-keeping was perceived to bring to businesses.

The Nature of the Benefits

Respondents to NAS (Q29) were asked to agree/disagree with each of seven statements of possible benefits to the firm and, where possible and appropriate, estimate the value of that benefit. In addition an open-ended question was included to cover 'Any other advantages', which respondents were also asked to describe.

The response to one of the statements, concerning useful extra cash, has already been discussed in Chapter 8. The other questions related to better-kept records of sales and purchases, more frequent claiming of discounts, saving money by doing own accounts, reduction of losses from bad debts and improved stock control.

Purchase and Sales Records

The two statements receiving the highest percentage agreement were those related to better-kept records: 32 per cent of respondents agreed that purchase records were better kept and 26 per cent that sales records were better kept. An analysis of the response by size and sector is given in Table 9.1.

As one would expect, the percentage agreement falls fairly consistently with size as measured by taxable turnover. For firms up to £100,000 over 40 per cent of respondents considered that their purchase records were better kept since VAT and 30 per cent or more that their sales records were better kept. For firms over £1 million these figures were down to about 10 per cent. That any of the big firms should be in this category is perhaps surprising; the explanation could be that VAT stimulated a change in accounting system (notably a move to computers) which resulted in better kept records; and/or it could be a result of the particular measure of size used. The business sectors with the biggest improve-

Table 9.1 Percentage of NAS respondents with better-kept records since VAT

Taxable turnover (£000 p.a.)	Primary	Manufacture and utilities	Construction	Transport and communication	Retail	Wholesale and dealers	Financial and business services	Professional and scientific services	Miscellaneous and public services	Overall
0– 9.9	57 / 48	26 / 16	44 / 33	57 / 50	26 / 18	21 / 21	14 / 14	32 / 26	43 / 36	42 / 34
10– 99.9	57 / 39	26 / 30	44 / 32	57 / 30	26 / 27	21 / 20	14 / 23	32 / 28	43 / 29	42 / 30
100–999.9	50 / 30	33 / 17	40 / 21	40 / 30	39 / 23	29 / 12	30 / 16	33 / 15	37 / 36	39 / 22
1000 and over	14[a] / 14	7 / 7	8 / 8	5 / 5	7 / 7	11 / 9	11 / 6	14 / 14	26 / 21	10 / 9
Overall	49 / 40	19 / 17	34 / 27	33 / 28	34 / 24	16 / 13	22 / 17	30 / 25	36 / 30	32 / 26

Note: Top left-hand: percentage agreeing with statement: '*My purchase records are better kept since VAT came in.*'
Bottom right-hand: percentage agreeing with statement: '*My sales records are better kept since VAT came in.*'
[a] Less than 10 respondents in cell.

ments in record-keeping are those we associated particularly with small firms, viz. primary, retail and miscellaneous and public services (see Appendix E5).

An interesting phenomenon is the way in which almost invariably the proportion of traders claiming better-kept purchase records is the same or higher than that claiming better-kept sales records. It bears out the view (Conservative Central Office 1977) that 'The trader finds much greater difficulty in keeping track of his input tax (on purchases) rather than in computing his liability on sales. The quarterly chore of listing inputs, based on a multitude of invoices in differing shapes and sizes – and not always correctly completed – is far greater than a simple totalling of (largely homogeneous) invoices issued or daily cash takings.' Thus, to comply with the VAT requirements, many traders would need to improve their input records.

Of the 851 NAS respondents who agreed that their purchases records had improved, 665 gave no value for the benefit and 122 gave a value of zero. Only 64 (7.5 per cent) gave a positive value for the benefit. The values given ranged from a nominal £1 up to £2,000; the average of the positive values was £128 in 1977/8. 680 respondents agreed that their sales records had improved. 542 gave no value, 86 a value of zero, whilst for 52 (7.5 per cent) the positive values ranged from £3 to £5,000. The average for the positive values came to £222. It is not clear just what the figures mean. It is very difficult to know how to value such an improvement and, indeed, the figures may attempt to take account of savings resulting from improved record-keeping, like saving an accountant's fees by doing one's own accounts. Most respondents who agreed with the statement did not attempt to value the benefit; and it is doubtful if much weight should be put on the value estimates.

Savings by Doing Own Accounts
It is all very nice to have better records. The real question is whether the records can be and are used to give increased managerial control and effect savings. One saving which, in principle, it should be possible to measure is a reduction in accountants' fees if a trader does more of his own accounts, and it was the statement on such saving which gained the next largest degree of support. Twenty-five per cent of respondents agreed with the statement. The responses, analysed by size and sector, are set out in Table 9.2.

The pattern is very much as expected, with the number of traders claiming a benefit diminishing as size of firm increased, the sectors with an above-average agreement being those in which small firms predominated (although, in this instance, primary and retail, whilst above the average, yield top places to construction and transport and communication). As was to be expected, in financial and business services and in professional and scientific services the scope for improvement of this kind proved more limited.

Twenty-two per cent (147), of the 654 respondents who agreed that they saved money on accountant's fees, gave a positive value for the benefit. It is not surprising that a higher proportion, compared to purchases and sales records,

Table 9.2 Percentage of NAS respondents who claim to save money by doing more of their own accounts

Taxable turnover (£000 p.a.)	Primary	Manufacture and utilities	Construction	Transport and communication	Retail	Wholesale and dealers	Financial and business services	Professional and scientific services	Miscellaneous and public services	Overall
0– 9.9	38	26	39	36	33	40	23	34	41	36
10– 99.9	25	34	37	41	28	31	24	18	29	29
100–999.9	15	21	24	24	22	15	4	4	18	18
1000 and over	0	9	9	5	10	12	6	0	10	9
Overall	27	20	32	30	26	19	17	18	27	25

should attempt to value the benefit; because there should be a direct and measurable reduction in the money paid out to accountants. Nevertheless 23 still gave a value of zero, and the rest of the values ranged from £1 to £2,000 with a mean of £150.

As with improvements in purchase and sales records it is, on the face of things, surprising that so many of the larger firms claimed a benefit from saving accountant's fees. It might have been expected that all the larger firms would employ their own fully qualified accounting staff. The explanation lies mainly in the particular measure of size used. Table 9.3 compares the average number of employees of firms agreeing and disagreeing with the statement 'I save money by doing more of my own accounts'; firms over £20,000 taxable turnover which agreed with the statement were smaller, as measured by average number of employees, than those which disagreed; for firms over £100,000 turnover the employment differences were very marked.

Table 9.3 Average number of employees of traders agreeing/disagreeing with statement: 'I save money by doing more of my own accounts.'

	Taxable turnover (£000 p.a.)					
	0–9.9	10–19.9	20–49.9	50–99.9	100–999.9	1000 and over
Agree	1.8	2.7	4.2	7.0	20.1	153.6
Disagree	1.9	2.5	4.9	7.2	51.7	665.4
Overall	1.9	2.5	4.7	7.1	46.0	616.5

Other Managerial Benefits

Improved stock control was claimed by 8 per cent of respondents, with the percentage response in each size band more or less the same up to £500,000 turnover but dropping to 2–3 per cent in firms above that size. Retail (12 per cent), miscellaneous and public services (11 per cent) and transport and communications (10 per cent) were the 'above average' sectors.

Six per cent of respondents agreed that they claimed discounts more frequently. The size dispersion showed no clear pattern except for a marked dropping away in the size bands above £500,000. The sector which stood out from the rest was primary where 13 per cent of firms (all below £500,000) agreed that they claimed more frequent discounts.

A reduction in losses from bad debts was claimed by 5 per cent of respondents overall, with again a somewhat uneven size distribution for firms up to £500,000 and a marked falling off thereafter. The professional and scientific services sector contained the largest proportion of agreements at 9 per cent.

Finally 4 per cent of respondents (94 by number) claimed other advantages. One, frequently mentioned, was to the effect that retailers were not subject to losses on stock (as with purchase tax). Other advantages had more to do with records and included: 'I now have a complete accounting system' and 'I now have a permanent record of all transactions'.

Views of Professional Advisers

Accountants interviewed were asked if the standard of book-keeping of their clients had improved as a result of VAT and, if so, whether this improvement had led to a reduction in their fee for preparing annual accounts (ADV, Q5a and b). The majority of accountants took the view that there had been improvement but most qualified their judgement with expressions such as 'initially', 'a little', 'for some firms', 'for small traders'. Several held that there had been no improvement. A majority took the view that there would be no reduction in their fee for other accounting work. Reconciliation has to be made with the VAT column and sometimes the client's efforts to do his own VAT work resulted in a mass of errors. A minority of accountants said there might be some reduction in their fee because, for example, less time might be spent in hunting for missing invoices.

The two firms specialising in a VAT service to small traders (p. 44) held that the information they supplied to clients constituted a useful management tool and that their clients benefited by reductions in the fees accountants charged them for annual accounting.

There would, indeed, appear to be three strands in a rather complex pattern. First, the existence of VAT puts up the annual accounting bills: there is extra work to be done in checking VAT transactions and making reconciliations. However, this effect may be offset or even more than offset by well-kept records (as a result of VAT). If, however, the VAT work is badly done, the result is still more work in the annual accounting in trying to effect reconciliations.

Table 9.4 Percentages of NAS respondents claiming particular number of benefits (n = 2,232)

No. of benefits	Taxable turnover (£ooo p.a.)							
	0 to 9.9	10 to 19.9	20 to 49.9	50 to 99.9	100 to 499.9	500 to 999.9	1000 and over	Total
0	4.8	7.1	8.1	6.5	8.2	2.7	10.1	47.5
1	2.7	3.2	3.6	3.2	3.7	1.2	4.2	21.8
2	2.3	2.6	3.3	2.1	2.5	0.6	1.0	14.4
3	1.6	1.7	1.7	1.3	1.0	0.1	0.6	8.0
4	1.2	1.0	1.1	0.7	0.6	0.0	0.1	4.7
More than 4	0.6	0.7	0.8	0.7	0.6	0.0	0.2	3.6
Overall[a]	8.4	9.2	10.5	8.0	8.4	1.9	6.1	52.5

[a] Column totals exclude those claiming no benefits.

Multiple Benefits

The above analysis, on a benefit-by-benefit basis, leaves one aspect unclear. How widely are the benefits spread amongst traders? The picture described above could represent a situation in which a smaller number of firms claimed a larger number of benefits each or a larger number of firms each claimed only one or two benefits.

Overall 47 per cent of the 2,232 respondents who replied to all the agree/ disagree statements on benefits said that they received no benefit at all from VAT. Twenty-two per cent recognised only one benefit. Eight per cent of firms perceived four or more benefits. The overall figures on number of benefits claimed, classified by size of firm, are given in Table 9.4. For purposes of this analysis the 'extra cash' benefit is also included. (A full analysis of the number of benefits claimed for each sector, classified by size group, is given in Appendix K.)

Perceptions of Benefit

It must be stressed that the NAS data gives us only stated *perceptions* of benefit which (as clearly demonstrated in the case of 'extra cash') are not necessarily the same as actual benefits. Benefits may be realised but not perceived; perceived but not realised; perceived and realised but not stated.

For those firms where VAT returns were completed by the proprietor, a partner or a director (in a company of less than three directors) information was collected in NAS (Q21) on whether the person completing the VAT returns had had any formal book-keeping training. Responses were in three categories: those who were qualified accountants; those with some book-keeping training; those with no book-keeping training, classified as 'self-taught'.

Table 9.5 shows that the more the training the less the benefit perceived. This may seem surprising; but, apart from the cash benefit, the more the training of

Table 9.5 Number of benefits perceived by proprietors, partners and directors of small businesses with different training (percentages)

| No. of benefits | Type of training | | | |
	Qualified accountant	Other book-keeping training	Self-taught	Overall
0	53	49	40	43
1	25	22	21	21
2	4	13	17	16
3	11	6	11	10
4	2	4	7	6
Over 4	4	5	4	5
Overall*a*	47	51	60	57

a Column totals exclude those claiming no benefits.
Columns do not always exactly total because of rounding.

the proprietor, the more we should expect the benefits of a managerial nature to have been achieved *before* VAT came in. Qualified accountants could be expected to keep better records than book-keepers who would keep better records than the self-taught; the introduction of VAT therefore could be expected to make most impact on those whose books were initially the worst and least impact on the qualified accountants.

Perhaps, in any case, perception depends less on training than on attitude – a subject we explore in Chapter 11.

Conclusions

Including the cash flow benefit, just over half the NAS respondents perceived at least one benefit from VAT. Whilst, as was shown in Chapter 8, the cash flow benefit markedly favours the large firms, the other benefits favour small firms. The managerial-type benefits stem from better record-keeping but depend on the use made of the records to increase control of the business, improve decision-making and effect economies in various directions. The NAS provides evidence of such improvement, but on a somewhat limited scale. Many small firms saw no benefits at all from VAT, not even a cash flow benefit. A major difficulty with the managerial-type benefits is that, whilst not unimportant, they are, of their nature, elusive and almost impossible to value realistically.

Introduction

In this chapter we seek to examine the effect on compliance costs of taking into account the benefits which traders receive as a result of VAT, in particular the cash flow benefits. (Such 'benefits' may of course be negative, as in the case of some repayment traders, with the result that net compliance costs are increased.) We analyse the outcome by business sector and by size and within each size/sector grouping, to obtain figures of *net* compliance costs for 1977/8. We then consider administrative costs and recognise that VAT administration may bring some social benefits. More significantly, however, the reduction of compliance costs by the value of the net 'loan' to traders from Customs & Excise has a counterpart in the cost of the 'loan' to the Exchequer (p. 17). That being so, the reduction in compliance costs of VAT as a result of the cash flow benefit makes little difference to total operating costs, but it does affect their distribution as between compliance and exchequer costs, and also affects the distribution of operating costs between firms in different sectors and of different sizes. Operating costs for 1977/8 are then calculated on the basis of some alternative assumptions.

Net Compliance Costs

The benefits of VAT to registered traders, as we saw in Chapters 8 and 9, were of two kinds: cash benefits and managerial benefits. Whilst reasonable values can be attributed to the first, assessing the extent and value of the second is much more difficult. There is a strong case for not attempting to put a monetary value on them, but for regarding them as unmeasurable benefits on the credit side of the VAT balance sheet, just as psychic costs are unmeasurable costs on the debit side.

A small minority of those respondents to NAS who perceived managerial benefits from VAT did put a monetary value on them, even if its meaing is unclear. There are, therefore, some data which could be used to attempt to put a figure on managerial benefits, whereas we have not even imperfect data with which to attempt to value psychic costs. But the number of valuations of managerial benefits is too few to enable us to look at their effect on a size within sector basis, as we can with the cash benefits. So in this section we shall treat managerial benefits as unmeasurable and modify our compliance cost figures only by the cash benefits. However, in the final section, in which we consider total operating costs of VAT on several different assumptions, we shall attempt a valuation of the managerial benefits, in aggregate and by size groups, so that we can see what difference their inclusion might make.

Table 10.1 shows the net compliance costs 1977/8 in aggregate and for various size ranges, derived by substracting the estimates of net cash benefit in each size range (Chapter 8) from the estimates of (gross) compliance costs (Chapter 5). Table 10.2 gives net compliance costs by sector. The figures from NAS data have been scaled down to be consistent with the estimate of cash benefit derived from aggregate (Customs & Excise) data. Two considerations should be recalled. First, nearly one-quarter of the benefit of the Customs & Excise 'loan' finds its way to the general public (through retail sales on credit) and to traders not registered for VAT, and is lost to registered traders. Second, the figure of the total net credit from Customs & Excise rests on the assumptions that payment traders pay at the end of the month following their VAT quarter and repayment traders receive their repayment a month after the month to which the repayment relates. In so far as these assumptions are incorrect, for example if payment is delayed (even by the device of posting the cheque to Customs & Excise on the last day of the month with a second-class stamp) the 'loan' from Customs & Excise is larger and the credit to traders bigger (p. 77).

Table 10.1 Net compliance costs: compliance cost minus cash benefits, 1977/8, analysed by size of firm (£ million)

Size range (£000 p.a.)	0– 9.9	10– 19.9	20– 49.9	50– 99.9	100– 999.9	1000 and over	Total
Compliance cost (NAS)	29.0	49.7	88.5	69.3	105.6	49.9	392.0
Value of cash benefit	0.2	0.7	1.7	1.9	2.2	49.4	56.1
Net compliance cost	28.8	49.0	86.8	67.4	103.4	0.5	335.9

Lines do not always exactly sum to totals because of rounding.

Table 10.2 Net compliance costs: compliance cost minus cash benefit, 1977/8, analysed by sector (£ million)

	Primary	Manufacture and utilities	Construction	Transport and communication	Retail	Wholesale and dealers	Financial and business services	Professional and scientific services	Miscellaneous and public services	Total
Compliance cost (NAS)	20.6	48.4	52.0	17.4	81.4	37.7	20.9	24.0	89.7	392.0
Value of cash benefit	−0.4	25.5	−0.6	0.1	23.6	0	0.4	1.3	6.2	56.1
Net compliance cost	21.0	22.9	52.6	17.3	57.8	37.7	20.5	22.7	83.5	335.9

Lines do not always exactly sum to totals because of rounding.

The effect of the cash benefit over size ranges is very small until the highest range is reached – then it is dramatic, virtually eliminating compliance costs, in aggregate, for that range (Table 10.1) despite the many repayment traders who suffer a cash flow disadvantage. The main sectors benefiting are manufacture and utilities, retail and, to a lesser extent, miscellaneous and public services (Table 10.2).

Table 10.3 Mean net compliance costs by sector and taxable turnover, 1977/8 (£)

Taxable turnover (£000 p.a.)	Primary	Manufacture and utilities	Construction	Transport and communication	Retail	Wholesale and dealers	Financial and business services	Professional and scientific services	Miscellaneous and public services	Weighted overall mean
0– 9.9	56	117	107	80[a]	163	72[a]	177	121	119	106
10– 19.9	88	270	196	199	146	213[a]	297	260	195	182
20– 49.9	98	275	280	233	229	352	340	466	303	254
50– 99.9	147	289	597	301[a]	307	309	650[a]	351	575	381
100–999.9	380	485	509	747	507	628	421	1093	594	557
1000 and over	1433[a]	−1038	2331	1943	−7654	854	3777	474[a]	492	15
Weighted overall mean	116	189	293	307	207	430	466	358	318	264

[a] Fewer than 10 respondents in cell.

Table 10.4 Net compliance costs as a percentage of taxable turnover, 1977/8 (means)

Taxable turnover (£000 p.a.)	Primary	Manufacture and utilities	Construction	Transport and communication	Retail	Wholesale and dealers	Financial and business services	Professional and scientific services	Miscellaneous and public services	Weighted overall mean
0– 9.9	1.04	1.80	1.74	1.05[a]	1.85	1.84[a]	3.65	1.77	1.83	1.69
10– 19.9	0.71	1.71	1.28	1.06	0.69	1.62[a]	2.17	1.53	1.21	1.13
20– 49.9	0.27	0.86	0.79	0.70	0.65	0.51	0.99	0.52	0.90	0.68
50– 99.9	0.21	0.47	0.56	0.21[a]	0.42	0.53	0.67[a]	0.58	0.78	0.50
100–999.9	0.21	0.15	0.24	0.26	0.23	0.18	0.19	0.30	0.28	0.22
1000 and over	0.02[a]	0.01	0.06	0.03	0.01	0.02	0.09	0.04[a]	0.04	0.03
Weighted overall mean	0.60	0.78	1.10	0.76	0.68	0.65	1.86	1.17	1.05	0.88

[a] Fewer than 10 respondents in cell.

Table 10.3 fills in some of the details by a size within sector analysis; it is directly comparable with the compliance cost figures in Table 5.3. Table 10.4 shows mean net compliance costs as a percentage of taxable turnover and is directly comparable with Table 5.4. The changes to compliance costs from allowing for cash benefits in conjunction with commercial credit periods are heavily concentrated on the larger firms in the three sectors already mentioned. In each the regressiveness of the burden of compliance is accentuated. Overall the average of compliance cost as a percentage of taxable turnover, which was forty times as high for firms in the smallest size range compared with those in the largest for (gross) compliance cost, rises to over fifty times as high with net compliance cost.

Reassessment of Administrative Costs

In Chapters 4 and 5 when we made provisional calculations of tax operating costs and their distribution we confined our attention to (gross) compliance costs and the official figures of administrative costs. We now have to consider, first, whether there are benefits to offset against administrative costs, as there have been with compliance costs; second, whether there are any additional costs to the Exchequer, particularly arising from our treatment of benefits under compliance costs.

There is one benefit of a social nature, extending beyond VAT alone, which may arise from its administration. In examining a trader's books VAT officers may collect information which, when co-ordinated with that collected by the Inland Revenue for income tax purposes, may serve to reveal (and thus ultimately to reduce) income tax evasion. The so-called 'Leeds experiment' is an exercise in such co-operation between Customs & Excise and Inland Revenue (*Hansard*, W.A., 17 February 1977, col 300). At the time of writing no report on the Leeds experiment has been published and any extension of the experiment awaits the outcome of a review of enforcement powers which the Government has decided on. But Sir Lawrence Airey, in evidence before the Public Accounts Committee, 4 June 1980, stated that the experiment had provided 'useful, although limited, information on evasion'. Any such benefit is unlikely to be measurable, although it could be an important offset to the social costs of VAT (p. 17).

An issue which does affect measurable costs is the treatment of the net 'loan' from Customs & Excise, which, in so far as it benefits traders (as distinct from non-registered persons) acts as an offset to compliance costs. In Chapter 2 (pp. 17–21) we argued that such a loan to the general community means an increase in the Public Sector Borrowing Requirement (PSBR) on which interest has to be paid. It is arguable whether the cost of this 'loan' should be termed an administrative cost (p. 21) but it should certainly be regarded as an additional cost to the Exchequer. Thus, when we take account of cash benefits, compliance costs are reduced but Exchequer costs are raised. We seem to be in a zero-sum game in which the total of operating costs remains the same but with a different balance between total Exchequer and compliance costs.

Whilst this is the essence of the situation, there are some important qualifications. First, as we have seen, nearly one-quarter of the net loan from Customs & Excise does not benefit registered traders but rather finds its way to non-registered traders and the general public. This sum represents an Exchequer cost without any corresponding compliance benefit to registered traders.

Second, because the government can normally borrow on more favourable terms than individual traders (because of its higher creditworthiness) it can be argued that the rate of interest used to measure the annual cost of the loan to the government should be lower than that used to measure the benefit of the loan to traders. The general validity of this argument is not open to doubt; where a trader is in permanent overdraft the credit benefit to him will certainly be more than the cost to the government. But not all traders will be in permanent overdraft and we should remember that the free credit which payment traders get from VAT flows in an irregular pattern which is not of a trader's own choosing, thereby having less value to him. In our calculations of traders' benefit (or detriment in the case of repayment traders) we have used the MLR rather than the overdraft rate (at least 2 per cent above MLR) and therefore it is not unreasonable, and is also very convenient, to use the same rate to assess the cost to the government, i.e. the additional Exchequer costs. In any case the calculations can readily be re-worked to accommodate a lower interest rate if this is considered the better procedure.

A final comment should be made about the managerial benefits of VAT to traders. In so far as they provide an offset to compliance costs, unlike the cash flow benefit, there is no corresponding increase in Exchequer costs; such benefits, therefore, constitute an overall reduction in operating costs.

Table 10.5 Exchequer costs: administrative costs plus net loan from Customs & Excise, 1977/8 (analysed by size of firm)

Size range (£000 p.a.)	0– 9.9	10– 19.9	20– 49.9	50– 99.9	100– 999.9	1000 and over	Total
Administrative costs (£m)	13.3	13.7	20.5	11.6	17.0	9.4	85.5
Net value of loan (£m)	0.3	0.9	2.0	2.5	8.8	58.9	73.4
Total Exchequer costs (£m)	13.6	14.6	22.5	14.1	25.8	68.3	158.9

The rows do not sum exactly because of rounding.

Tables 10.5 and 10.6 show the revised composition, by size and sector, of Exchequer costs, allowing for the effects of the 'loan' from Customs & Excise which is allocated across the sectors and size ranges in proportions derived from Table 8.5 (but scaled down to be consistent with the total from the aggregate data in the

Table 10.6 Exchequer costs: administrative costs plus net loan from Customs & Excise, 1977/8 (analysed by sector)

	Primary	Manufacture and utilities	Construction	Transport and communication	Retail	Wholesale and dealers	Financial and business services	Professional and scientific services	Miscellaneous and public services	Total
Administrative costs (£m)	9.3	11.1	11.0	3.7	18.2	8.4	3.0	3.7	17.4	85.5
Net value of loan (£m)	−3.7	55.1	−1.2	0.6	12.0	5.5	2.0	2.5	0.5	73.4
Total Exchequer costs (£m)	5.6	66.2	9.8	4.3	30.2	13.9	5.0	6.2	17.9	158.9

The rows do not sum exactly because of rounding.

Customs & Excise report). It was considered appropriate to allocate the whole of the Customs & Excise 'loan' to registered traders even though some of it is lost to them (to non-registered firms and the general public) through the operations of commercial credit. First and foremost the 'loan' consists of 'delayed' tax payment by registered traders only, to Customs & Excise; from the Revenue side the liability is placed wholly on registered traders. Secondly, in so far as registered traders 'lose' this benefit to their non-registered customers, it is through the operation of commercial credit which in turn is part of the complex network of payments in exchange for goods and services, and the firm may get compensating benefits: for example, credit terms to retail customers may be associated with a somewhat higher price level, or be used as a means of increasing profit margins by promoting higher turnover. The allocation of administrative costs other than the 'loan' is the same as in Chapter 5 (pp. 53–5).

As was to be expected, the really big differences in total Exchequer costs occur in relation to the big firms which are the main beneficiaries of the 'loan'. Amongst the sectors by far the biggest change, absolutely and proportionately, is in manufacture and utilities. There is a substantial increase in Exchequer costs in retail and a very marked reduction in primary industry because of the net 'loan' to Customs & Excise.

Net Operating Costs

We are now in a position to combine the figures of net compliance costs (Tables 10.1 and 10.2) and Exchequer costs into a new figure of tax operating costs (hereafter called net operating costs). In Table 10.7(a) and (b) we compare net compliance cost and Exchequer cost analysed by size and sector and in Table 10.8(a) and (b) we compare net operating cost with tax revenue also by size and sector.

Table 10.7 Comparison of net compliance and Exchequer costs, 1977/8

	Exchequer cost (EC) (£m)	Net compliance cost (NCC) (£m)	Ratio $\dfrac{NCC}{EC}$
(a) By sector			
Primary	5.6	21.0	3.8
Manufacture and utilities	66.2	22.9	0.3
Construction	9.8	52.6	5.4
Transport and communication	4.3	17.3	4.0
Retail	30.2	57.8	1.9
Wholesale and dealers	13.9	37.7	2.7
Financial and business services	5.0	20.5	4.1
Professional and scientific services	6.2	22.7	3.7
Miscellaneous and public services	17.9	83.5	4.7
Total	158.9	335.9	2.1
(b) By range of taxable turnover (£000 p.a.)			
0– 9.9	13.6	28.8	2.1
10– 19.9	14.6	49.0	3.4
20– 49.9	22.5	86.8	3.9
50– 99.9	14.1	67.4	4.8
100–999.9	25.8	103.4	4.0
1000 and over	68.3	0.5	*
Total	158.9	335.9	2.1

The columns do not sum exactly because of rounding.
* Less than 0.05.

Table 10.7 can be directly compared with Table 5.8 which shows the relationships between compliance and administrative costs before modification. The effect of the 'loan' from Customs & Excise in reducing compliance costs and increasing Exchequer costs has the effect of evening out the ratios of compliance costs to Exchequer costs. Particularly notable is the big reduction in the ratio for manufacture and utilities and for the largest firms overall.

Table 10.8 (which can be directly compared with Table 5.9) shows net operating costs as a percentage of net tax collected. The overall operating costs are some £17 million larger because the cost of the 'loan' from Customs & Excise is more than the value to traders as a result of the 'loss' to the general public and non-registered traders; but the readjustments between sectors and across the size ranges are not startling. The effect on the main feature of the table – the disproportionate operating costs to tax revenue amongst the medium and smaller firms – remains as pronounced as ever, indeed is very slightly accentuated. The compliance costs of the smaller firms are virtually unchanged when allowance is made for the 'loans' to and from Customs & Excise, whilst Exchequer costs are somewhat higher.

Table 10.8 Comparison of net operating costs with tax revenue, 1977/8

	No. of registered traders (000s)	Net tax paid[a] (£m)	Net operating costs (£m)	Net operating cost as % of net tax collected (where positive)
(a) By sector				
Primary	179.9	−217	27	n.a.[b]
Manufacture and utilities	120.8	2268	89	3.9
Construction	179.2	−252	62	n.a.[b]
Transport and communication	56.4	206	22	10.7
Retail	280.2	338	88	26.0
Wholesale and dealers	87.7	976	52	5.3
Financial and business services	44.0	228	26	11.4
Professional and scientific services	63.2	194	29	15.0
Miscellaneous and public services	262.9	507	101	19.9
Total	1274.2	4235[c]	495	11.7
(b) By range of taxable turnover (£000 p.a.)				
0– 9.9	270.7	15	42	280.0
10– 19.9	269.5	55	64	116.4
20– 49.9	340.9	120	109	90.8
50– 99.9	177.7	140	82	58.6
100–999.9	185.4	600	129	21.5
1000 and over	30.0	3305	69	2.1
Total	1274.2	4235[c]	495	11.7

The columns do not sum exactly due to rounding.
[a] Source: HM Customs & Excise, *69th Annual Report*.
[b] n.a. Not applicable.
[c] Includes £48m allocated by size but not by sector.

In the judgement of the research team, the various cost figures in Tables 10.7 and 10.8 represent the most realistic statement of the situation in 1977/8. But it is necessary to re-state some of the limitations of the data.

Because 1977/8 was a year of little change in VAT and because the survey was restricted to traders who had been registered for at least a year, the data from NAS would tend to under-estimate annual compliance costs. Conversely, because of the known higher response from larger firms, which might well also apply within a size/sector group, the grossed-up sample might tend to overstate compliance costs.

On the benefit side, the tendency of firms to pay their VAT late would mean some over-estimation of net compliance costs; but this would have a counterpart in an under-estimate of the value of the 'loan' component in Exchequer costs and so would have little effect on total operating costs.

In these calculations, psychic costs, social costs, social benefits and managerial-type benefits have not been treated as measurable.

It is useful, however, to offer some alternative estimates of net compliance and net operating costs which could be taken as representing lower limits to these costs based on alternative principles. Two such estimations have been made. Alternative A reduces both compliance costs and operating costs by a valuation of managerial benefits. Alternative B is based on the charges of one of the professional firms offering a special VAT service which resulted in the lower aggregate compliance costs (Firm B, see pp. 44–5). These were applied to firms up to £100,000 taxable turnover. The 'other costs' associated with that service (distributed over the size ranges in proportion to the number of registered traders) were then added. The net cash benefit, as previously calculated, was then deducted to give the alternative estimate of net compliance cost.

There remains the question of how the managerial benefits have been calculated. As already discussed (p. 91) of those who recognised a managerial-type benefit, only a small minority put a value on it. Moreover, where a respondent recognised and valued a number of benefits it is not clear whether or not the valuations are mutually exclusive. For example, if a valuation of £100 per annum is put on the improvement in purchase records and a valuation of £30 is put on more frequently claimed discounts, it is unclear whether the former includes the latter.

However, it was decided that it would be more useful to overstate rather than understate the value of the benefits so that the compliance cost figure resulting could more effectively serve as a lower limit. The valuations were therefore treated as mutually exclusive.

Similarly, of the various procedures open for weighting the value of benefits amongst the total of registered traders, that one which maximised the benefit was followed. This method took the mean of each benefit* from those valuing the benefit in each size group within a sector (including those – the majority – who valued it at zero); multiplied this figure by the proportion in each group who recognised the benefit; and then grossed-up by the number of registered traders in that size/sector group for each benefit, summing the benefits to give an overall figure. (This method, in effect, involved valuing the benefits of those who did not place a value on them at the same figure as comparable traders who did.) The aggregate value of the benefits by this method was £51 million.

An alternative, at the other extreme, would have been to have followed a similar procedure but have valued at zero the benefits of those who recognised but did not value a benefit. This method would have given an overall value of £29 million. A third and intermediate method would have been to omit from the reckoning altogether, for each benefit, those who recognised the benefit but put no value

---

* The cash benefit was omitted (because this was separately estimated to give a larger figure than would have emerged from the traders' estimations) as was the 'other advantages' where the number of benefits valued was very small and only aggregated to a total of £0.3 million.

Table 10.9 Alternative measures of the cost of operating VAT – alternative A

Range of taxable turnover (£000 p.a.) (1)	Net compliance cost (£m) (2)	Value of managerial benefits (£m) (3)	Net CC (alternative A) (£m) (4) = (2) − (3)	Exchequer cost (£m) (5)	Operating cost (alternative A) (£m) (6) = (4) + (5)
0– 9.9	28.8	9.8	19.0	13.6	32.6
10– 19.9	49.0	7.2	41.8	14.6	56.4
20– 49.9	86.8	11.7	75.1	22.5	97.6
50– 99.9	67.4	6.5	60.9	14.1	75.0
100–999.9	103.4	15.6	87.8	25.8	113.6
1000 and over	0.5	0.5	0	68.3	68.3
Total	335.9	51.3	284.6	158.9	444

Table 10.10 Alternative of the cost of operating VAT – alternative B

Range of taxable turnover (£000 p.a.) (1)	CC using outside advisers[a] (£m) (2)	Value of cash benefit (£m) (3)	Value of managerial benefit (£m) (4)	Net CC (alternative B) (£m) (5) = (2) − (3) − (4)	Exchequer cost (£m) (6)	Operating cost (alternative B) (£m) (7) = (5) + (6)
0– 9.9	40.4	0.2	9.8	30.4	13.6	44.0
10– 19.9	40.2	0.7	7.2	32.3	14.6	46.9
20– 49.9	50.9	1.7	11.7	37.5	22.5	60.0
50– 99.9	40.3	1.9	6.5	31.9	14.1	46.0
100–999.9	105.6	2.2	15.6	87.8	25.8	113.6
1000 and over	49.9	49.4	0.5	0	68.3	68.3
Total	327.3	56.1	51.3	219.9	158.9	379

[a] Figures derived from Appendix F3 for firms with a taxable turnover less than £100,000 p.a. Special problem and other costs were allocated on a per capita basis.

Table 10.11 Cost of operating VAT compared with tax revenue

Range of taxable turnover (£000 p.a.)	Number of registered traders (000s)	Net tax paid (£m)	Costs of operating VAT			Cost of operating VAT as percentage of net tax		
			Net operating cost (Table 10.8) (£m)	Alternative A (Table 10.9) (£m)	Alternative B (Table 10.10) (£m)	Net operating cost (%)	Alternative A (%)	Alternative B (%)
0– 9.9	270.7	15	42	32.6	44.0	280.0	217.3	293.3
10– 19.9	269.5	55	64	56.4	46.9	116.4	102.6	85.3
20– 49.9	340.9	120	109	97.6	60.0	90.8	81.3	50.0
50– 99.9	177.7	140	82	75.0	46.0	58.6	53.6	32.9
100–999.9	185.4	600	129	113.6	113.6	21.5	18.9	18.9
1000 and over	30.0	3305	69	68.3	68.3	2.1	2.1	2.1
Overall	1 274.2	4235	495	444	379	11.7	10.5	9.0

on it (i.e. counting them neither as receiving a benefit with an average value, the first method, nor as receiving a value with a zero benefit, the second method). The aggregate value of the benefits by this method would have been £33 million.

Tables 10.9 and 10.10 show the effects of those calculations. Including managerial benefits (on the maximum value basis) brings net compliance costs down from £336 million to £285 million; using outside advisers as well, reduces net compliance costs to £220 million. In both cases the reductions are con- centrated on the small and medium-sized firms.

Finally Table 10.11 compares the three estimates of operating costs with each other and with tax revenue. Alternative B brings down the total operating costs significantly, but overall they still represent 9.0 per cent of tax revenue. Moreover, although alternatives A and B reduce costs primarily amongst the medium and smaller firms, the general picture, of costs disproportionate to revenue for those firms, remains unchanged.

Introduction

As indicated in Chapters 5 and 6, many factors contribute to a trader's VAT compliance cost, such as the nature of the business, its size, the type of book-keeping system, and so on. We cannot measure directly every single factor, especially since pertinent questions have had to be omitted from NAS to reduce the length of the questionnaire. But traders' attitudes, which we consider in this chapter, may serve as a proxy for many such factors and several of the case studies (Chapter 13) strongly suggest the importance of attitude.

In this chapter we first attempt to construct an attitude scale based on response to a series of statements in NAS (Q25). We then relate attitudes, as measured by the scale, to compliance costs, benefits perceived, and difficulties encountered. In the final section we analyse, as best we may, the free comments on VAT made by respondents to NAS.

Likert Attitude Scale

A Likert attitude scale (Oppenheim 1979) is an attempt to produce a single measure which sums up attitudes to a particular phenomenon. The scale is based on responses to a wide range of statements which have been expressed as unambiguously as possible.

The scale used here to sum up attitudes to VAT is based on responses to eight statements about VAT in NAS (Q25) which could be arranged as four matched pairs* (Table 11.1). (Fourteen statements had been tested in the pilot survey

Table 11.1 Matched pairs of statements on VAT

Pro-VAT	Anti-VAT
VAT is a simple method of collecting tax (1)	As it stands, VAT is unreasonably complicated (5)
I do not mind doing VAT work (4)	Pressure of VAT work means that other aspects of the business suffer (2)
Keeping VAT accounts helps to control purchases and sales efficiently (6)	Considering how much VAT I pay, I spend too much time on VAT accounts (8)
VAT works satisfactorily for all concerned (7)	Most other taxes work more efficiently than VAT (3)

The figures in brackets give the order in which the statements appear on NAS.

* This arrangement enabled inconsistencies in answers to be more easily detected. Strong negative correlation coefficients between the pairs suggest the consistency of the response. Tests on the scale, using factor analysis and reliability measures, supported its robustness.

and the eight chosen for NAS were those which generated the most consistent replies.)

Respondents were asked to indicate whether they 'agreed', 'strongly agreed', 'disagreed', 'strongly disagreed', or were 'uncertain' whether they agreed or disagreed. Agreement or disagreement received a score of one, while strong agreement or disagreement received a score of 2. The 'indifferent' responses of those who neither agreed nor disagreed were accorded a zero score. Pro-VAT responses were scored positively, anti-VAT responses were scored negatively, so that when the scores on the individual statements were added together they fell within the range − 16 (every response very anti-VAT) to + 16 (every response very pro-VAT).

Table 11.2 shows few large deviations from the overall mean of − 2 (meaning slightly anti-VAT), and generally the scores are consistent within sector but show differences between sectors. The main exception is the retail sector which, from a notably unfavourable attitude amongst the smaller and medium-sized firms, shows a marked rise in score for firms above £1 million. This change in attitude doubtless owes much to the large cash benefit gained by larger firms.

The sector most well disposed to VAT was manufacture and utilities. The relatively low compliance costs of the larger firms in this sector, because they generally trade in bulk with other registered traders at a single VAT rate and the substantial cash benefit many receive, may well explain their attitude.

Table 11.2 Mean attitude score by size and sector

Taxable turnover (£000 p.a.)	Primary	Manufacture and utilities	Construction	Transport and communication	Retail	Wholesale and dealers	Financial and business services	Professional and scientific services	Miscellaneous and public services	Overall
0– 9.9	−1	−2	−3	0	−3	0	−1	−3	−2	−2
10– 19.9	−2	−2	−4	−3	−3	−2	−2	−4	−3	−3
20– 49.9	−2	−1	−3	−2	−4	−3	−4	−2	−3	−3
50– 99.9	−1	0	−3	+1	−4	−3	0	−2	−2	−2
100–999.9	−1	0	−2	−1	−3	−2	−3	−3	−2	−2
1000 and over	−1	0	−2	−4	0	−1	−3	−3	−2	−2
Overall	−1	0	−3	−2	−3	−2	−2	−3	−2	−2

Note: The mid-point is zero. The scale range is from − 16 to + 16.

The primary sector also appears to be relatively well disposed towards VAT. We have seen evidence (Chapter 5) that compliance costs are lowest in this sector. The fact that most farmers are eligible for repayments of VAT may also influence their attitudes favourably to some extent.

The degree to which most sectors show an anti-VAT attitude is by and large predictable; the sectors where the strongest views are expressed are (not un-expectedly) construction, retail (except the largest firms), and (perhaps more surprising) professional and scientific services. Retailers often deal in large volumes of low-priced goods, often in more than one tax category and the high anti-VAT score comes as no surprise. The construction industry tends to suffer from difficulties with liability borderlines (see Chapter 7) and the problems caused are doubtless reflected in traders' attitudes. Some respondents in professional services had experienced difficulties with partial exemption which are likely to have increased their dissatisfaction with VAT.

One oddity which deserves some comment is the highly anti-VAT attitude of the largest transport firms. The complexities associated with exporting (in which they are heavily engaged) could account for their anti-VAT attitudes.

There was a slight tendency for attitudes to be more favourable as the size of firm increased. This tendency would have been much more clear cut had it not been for the marked anti-VAT attitude of the largest transport firms.

An overall score on the scale which is near the central 'indifference' point may arise because most respondents do not feel strongly either way or because many respondents hold extreme views which cancel out. Although there were many more respondents in the very anti-VAT category than very pro-VAT it is clear that the vast majority of respondents did not take an extreme view and the overall picture of slight antagonism to VAT reflects a typical view (see Figure 11.1).

To be put in perspective this finding needs to be given a comparative dimension. It is unreasonable to expect people to like a tax and what one would like to do

Table 11.3 Responses to '*Most Other Taxes Work More Efficiently Than VAT*'

By sector	Mean of responses	Preference	By size: taxable turnover (£000 p.a.)	Mean of responses	Preference
Primary	− 0.02	Others	0– 9.9	− 0.24	Others
Manufacture and utilities	0.25	VAT	10– 19.9	− 0.14	Others
Construction	− 0.20	Others	20– 49.9	− 0.17	Others
Transport and communication	0.05	VAT	50– 99.9	− 0.05	Others
Retail	− 0.17	Others	100–499.9	− 0.02	Others
Wholesale and dealers	− 0.03	Others	500–999.9	0.25	VAT
Financial and business services	0.15	VAT	1000 and over	0.12	VAT
Professional and scientific services	− 0.08	Others	Overall	− 0.06	Others
Miscellaneous and public services	− 0.21	Others			
Overall	− 0.06	Others			

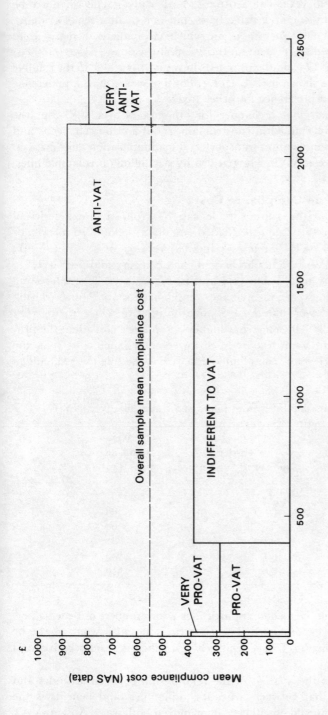

Figure 11.1 *Compliance costs related to attitudes to VAT and the number of respondents with those attitudes.*

is to compare attitudes to VAT with attitudes to other taxes. This could not be done within NAS on any comprehensive basis, but one small piece of evidence is available. One of the statements (3) on which respondents were asked to express their agreement/disagreement on the five-point scale was '*Most other taxes work more efficiently than VAT*' and the responses may give some clue to the relative attitude. The results are shown in Table 11.3. Positive scores show a preference for VAT and negative a preference for other taxes.

Overall there is a marginal preference for other taxes over VAT but the preference is much more marked in construction, retail and miscellaneous and public services whilst manufacture, transport and communication and financial and business services prefer VAT. The pattern by size follows predictable lines.

Attitudes in Relation to Compliance Costs
The scores derived from the attitude scale can be grouped into a series of categories. The range of the scale was divided equally as follows: 16 to 11 very pro-VAT; 10 to 5 pro-VAT; +4 to −4 indifferent; −5 to −10 anti-VAT; −11 to −16 very anti-VAT. The numbers in each category and their average compliance costs are given in Table 11.4 and in Figure 11.1. It is interesting that whilst, as one would expect, the average compliance costs of those favouring VAT was substantially lower than those opposed to it, at the extremes the very pro-VAT traders actually had somewhat higher compliance costs than the pro-VAT, and the very anti-VAT traders have lower compliance costs than the anti-VAT. Clearly the level of compliance cost is not the sole determinant of attitude.

Table 11.4 Relationship between attitudes and compliance cost (NAS)

Attitude to VAT	Traders Number	Per cent	Average compliance cost (£)
Very pro	14	0.6	391
Pro	371	15.9	288
Indifferent	1098	47.0	397
Anti	634	27.1	881
Very anti	221	9.5	799
Overall	2338	100	549

Figure 11.2 and Table 11.5 compare attitudes with numbers of benefits perceived and difficulties experienced. The pattern is broadly what might be expected. Those favouring VAT have relatively few difficulties and perceive most benefits and vice versa.

What is unclear from the analysis of the relationship between attitudes and compliance costs and that between attitudes, difficulties, and benefits is the direction of causality. It could go either way or indeed both ways. An anti-VAT

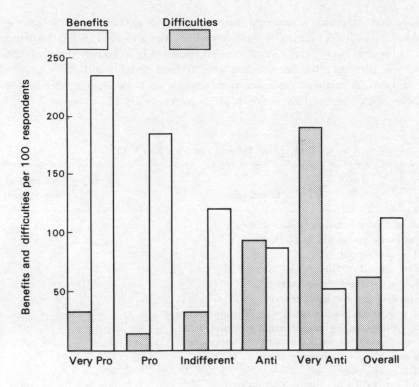

Figure 11.2   Attitudes to VAT of NAS respondents related to difficulties experienced and benefits perceived

Table 11.5 Comparison of attitudes with difficulties and benefits

Attitude to VAT	No. of difficulties experienced (expressed per 100 respondents)	No. of benefits experienced (expressed per 100 respondents)
Very pro	33 (18)	236 (14)
Pro	13 (411)	186 (334)
Indifferent	32 (1224)	119 (1009)
Anti	93 (711)	87 (614)
Very anti	189 (256)	51 (226)
Overall	61 (2620)	114 (2197)

The number of respondents is in brackets.

attitude may help to generate high compliance costs and high compliance costs reinforce an anti-VAT attitude. Similarly difficulties and benefits affect attitudes and attitudes affect difficulties and the perception of benefits. Furthermore difficulties will directly influence compliance costs and benefits will affect net compliance costs. A further analysis of the relationship between attitudes and the variables considered in this section is given in Appendix L.

Table 11.6a Critical comments on VAT

Comment	Number of respondents
Consumes too much time and/or money	175
Resent being an unpaid tax collector	113
VAT is too complicated	79
General critical comment (e.g. 'Abolish it!')	76
Prefer a return to purchase tax	68
Official booklets and literature criticised	59
VAT is an unnecessarily costly way of raising revenue	58
Payment between registered traders is pointless	50
Too much work involved compared to respondent's VAT payment	48
Cash flow has been adversely affected	44
VAT is too cumbersome	39
Customs & Excise have excessive powers	30
VAT officers criticised	28
Old VAT return form criticised	27
Problems with bad debts	24
VAT is bureaucratic madness	20
Zero rating and exemption criticised	17
Construction industry borderline problems	14
Competition from small unregistered firms is unfair	12
VAT is crippling small businesses	11
Secondhand schemes criticised	11
Rules and rates change too often	10
General borderline problems	9
Partial exemption criticised	8
Import and export paperwork criticised	8
Difficult or uneconomic to get VAT invoices on purchases	6
Rebates delayed	6
Retail schemes criticised	5
Group registration problems criticised	5
Higher rate criticised	5
Other critical	31
Total	1096

NAS Respondents Comments on VAT

At the end of NAS (Q34) respondents were invited to make general comments on the VAT system. Not all such comments reflect a particular *attitude* to VAT, but they can all conveniently be considered at this point. 1539 respondents offered 1733 such comments, some respondents making more than one point. The majority (1096) of these comments were critical of the VAT system (see Table 11.6a); 224 were favourable to the tax (Table 11.6b); and the remainder (413) were neutral comments on particular aspects of the tax, or suggestions for improvement of the system (Table 11.6c). There is, inevitably, an element of subjectivity in the grouping of such diverse remarks and also some element of overlap between categories (e.g. criticism of the higher rate appears as a critical comment whilst the plea for a single rate is classed as a general comment). Whilst the number of comments on a particular topic can often be rightly taken as an indication of the strength of opinion on that subject, some caveats must be made. Some topics which might otherwise have figured more prominently in the comments were the subject of special questions, like common difficulties (Q23b) special problems (Q24b) or advantages (Q29). Also comments were specifically invited on the VAT officer's visit (28d). Finally, the inclusion of a question on claim (Q33) on the same page of the questionnaire as the invitation to make a general comment may have encouraged rather more people to suggest that they should be paid to collect VAT. Finally, it should be recalled that, in general, respondents are more likely to comment if they are critical of a tax than if they are satisfied with it – and, indeed, it is the very nature of taxation that we tend to criticise the beast! To quote the aphorism of Edmund Burke – 'To tax and to please, no more than to love and to be wise, is not given to men.'

Table 11.6b Favourable comments on VAT

Comment	Number of respondents
Generally favourable comment (e.g. 'straightforward')	143
Record-keeping improved	27
VAT officers helpful	15
Zero rating a good idea	12
Cash flow improved	10
Prefer VAT to purchase tax	9
VAT helps to reduce evasion	4
Other favourable comments	4
Total	224

Table 11.6c Other comments

Comment	Number of respondents
Would prefer a single rate VAT	123
Traders should be paid for VAT work done	61
VAT should replace direct taxation	42
VAT should be modified into a retail sales tax	41
The minimum registration limit should be increased	20
Agricultural supplies should be zero-rated	19
Accounting should be done annually	16
VAT should be altered into a tax on turnover	14
Customs should provide more assistance (e.g. by supplying record-keeping books)	12
There should be a switch from invoice basis to payments basis	9
The minimum registration limit should be reduced	9
VAT officers need more book-keeping training	8
Direct taxation should replace VAT	8
More use should be made of higher rate(s)	7
Other	24
Total	413

Critical Comments

Many respondents felt strongly that, as one put it: 'VAT contravenes at least one of Adam Smith's maxims of taxation – that there should be economy of collection.' 'In my opinion,' the respondent said, 'the VAT system falls very short of this principle. Its operation is both time consuming and costly, not only for the organisations or persons paying but also for the Customs & Excise officers collecting.' Strong resentment was expressed at the accounting requirements imposed on the traders, e.g. 'The system depends on slave labour', 'Governments should not force anyone to do civil servants' work for no remuneration', 'We describe ourselves as *merchants* but in reality we are *unpaid tax collectors*!'. There was also considerable anxiety about the complexity of VAT regulations, e.g. 'It is unnecessarily complicated for many types of business', 'It is slowly growing more cumbersome as a gradually increasing amount of amendments are made.' Many more respondents compared VAT unfavourably with purchase tax (63) than the reverse (9), adding such comments as: 'I think VAT is a very complex and complicated system – the old purchase tax system was much superior in every way', 'Purchase tax was more effective, less cumbersome, more easily administered, less capable of being evaded and should replace VAT as soon as possible', 'Purchase tax must have been much easier and much less costly to administer', 'the irony is that there is no chance of going back to previous methods – the word that is used I think is "progress".'

Many respondents were bothered by the fact that: 'An enormous amount of work is done by traders and industry in handing money backwards and forwards to no purpose whatsoever.' Some added comments such as: 'It seems undesirable that wholesalers such as ourselves need to get involved in playing "pass the parcel" with other registered traders.' 'It all seems to be a rather pointless exercise as all our customers are in a position to claim back all the VAT collected by us from them, and similarly we can claim back all the VAT charged to us by our suppliers.' In several cases the point was made that: 'The amount of work involved in VAT accounting when equated against the tax which I end up paying is totally ridiculous'; 'The amount of work involved for the amount of tax collected is both ludicrous and unjust.'

Traders whose outputs were zero-rated or exempt from VAT were especially dissatisfied with the system, e.g.:

My business, *insurance and investment of funds*, is exempt from VAT, however, there are peripheral activities which bring us within the scope of the VAT system. Since 1973 up to June 1978 we have recovered £2,176 from Customs & Excise on a turnover of over £1,000 million.

As a *retail chemist* we have to pay VAT on suppliers' invoices, but as NHS drugs are zero-rated we have to finance the Customs & Excise for a month for the VAT payable to suppliers. It ought to be possible to zero rate the supply of prescription only medicines to us.

As *fruit importers* we consider the system of paying VAT on imports, keeping records and claiming back all inputs to be needless extra work, not only for ourselves but for the people we trade with in the same business. Presumably we are all paying VAT and claiming back VAT to produce a nil result.

There were once again a number of criticisms of official VAT literature, such as:

VAT is basically a simple method made complicated by the continual issue of revised booklets which at first I could not understand and now do not bother to read.

Information given in VAT notices is both vague and badly worded.

The literature is unnecessarily complicated and in many cases is irrelevant to the people it is sent out to.

Cash flow difficulties were mentioned by several respondents:

The system where VAT is due on invoice rather than on receipt of payment is hard on a small business where payment can stretch as long as four months or longer.

The present system encourages big companies to delay paying for purchases although claiming rebate for these as inputs, thereby obtaining substantial loans at the expense of small companies and the Government.

Most businesses either give or receive interest free loans on account of VAT. This encouragement to some and discouragement to others is quite regardless of their value to the economy.

A number of respondents were worried that: 'VAT officials have too much power', 'Although I have found the Customs & Excise officers usually helpful, it is *very* worrying that in some circumstances they have greater powers than the police.' Another trader described the system as: 'Bureaucratic, petty-Hitler breeding, and overadministered'.

Favourable Comments

In contrast, some respondents found VAT: 'Quite easy to cope with and not very time consuming', 'Simplicity itself in operation', 'Additional book-keeping for VAT is negligible.' Typical comments were that: 'Being computerised, the main problem with VAT was setting up the system. Now that it is running there are very few problems.' 'Installation of systems to record VAT are expensive, but once integrated into the system, VAT becomes a minor part of book-keeping.'

Some traders commented specifically on the managerial benefits obtained, e.g.:

> The VAT system has made us keep better and clearer records of our purchases and sales and as far as it affects my business the extra work involved in filling in the quarterly return forms and keeping records is worthwhile for that reason.

A very few respondents mentioned cash flow benefits, e.g. 'We probably make a small profit out of VAT as a result of the cash flow advantage due to debtors paying promptly' . . . but again this benefit did not appear to be widely recognised (see Chapter 8).

Other Comments

There was a strong desire for the reinstatement of the single positive rate (which has since taken place): 'A single rate of VAT instead of the existing 8 per cent and 12.5 per cent would be much simpler', was a typical comment, and several respondents also suggested the abolition of zero rating, e.g. 'Place a 10 per cent VAT rate on all goods, food, etc. included.' Such comments were frequently coupled with an appeal for reduction or abolition of direct taxes:

> If it were used to replace all other taxes regardless of rate needed it would ensure that everyone from crook to prime minister paid tax. Nobody would moan about tax as the tax content of any purchase is never remarked on, but income tax is.

> I wouldn't mind doing VAT if it had replaced income tax, but to have another top heavy highly paid Civil Service overhead is ridiculous.

Many readers suggested that they deserved some payment for VAT work, e.g.

> I think it would be some compensation for time spent on this work if a flat rate tax allowance were introduced.

> If recompense were made for time spent doing VAT, I would be more prepared to keep on top of the job and up to date with developments.

Another frequent suggestion was that:

> VAT should be replaced by a flat rate sales tax at the retail point of sale only.

Work carried out for a registered trader should be zero-rated to save work on both sides.

There was evidently considerable disquiet over the fact that: 'for all registered businesses, VAT is a sterile, circular tax'; 'The present system is a sheer farce only of benefit to the paper industry.'

Other suggestions included increasing the minimum turnover for registration (though some respondents wanted *all* traders to be registered down to the smallest); zero rating of supplies to farmers having all zero-rated outputs; and a possible option for annual accounting.

12 Advice on VAT

Introduction

How well traders cope with the compliance work arising from VAT, how much compliance cost they incur and how they perceive the benefits of VAT partly depends on the advice they receive. In this chapter we examine the sources of advice and the perceived usefulness of these sources, we seek to throw some light on which sources are most helpful and we include an analysis of the readability and comprehensibility of the VAT official booklets.

Sources of Advice

The NAS questionnaire (Q27) listed eight sources of advice (including an 'other' category) and asked respondents if they had used them and how helpful, or otherwise, they had found them. Table 12.1 gives the response to the first part of this question. Most respondents used a number of sources (three on average). Four sources of advice have been more widely used than the rest and our more detailed analysis will concentrate on them. The order of frequency in which the first five sources were used was common to almost all business sectors. The exceptions were construction, where marginally more respondents used the visiting VAT officers than used the official booklets and the primary, retail and miscellaneous and public services sectors where accountants were used more frequently than the local VAT office.

Table 12.1 Sources of advice on VAT

Source of advice	Respondents who had used the source	
	Number	Percentage
Official VAT booklets	2136	76.3
Visiting VAT officer	1982	70.8
Local VAT office	1332	47.6
Accountant	1293	46.2
Other tax guide books and journals	501	17.9
Trade association	240	8.6
VAT headquarters	189	6.8
Other sources	108	3.9

In the analysis which follows we look first at the three official sources of advice which head the list: the VAT booklets, the visiting VAT officer and the local VAT office; and then, more briefly, examine the unofficial sources. The 'others' category covered a wide variety of sources, including courses at local colleges, other businesses, and consultants associated with a particular industry.

Official Sources

Perhaps the outstanding feature about the use of official sources to emerge from Table 12.2 is that primary industry makes least use of all three sources – booklets, officers' visits and local office. Next in line for lowest use of all three is retail. Thereafter the differences in use are not very pronounced. Manufacture and utilities make the most use of the VAT booklets; construction, and transport and communication make the most use of the visiting officer; construction also makes marginally more use of the local VAT office.

Table 12.2 Respondents in each business sector who have used official sources and found them helpful (percentages)

Sector	VAT booklets		Visiting officer		Local office	
	Respondents who have used	Users finding helpful	Respondents who have used	Users finding helpful	Respondents who have used	Users finding helpful
Primary	61	62	58	77	26	72
Manufacture and utilities	87	72	74	85	55	86
Construction	78	65	80	86	59	80
Transport and communication	83	60	80	82	52	83
Retail	72	61	69	79	43	78
Wholesale and dealers	82	67	76	84	58	83
Financial and business services	79	65	75	79	58	77
Professional and scientific services	85	63	69	81	53	74
Miscellaneous and public services	77	60	70	82	50	83
All	76	64	71	82	48	80

Assessed by helpfulness the VAT booklets are bottom of the list for every trade sector; there is little to choose between the perceived helpfulness of the visiting officer and the local office. As between sectors, perhaps the figure to stand out most was the *relatively* high assessment of helpfulness to be given to the VAT booklets by the manufacture and utilities sector – distinctly above every other sector on the booklets, but still low compared with the ratings of the VAT officers and the VAT office.

Considerably more light is shed on the picture by the analysis of respondents by size range in Table 12.3. The proportion of respondents who have used the

Table 12.3 Respondents in each size range who have used official sources
and found them helpful (percentages)

Taxable turnover ($£000$ p.a.)	VAT booklets		Visiting officer		Local office	
	Respondents who have used	Users finding helpful	Respondents who have used	Users finding helpful	Respondents who have used	Users finding helpful
0– 9.9	63	59	63	87	34	84
10– 19.9	68	66	66	85	35	84
20– 49.9	68	61	63	83	36	80
50– 99.9	73	64	60	87	46	87
100–999.9	80	65	69	87	52	85
1000 and over	93	79	83	89	71	87
All	72	66	65	86	44	85

Note: Some traders did not indicate their taxable turnover band; they are excluded from this table but included in the analysis by business sector (Table 12.2).

VAT booklets rises steadily with size and the largest firms get the most help from the booklets. A similar pattern of increasing use with size applies to the local office, though here there is little difference across the size ranges in the perceptions of the helpfulness of the VAT office. With the visiting VAT officer the progression with size is not quite so clear cut but the largest firms used the VAT officer more as a source of help and more of them found him more helpful than the medium and small firms.

The differing pattern according to size partly explains the differences by sector. Primary industry has the largest concentration of small firms (see Appendix E5), and that is the sector which makes strikingly least use of the official sources. Conversely manufacture and utilities, which makes the most use of the VAT booklets and above-average use of the other two official sources, has the highest concentration of large firms. On the face of things retail appears to contradict the pattern; next to the primary sector retailers make least use of all the official sources, yet, as measured by taxable turnover, the sector does not stand out as predominantly weighted by small firms. The explanation lies in the measure of size, which imparts an increasing upward bias the nearer the stage of production to the final consumer (p. 48); at the retail stage this bias is at a maximum. If employment is used as a measure, retailing shares with the primary sector the characteristic of having by far the highest concentration of small firms (Appendix G2). The construction sector appears to be something of an exception to the finding that small firms make least use of the official sources. Forty-seven per cent of the firms in the sector have a taxable turnover of under $£20,000$ and 65 per cent of under $£50,000$ against figures for the NAS as a whole of 35 per cent and 57 per cent; yet the sector shows an above average use of the VAT booklets and is amongst the top users of the visiting officer and the highest user of the VAT office. The higher usage of VAT booklets may be explained by the existence of two booklets (numbers 708 and 715) addressed exclusively to the construction industry. The more frequent reference to the VAT officer and the VAT office may be a product of the need for advice because of the borderline problems in the industry (Chapter 7).

A relationship can also be traced between the use and usefulness of particular sources and the education and training of sole proprietors and partners in small firms filling in their own VAT returns. The professional and scientific services sector is notable for small firms, 63 per cent having a taxable turnover of less than £50,000, but the proportion of the firms in that sector who had used the VAT booklets was well above average whilst the proportion of users finding it helpful was about average. However, 30 per cent of the sole proprietors, partners or directors of small firms who fill in their own VAT returns in the professional and scientific services sector are qualified accountants, as against only 1 per cent in the primary sector. In general over three-quarters of respondents with account-ing qualifications who were sole proprietors etc., and filled in their own VAT returns found the booklets useful, as compared with less than half of those who had had no accounting or book-keeping training.

Apart from the more specialist book-keeping training, we would also expect there to be a relationship between the general education of sole proprietors etc. filling in their own VAT returns and the use they made of, and the help obtained from, the VAT booklets. Such a relationship is clearly revealed in Table 12.4. The longer the period of full-time education, the more use had been made of VAT

Table 12.4 Relationship between education of proprietors, partners and directors of small firms and their use of VAT booklets

NAS respondents	Age in years at end of full-time education			
	15 and under	16–18	19–21	22 and over
Percentage using VAT booklets (n)	73 (375)	82 (453)	83 (77)	87 (72)
Percentage of users who found them:				
Very helpful	8 } 62	6 } 66	10 } 67	4 } 69
Helpful	54	60	57	65
Unhelpful	7 } 14	8 } 14	12 } 15	11 } 15
Very unhelpful	7	6	3	4
Neither helpful nor unhelpful	24	20	18	15
	100	100	100	100

booklets, and the more they were found to be helpful.

As a final comment on this section it should be recalled that 'Understanding VAT instructions' emerged as the NAS respondents' most common difficulty (Chapter 7, p. 67).

Readability and Comprehensibility of Official VAT Literature
The general picture to emerge from the NAS data was that although the VAT
booklets had been widely used, proprietors of small firms and the least well
educated got least help from them. Overall 5 per cent of NAS respondents who
had at some time used the VAT booklets put them in the extreme category of
'Very unhelpful' (a much higher proportion than respondents gave for the
visiting VAT officer or the local office). About a quarter of the accountants
interviewed (ADV) in response to general questions about the administration of
VAT (Q8) or how it might be simplified (Q17) were critical of the booklets,
whilst some 10 per cent of the interviewees (FOL(P)) volunteered adverse
comment on them. To quote the strong view expressed by one accountant: 'You
read the VAT booklet three times and your mind boggles at what they are trying
to get at.'

In the light of these views and comments it was decided to conduct a readability
and comprehensibility analysis* of some of the official VAT literature. Whether
a guide or explanation is comprehensible depends on many considerations such
as size of print, number and presentation of headings as well as matters of style,
syntax and semantics. But an essential prerequisite of comprehensibility is readability: before any written communication can be understood it must be read.
One way of testing whether a piece of literature is easy to read is to employ
reading measures which offer an objective assessment of readability using formulae
incorporating the length of sentences, number of syllables in the words and so
on. Amongst the most widely researched and respected of these measures are
the Flesch (1948), Fry (1968) and Smog (McLaughlin 1969) indices. Smog stands
for 'simple measure of gobbledegook'. The formulae provide a 'reading age' i.e.
what the average child of that age could be expected to be able to read. Reading
ages are put in perspective if it is recalled that two million adults in the United
Kingdom are illiterate, when literacy is defined as a reading age of nine (Clyne
1973). (The number whose reading age is below the UNESCO level of literacy,
thirteen years, is unknown.) Another useful point of reference is the reading age
of national newspapers – the major source of reading material for the mass of
the general public. On the basis of the Fry measure it has been calculated that,
as one might expect, *The Times* is the most difficult, with a reading age of 16.9,
The Guardian scores 15.5, *Daily Mirror* 12.8 and *Sun* 12.3.†

Table 12.5 shows how some of the VAT literature scores on the basis of the
three indices. It gives the reading ages for the treatment of the General Explanation of VAT and the VAT Account from the *General Guide* (No. 700) comparing
the old (September 1975) which would have been familiar to our respondents,
with the new (October 1979) introduced since NAS but well before the interviews

---

* This section was completed with the help and advice of Dr Alan Lewis of the Centre for Fiscal
Studies, University of Bath and Mr Colin Harrison, Department of Education, University of Nottingham, whose computer program was used for the analysis.

† The authors are indebted to Donald Moyle, Reader in Education at Edge Hill College of
Education, for these calculations.

with professional advisers. The personal interviews took place during the transition and it is probable, but not certain, that comments related to the earlier version. The old and new instructions for VAT form 100 (the VAT return) are also compared.

Table 12.5 Reading ages for VAT literature

| | Reading measures | | |
	Flesch	Fry	Smog
General explanation of VAT	15 　　15	14 　　14	16 　　16
VAT Account	16 　　14	14 　　10	16 　　14
The VAT return (Form VAT 100) instructions	15 　　14	14 　　13	15 　　13

Note: earlier version in top left hand; later in bottom right hand.

Table 12.5 shows that the reading level of the old guides was considerably above that which the majority of the population are used to. The instructions for the new VAT return form and the explanation of the VAT Account have been significantly simplified in the later version, but parts of them remain at a 'high' reading level and the general explanation of VAT remains as difficult as it was before.

VAT Booklet No. 727, *Special Schemes for Retailers* (as revised October 1977) has often been singled out as one of the most difficult of the guides and Table 12.6 gives the reading age for various sections of it and for the booklet as a whole. The figures do not suggest that VAT 727 is significantly more difficult to read than the *General Guide*. However, we must qualify this judgement because of the variability from section to section; parts of Section IV 'Special Schemes' become very complicated, paragraph 21 having a Smog score of 19.0 years.

Table 12.6 Readability of VAT Booklet No. 727, *Special Schemes for Retailers*

| | Reading measures | | |
	Flesch	Fry	Smog
I Introduction 　(paragraphs 3–7 and 9)	14	13	15
II Rates Fraction and Changes 　(paragraphs 10 and 12–13)	13	12	15
III Gross Takings 　(paragraphs 15 and 19)	14	14	16
IV Special Schemes and How to Choose 　Between Them 　(paragraphs 20–21 and 24)	15	14	17
VAT 727 overall	14	13	16

Comments on VAT Officers' Visits

Respondents to NAS were invited to comment on the visit of the VAT officer (Q28d) and 722 (about a quarter) took up the invitation. Of those who commented 414 (57 per cent of respondents to this question and 15 per cent of total respondents) found the visits helpful and their remarks suggest that, as VAT has become established, so relations between registered traders and visiting officers have improved. Adverse comments came from 308 (43 per cent of respondents to this question and 11 per cent of total respondents). Table 12.7 attempts to classify the comments.

Table 12.7 Comments on VAT officer visits

Favourable comments (e.g. 'co-operative', 'helpful', 'constructive', 'pleasant' and 'friendly')		414
Adverse comments of which:		308
General (e.g. 'very disturbing', 'not pleasant', 'irritating', 'inconvenient time')	53	
Dictatorial/offensive	44	
Inconsistent/incompetent	22	
Uneconomic[a]	30	
Waste of traders' time	159	
Total		722

[a] By uneconomic was meant that the amount of time and effort expended by Customs & Excise was unduly large compared with the net tax paid.

An analysis of complainants, by size and sector, revealed a disproportionately large number of respondents (as compared with the sample distribution) in the size groups £10,000–£50,000; in those sectors concerned with distribution and services; and (marginally) in the construction sector. Complaints were significantly fewer in the (low compliance cost) primary sector.

The interviews with respondents FOL(P) and with accountants (ADV) provided occasions for probing causes of complaint more fully. It should be recalled (p. 34) that just over half of the sample for FOL(P) were chosen because they had special problems with VAT; thus it might be expected that the sample would be biased towards complainants.

In FOL(P) about as many said that they had found VAT officers helpful as claimed that they were unhelpful. Amongst the accountants (ADV) the general balance was more favourable to Customs & Excise, but there were a number of exceptions, which often took the form of complaints about *particular* officers who were contrasted with a generally favourable view of the local VAT office. Of the more specific points, that which occurred most frequently both amongst NAS interviewees (FOL(P)) and accountants, was the view that VAT officers lacked adequate book-keeping training. (Sometimes a contrast with the Inland Revenue inspector was painted.) Other complaints were of a reluctance on the part of officers to give written rulings, variable interpretations of the rules by different officers and an unwillingness to accept the accountant as the trader's agent. There were also complaints about the time taken for refunds to come through when there was some abnormality about the situation, e.g. the trader was changing his address or was de-registering, but it was generally agreed that refunds were promptly made in normal circumstances. An occasional criticism was directed at the local office or at Southend (e.g. 'They lost my cheque and then threatened Court action'). Several accountants confirmed the view derived from NAS (p. 126) that the general competence of VAT officers was 'improving'.

Unofficial Sources

The predominant source of unofficial advice was the accountant, who came close behind the VAT office in frequency of use. Forty-six per cent of all respondents had used an accountant at some time or another for advice on VAT, which contrasts with the 13 per cent of NAS respondents who, in 1977/8, paid fees to accountants for VAT work (p. 37). The ADV interviews made clear that some traders had used accountants for their early VAT work, which they then (often encouraged by the accountant) took over themselves. Further, the accountant who did a firm's accounting and auditing for other purposes was often consulted on VAT problems on an *ad hoc* basis by traders who generally did their own VAT work. Table 12.8 analyses, by size and sector, respondents who had sought advice from accountants.

Table 12.8 Respondents who have used accountants and found them helpful

(a) Analysed by business sector (b) Analysed by size

Sector	Respondents who have used (%)	Users finding helpful (%)	Size: taxable turnover (£000 p.a.)	Respondents who have used (%)	Users finding helpful (%)
Primary	52	85	0– 9.9	44	89
Manufacture and utilities	38	88	10– 19.9	45	94
Construction	46	86	20– 49.9	46	93
Transport and			50– 99.9	44	94
communication	38	91	100–999.9	49	95
Retail	47	80	1000 and		
Wholesale and dealers	40	89	over	23	98
Financial and business					
services	53	80	All	41	93
Professional and					
scientific services	42	82			
Miscellaneous and					
public services	52	90			
All	46	86			

Note: Some traders did not indicate their taxable turnover band. They are included in the analysis by business sector but excluded from the analysis by size.

Financial and business services, the primary sector, and miscellaneous and public services made most use of accountants and, in every sector except one, a higher proportion of users found them helpful than was true of the three official sources; in the one exception, construction, the helpfulness rating was the same as that of the visiting VAT officer, the highest of the official sources. The same feature was true of all the size ranges; a larger proportion of those firms in each size group who had used the source had found the accountant helpful than was true of any of the official sources. The extent to which accountants were used varied little in the size ranges up to £1 million but dropped markedly amongst firms with a taxable turnover above £1 million.

The other sources of unofficial advice were not used widely enough to justify a detailed analysis, but a few comments can be made. It is noteworthy that the percentage of respondents using tax guide books and journals and trade associations tended to increase with size of firm.

An above average use of tax books and journals, as one might expect, occurred in the professional and scientific services sector and in financial and business services. Manufacture and utilities also made above average use of these sources.

Trade associations vary considerably in the VAT guidance (if any) they provide. Some made a particular attempt to help their members at the start of VAT. Others offer a continuous advice service. The sector with the largest proportion of traders who had used a trade association for advice was retail, at 19 per cent.

Conclusions

Although the majority of respondents used more than one source, a comparative analysis of the various forms of advice revealed two distinct groups – those using accountants and those using official sources. There are also strong positive associations between all the official sources – the booklets, visiting officers and the local office; and a marked association between the use of official VAT booklets and other tax guide-books and journals.*

The other main conclusion is the degree of dissatisfaction with the VAT booklets, which ranked low for helpfulness, especially amongst the less well-educated, and were the subject of critical comments from NAS interviewees (FOL(P)) and accountants (ADV). The readability measures supported the view that the criticisms had substance.

---

* These associations are shown very clearly in a correlation matrix in Appendix M.

Introduction

So far, with the exception of some comments of NAS respondents and professional advisers, this study has rested heavily on aggregate data. It is the nature of the project that this should be so. But in this chapter we seek to redress the balance somewhat by examining case studies drawn from the NAS. These case studies illustrate many of the features with which the earlier chapters have been concerned: the varying levels of compliance cost by size and sector; some of the features influencing compliance costs; the perception and realisation of benefits; differences in attitudes to VAT – and so on.

Case studies have the merit of increasing the reality of the picture. Their import is often easier to grasp than that of large aggregates. However, they must be used with care; there is a danger of generalisation on the basis of one or two examples. Given the background against which the cases are set, this danger should not prove serious. But the case studies are brief and, in the complex and variegated pattern of economic life, they are an over-simplification from which significant factors may have (inadvertently) been omitted. Moreover, the selection has often been made in order to highlight particular features; whilst some firms have been chosen because, in most respects, they appear typical for their size and sector, others have been chosen specifically to paint a contrast.

The cases are set out in order by sector, but no attempt has been made to cover every sector nor to restrict the number of studies drawn from any particular sector.

Notes to the Summary Details

Abbreviations

In the summary details of the case studies the following abbreviations will be used where convenient.

Of VAT Categories: S = standard
H = higher
Z = zero
X = export
E = exempt
Taxable turnover = TT
Customs & Excise = C & E
Credit Period = CP

Measures

Loans are valued at a rate of interest of 7.0 per cent. Commercial credit periods are calculated as described on p. 83. The attitude scaling and scores are as calculated in Chapter 11. Compliance costs, and all other magnitudes which relate to a time period, are for twelve months in 1977/8, unless stated otherwise. Net commercial credit points are positive when the average credit period on purchases exceeds that on sales and negative where the reverse holds true. It is assumed that VAT payments to Customs & Excise (and repayments) take place one month after the end of the collection period.

Firm A: Small to Medium-Sized Farmer

Summary of Relevant Details 1977/8

Taxable turnover:	£20,000–£50,000
VAT categories:	
Input	$\frac{1}{2}$–$\frac{3}{4}$ S, other mainly Z
Output	Over $\frac{3}{4}$ Z, rest S
Net tax paid:	–£1,526
Credit:	
From C & E	–£191
Value	–£13
Net commercial CP	19 days
Effective value	–£3
Accounting system:	Handwritten
Invoices and sales:	
Average sales value	Over £1,000
Number of invoices –	
purchases	Under 500
sales	Under 500
Compliance cost:	£30
As % of TT	0.09
Net compliance cost	£33
Benefits perceived	Nil
Attitude:	Indifferent (0)

Comment

Firm A is a small to medium-sized farmer producing general agricultural produce, with three full-time employees and one part-time. Typically for a farmer compliance costs are low. The farmer, as a net repayment trader, makes a 'loan' to Customs & Excise which cost him £13 in 1977/8. However, because the credit period for purchases is much longer than that for sales, he is able to offset most of this cost.

The farmer left school at the age of 19, has some book-keeping training and has no difficulties with the VAT system. Untypically for a farmer he uses both the official VAT booklets and the visiting VAT officer as sources of advice and

finds both helpful. Unlike most farmers he does not use his accountant for advice
on VAT. He sees no benefit from the VAT system and his attitude is indifferent.

Firm B: Very Large Manufacturer
Summary of Relevant Details 1977/8

Taxable turnover:	£550 million
VAT categories:	
Input	$\frac{1}{2}$–$\frac{3}{4}$ S: also H, Z and E
Output	Over $\frac{3}{4}$S: also H, X and E
Net tax paid:	£25,115,000
Credit:	
From C & E	£5,232,000
Value	£366,240
Net commercial CP	3 days
Effective value	£218,000
Accounting system:	Fully computerised
Invoices and sales:	
Average sales value	36% up to £10 (retail), rest £100–£1,000
Number of invoices –	
purchases	Over 100,000
sales	Over 100,000
Compliance cost:	£61,750
As % of TT	0.01
Net compliance cost	– £156,260
Cash benefit perceived:	Yes
Managerial benefits perceived:	Nil
Attitude:	Anti-VAT (– 5)

Comment

Firm B is typical of large manufacturers with its fully computerised accounting
system, very low compliance cost as a percentage of taxable turnover (despite
the range of VAT rates), substantial 'loan' from Customs & Excise, reduced by
the operation of commercial credit, but still giving a benefit which swamps the
compliance cost. It is untypical in that 36 per cent of its output is sold retail
(which increases its credit benefit from VAT) and unusual for its size and sector
in its anti VAT views. Several specific difficulties were mentioned in the questionnaire (e.g. obtaining tax invoices for small amounts), there was criticism of some
VAT officers and the general comment was that the system could be simplified
and the booklets written in simpler language.

Firm C: Very Large Net Repayment Manufacturer
Summary of Relevant Details 1977/8

Taxable turnover:	£300 million
VAT categories:	
Input	$\frac{1}{2}$–$\frac{3}{4}$ Z: also S, H and E

Output	Over ¾ Z: also S, H and E
Net tax paid:	−£4,488,000
Credit:	
From C & E	−£561,000
Value	−£39,270
Net commercial CP	1 day
Effective value	−£22,080
Accounting system:	Fully computerised
Invoices and sales:	
Average sales value	£1,000 or more
Number of invoices –	
purchases	Over 100,000
sales	Over 100,000
Compliance cost:	£12,100
As % of TT	0.004
Net compliance cost	£34,180
Benefits perceived:	Nil
Attitude:	Indifferent (2)

Comment

Firm C, in common with most large firms, has no difficulty in operating VAT, and has a very low compliance cost as a percentage of taxable turnover. The firm effectively makes a substantial 'loan' to Customs & Excise because its outputs are predominantly zero-rated. Although part of the cost of this loan is passed on to suppliers, through the effect of commercial credit periods, the firm's net compliance cost is nearly three times the reported cost. Despite this the trader is not anti VAT, and the only criticism mentioned in the questionnaire was too many visits from VAT officers at (sometimes) inconvenient times.

Firm D: Small Construction Firm

Summary of Relevant Details 1977/8

Taxable turnover:	£20,000–£50,000
VAT categories:	
Input	Over ¾ S, other H
Output	½–¾ S, other Z
Net tax paid:	£830
Credit:	
From C & E	£173
Value	£12
Net commercial CP	− 10 days
Effective value	£4
Accounting system:	Handwritten
Invoices and sales:	
Average sales value	£100–£1,000

Number of invoices –	
purchases	Under 500
sales	Under 500
Compliance cost:	£393
As % of TT	1.12
Net compliance cost	£389
Cash benefit perceived:	No
Managerial benefit perceived:	Yes
Attitude:	Indifferent (1)

Comment

Firm D is a small construction firm with a mixture of VAT rates and a relatively high burden of compliance cost. All VAT work is undertaken by the proprietor who left full-time education at the age of fifteen and received part-time education for a further seven years. He has received no formal book-keeping training, but has no problems with VAT and finds the official VAT booklets and other tax guide-books and journals helpful.

The business received a 'loan' from Customs & Excise of £173 in 1977/8, which was valued at £12. However, adverse commercial credit periods reduced the value to £4, leaving a net compliance cost of £389.

Firm E: Large Construction Company

Summary of Relevant Details 1977/8

Taxable turnover:	£1 million–£5 million
VAT categories:	
Input	¾ or more S; also Z
Output	All Z
Net tax paid:	– £56,000
Credit:	
From C & E	– £7,000
Value	– £490
Net commercial CP	57 days
Effective value	£316
Accounting system:	Machine
Invoices and sales:	
Average sales value	£1,000 or more
Number of invoices –	
purchases	1,000–10,000
sales	under 500
Compliance cost:	£400
As % of TT	0.01
Net compliance cost	£84
Benefits perceived	Nil
Attitude:	Anti-VAT (– 5)

Comment

Firm E is a large construction company concerned with house building and is a net repayment trader. Compliance costs are low, both absolutely and as a percentage of taxable turnover, and the firm makes a 'loan' of around £7,000 to Customs & Excise. No particular difficulties were mentioned in the questionnaire other than the problem of ensuring that all items of VAT to be claimed were accounted for (particularly petty cash vouchers and other items outside the main system of book-keeping).

An interesting feature of this firm is the very long credit period. Although the firm makes a 'loan' to Customs & Excise, it is able to claim the tax back *before* paying the bills. Thus the firm is able to gain a net *benefit* from the cash flow, which offsets three-quarters of the reported compliance cost.

Firm F: Small to Medium-sized Retailer

Summary of Relevant Details 1977/8

Taxable turnover	£50,000–£75,000
VAT categories:	
Input	Over $\frac{3}{4}$ S, other Z
Output	Over $\frac{3}{4}$ S, other Z
Net tax paid:	£970
Credit:	
From C & E	£200
Value	£14
Net commercial CP	24 days
Effective value	£20
Accounting system	Handwritten
Invoices and sales:	
Average sales value	Under £10
Number of invoices –	
purchases	500–1,000
sales	1,000–10,000
Compliance cost:	£494
As % of TT	0.79
Net compliance cost	£474
Cash benefit perceived:	Yes
Managerial benefit perceived:	No
Attitude:	Very anti-VAT (−13)

Comment

Firm F is a small to medium-sized retailer who is very anti-VAT. Compliance costs as a percentage of taxable turnover are relatively high. Comments on the questionnaire included criticism of the taxation of payments between registered traders, and the complaint that administrative costs alone gave a false impression of total operating costs.

Scheme D is used, which covers all output tax and is regarded as the best scheme for the business. The firm has no difficulties in operating the system.

The firm receives a 'loan' of £200 from Customs & Excise, which is valued at £20 after taking into account the net commercial credit period.

Firm G: Medium-sized Retailer
Summary of Relevant Details 1977/8

Taxable turnover:	£75,000–£100,000
VAT categories:	
Input	All S
Output	All S
Net tax paid:	£3,300
Credit:	
From C & E	£684
Value	£48
Net commercial CP	– 1 day
Effective value	£34
Accounting system:	Handwritten
Invoices and sales:	
Average sales value	£10–£100
Number of invoices –	
purchases	500 to 1,000
sales	under 500
Compliance cost:	£20
As % of TT	0.02
Net compliance cost	– £14
Cash benefit perceived:	Yes
Managerial benefit perceived:	No
Attitude:	Very pro-VAT (11)

Comment
Firm G is a medium-sized retailer with handwritten records, relying on official VAT booklets and the visiting VAT officer for advice. All transactions are standard rated. The trader uses Scheme A and has no problems. The advice obtained is helpful, and he regards the VAT system as 'very efficient and quite painless'. He receives a small 'loan' from Customs & Excise which, taking account of commercial credit periods, is sufficient to offset the low reported compliance cost and leave the firm with a small net benefit.

Firm H: Small Firm of Accountants
Summary of Relevant Details 1977/8

Taxable turnover:	£10,000–£20,000
VAT categories:	
Input	$\frac{1}{2}$–$\frac{3}{4}$ S, other H, Z, E
Output	$\frac{1}{2}$–$\frac{3}{4}$ S, other E, Z, X
Net tax paid:	£897

Credit:

From C & E	£187
Value	£13
Net commercial CP	0
Effective value	£12
Accounting system:	Handwritten
Number of invoices –	
purchases	Under 500
sales	Under 500
Compliance cost:	£630
As % of TT	4.2
Net compliance cost	£618
Benefits perceived:	Nil
Attitude:	Anti-VAT (−9)

Comment

Firm H is a small firm of accountants specialising in audit and taxation work, with one full-time and one part-time employee. In common with many small firms, compliance costs are very high both in relation to taxable turnover and also to the net tax paid. The business is partly exempt from VAT, which regularly causes difficulties.

All sales and purchase invoices are settled within a week, giving zero net commercial credit, but reducing the already small value of the loan from Customs & Excise.

No benefits arising from the VAT system are perceived by the firm, and the attitude expressed is anti-VAT.

Firm I: Small Servicing Garage

Summary of Relevant Details 1977/8

Taxable turnover:	£10,000–£20,000
VAT categories:	
Input	Over ¾ H, other S
Output	Over ¾ H, other S
Net tax paid:	£255
Credit:	
From C & E	£53
Value	£4
Net commercial CP	− 15 days
Effective value	£2
Accounting system:	Handwritten
Invoices and sales:	
Average sales value	£100–£1,000
Number of invoices –	
purchases	1,000–10,000
sales	Under 500

Compliance cost:	£400
As % of TT	2.67
Net compliance cost	£398
Cash benefit perceived:	No
Managerial benefit perceived:	Yes
Attitude:	Pro-VAT (5)

Comment

Firm I is a one-man garage carrying out servicing work and selling secondhand cars. The proprietor considers the VAT system 'a nuisance' but recognises that it does confer some benefits on his business – particularly with record-keeping and stock control. He also saves money by doing more of his own accounting and his overall attitude score is favourable. He regards the official VAT booklets as very unhelpful and has difficulty understanding VAT instructions.

Commercial credit periods work against this firm, halving the (negligible) value of the 'loan' from Customs & Excise, leaving the relative burden of compliance costs high (without allowing for the managerial benefits).

Firm J: Small to Medium-sized Catering Establishment

Summary of Relevant Details 1977/8

Taxable turnover:	£50,000–£75,000
VAT categories:	
Input	Over $\frac{3}{4}$ Z, other S
Output	$\frac{3}{4}$ S, other Z
Net tax paid:	£4,670
Credit:	
From C & E	£972
Value	£68
Net commercial CP	27 days
Effective value	£71
Accounting system:	Handwritten
Invoices and sales:	
Average sales value	Under £10
Number of invoices –	
purchases	Under 500
sales	Not issued
Compliance cost:	£900
As % of TT	1.44
Net compliance cost	£829
Cash benefit perceived:	No
Managerial benefit perceived:	Yes
Attitude:	Indifferent (3)

Comment

Firm J is a small to medium-sized catering establishment with a turnover in the range £50,000–£75,000 with four full-time and three part-time employees. VAT returns are completed by a director who continued full-time education to the age of 22 and is a qualified accountant. The trader experiences no difficulties with VAT, and the only source of advice used is the official VAT booklets, which are considered not particularly helpful.

The trader believes that VAT accounting constitutes half of their internal accounting costs, but claims that this work reduces *outside* accounting fees.

The trader gains from the 'loan' from Customs & Excise and the value of this 'loan' is increased slightly by the effect of commercial credit periods. However the effective value of the credit, £71, does little to offset the reported compliance cost of £900.

Conclusion

The main conclusion to be drawn from this clutch of case studies is the wide variety of ways in which VAT may affect traders – according to size, payment/repayment situation, credit periods and so on. Attitude to VAT is often a product of the net benefit or disbenefit from these features, but by no means wholly so.

Changes in Administrative and Compliance Costs since 1978

Introduction

In this chapter we try, as far as maybe, to update the main findings of the research. We describe the main changes in VAT in the UK since the National Survey and endeavour to assess their likely implications for net compliance, administrative and operating costs.

Main Changes in the United Kingdom VAT since NAS

A number of changes in the VAT system were made as a consequence of the review of the tax undertaken by the Department of Customs & Excise in 1977/8 (Cmnd 7415, 1978). The rules concerning partial exemption were modified so that the number of traders who have to apply restrictions to their deduction of input tax was reduced from about 20,000 to about 3,000. Largely because of this change, it was also possible to simplify the VAT return form, which was reduced in size from a double to a single sheet. The remaining 3,000 partly exempt traders had more complicated compliance duties than before, but were generally large businesses with adequate accounting systems.

Certain businesses were previously not allowed to align their 'VAT year' with their financial year; these restrictions have been lifted. Small businesses are now being encouraged to adapt their cash book record to serve also as the VAT record of purchases. The maximum value of a supply by a retailer for which a less detailed tax invoice might be issued was raised from £10 to £25. Finally, where a debtor had become formally insolvent, the trader was (for the first time) entitled to reclaim any VAT paid on bad debts. All these simplifications were implemented during 1978, but in general NAS respondents would not have had sufficient experience of them to take them into consideration in their replies.

The minimum turnover for compulsory registration has been raised firstly from £7,500 to £10,000 (in April 1978), and more recently from £10,000 to £13,500 (in March 1980). Several of the VAT booklets, notably the *General Guide*, have been rewritten in a simpler manner (see Chapter 12).

It is interesting to note that the most common suggestion for simplification made in submissions to the review body was for a return to a single positive rate of VAT, and this recommendation was, of course, implemented in June 1979.

Certain other modifications to VAT were proposed during 1977/8, but not implemented. The Conservative Party VAT Task Force (Conservative Central Office 1977) and the Consultative Committee of Accountancy Bodies (Memorandum TR 260, 1977) both considered the possibility of an option to account for VAT annually. The CCAB proposal was that the VAT year should always line up with the financial year, and that quarterly returns should be submitted on the understanding that they were subject to annual adjustment following a reconciliation. They emphasised that the improvement in small business records brought about by VAT regulations was a major justification for retaining the quarterly return.

The Conservative proposals were more radical, recommending that for businesses with a turnover of up to £1 million per annum an option to calculate VAT liability from annual financial accounts should be provided. Each business would make quarterly payments (by direct debit to minimise collection costs) on the basis of the previous year's accounts, plus a premium to allow for inflation and to ensure that such businesses did not obtain any unfair advantage. There would then be a retrospective adjustment for the previous year when the accounts were filed, with an interest penalty for late filing.

The Financial Secretary to the Treasury rejected any move towards annual accounting on the grounds that it 'would make it more difficult for small firms to keep their records up to date and would complicate rather than simplify the administration of the tax', (*Hansard* 12 April 1978, col 1537). However, it would appear that at the time of writing Customs & Excise still have this possibility under consideration.

Other proposals made by the Conservative Task Force were that charities should be relieved of VAT on their non-trading activities; that Customs & Excise powers should be harmonised with those of Inland Revenue as far as possible, including the requirement that entry powers should be approved by a circuit judge; and that a House of Commons Select Committee on the administration of VAT should be set up.

A second CCAB proposal (Memorandum TR 277, 1978) was for the elimination of VAT between registered businesses. It was argued in the memorandum that:

> there is a large volume of outputs by registered traders, on which VAT is paid, which are inputs of other registered traders, on which VAT is, in effect, repaid. This volume involves a very considerable administrative burden on industry, commerce and Customs & Excise.

The President of the UK VAT Tribunals, Lord Grantchester, is quoted (*Lords Hansard* 7 December 1976) as saying, 'The whole tax could be made a lot more efficient if most transactions between registered traders were excluded from the tax because it is collected at the end of the line.' Accordingly, the Committee recommended that any registered trader should be entitled to apply for a certificate of exemption and become a non-taxable business. Business customers who could prove they were non-taxable (by reference to their exemption certificate) would be invoiced without the VAT charge. Registered traders retailing or supplying services to the general public would continue to charge VAT on all sales, and registered customers of such traders would have to obtain VAT invoices and reclaim VAT input tax as at present.

A working party on this proposal was set up including representatives from the CCAB, the Confederation of British Industry, the Retail Consortium, the Federation of Wholesale and Industrial Distributors, and HM Customs & Excise and reported in April 1979. CCAB received no support from any of the other parties. Customs & Excise pointed out that about three-quarters of registered traders make at least some regular supplies to final consumers, and 600,000 of these predominantly supply neither registered traders nor final consumers. It was argued that these traders (almost half of the registered population) would have considerable administrative problems in identifying their customers' eligibility for tax. Shifting the collection of VAT entirely on to retailers would place the burden on the category of traders containing the highest proportion of those ill-equipped to cope with it. The incentive to declare purchases which exists at present would disappear, and a problem could arise with unregistered persons fraudulently representing themselves as registered in order to obtain VAT-free goods and services.

It is interesting in view of the findings on cash flow benefits (Chapter 8) that the CBI considered the loss of this benefit to manufacturers and wholesalers (which the proposal would entail) to be 'the fundamental objection to the CCAB proposals'. Intriguingly, the Retail Consortium, whose members might have been expected to benefit from this redistribution of cash, believed that the proposals would result in a switch from quarterly to monthly tax payments. It is not clear how they arrived at this view; presumably they considered that the large sums being remitted by retailers, and the increased control effort required at the retail stage, would necessitate this measure.

In Chapter 11 the disquiet of many NAS respondents over the 'money merry-go-round' was recorded, and one respondent suggested a system similar to that proposed by CCAB:

> This could be done on a card system similar to Barclaycard. When making a purchase I could present my card and the vendor would have a receipt showing my name, address, and registration number. The sum total of these receipts would be deducted from the vendor's takings as VAT free sales. The whole system could easily be computerised and frauds would be quite easy to spot.

The rejection of the CCAB proposal by the Working Party has presumably made it unlikely that any move in this direction will be further considered in the near future.

The Significance of Changes for Operating Costs
Cash Flow Effects
Since the distribution of the NAS questionnaire, VAT has increased substantially – from 8 per cent to 15 per cent on goods and services which were standard rated (an increase of 87.5 per cent) and from 12.5 per cent to 15 per cent on goods and services which were formerly higher rated (an increase of 20 per cent).

Of itself, this increase accentuates the cash flow effects considered in Chapter 8. The size of the 'loan' from Customs & Excise to payment traders rises as does the 'loan' from repayment traders to the revenue authorities. Traders in a relatively favourable commercial credit position will receive still larger benefits. When this change is valued an even more accentuated effect arises because of the substantial increase in UK interest rates between 1977/8 and 1979/80.

Revenue Effectiveness

As observed earlier (p. 9) an increase in tax rates does not normally involve a proportionate increase in operating costs, and hence the 'revenue effectiveness' of each pound spent on operating the tax rises.

Unification of Positive Rates

The replacement of the 8 and 12.5 per cent VAT rates by one of 15 per cent will certainly have simplified the operation of the tax, both for registered traders whose inputs and outputs had been at more than one positive rate, and also for the administration. However, costs may have risen for all traders during the period of transition from the old to the new rate structure.

An open-ended question (FOL(P) and (T)) was asked on whether the changes had made VAT work easier. The main problem eliminated was that of calculating input tax on petrol separately from other input calculations. Most of the professional advisers interviewed (ADV) also agreed that abolition of the higher rate was an improvement; and the evidence obtained during the project suggests that, overall, compliance costs will have been reduced by something in the order of £32 million (1978 prices) because of this change, assuming that after abolition, all traders previously operating with higher rated outputs will have had their compliance costs reduced to the average reported by other traders of the same size and sector.

However, 30 per cent of interviewees had experienced transitional difficulties with the changing of rates; repricing of goods and services was the most frequent difficulty, especially amongst retailers, one of whom complained that there were 'a lot of difficulties, involving 4 days' work for 3 people, including hiring staff at expensive Sunday wage rates'. There were particular difficulties of customer resistance with price 'flashed' sweets such as Mars Bars: 'I could *not* raise prices; people do not understand that prices go up on old stock. Regulars trust you but there are problems with passing trade'. It was noticeable that, of the transitional difficulties involving at least 2 hours' extra work, 80 per cent were reported by respondents in the distribution and services sectors.

There were also a number of problems caused by the change of rates in the middle of the month (18th June). Several respondents had difficulties with apportioning June records correctly between the old and the new rates, and many of them suggested that, 'If changes had to be made, they should start from the beginning of the month.'

The only other frequently-reported difficulty was with long-term contracts. One accountant explained 'we bill clients by the calendar year and render fees on account monthly. The change caused a horrendous amount of paperwork; we are still doing it for some clients, six months after the change. It would have been much simpler if everything *billed* after 18th June had been at the new rate, rather than the existing tax point system'.

Partial Exemption

The reduction in the number of traders required to register as partly exempt from 20,000 to 3,000 (i.e. from 1.5 per cent to one-fifth of one per cent of the registered population) will have reduced compliance costs substantially for the 17,000 traders removed from this category, although, as they were few in number, the overall effects on compliance costs will not be marked. It is likely that the improvement will have been concentrated in the financial and business services sector. Little evidence on partial exemption was obtained from the follow-up interviews but one accountant did comment that several of his clients had benefited from the change.

New Return Form

The liberalisation of partial exemption made simplification of the VAT return form possible; costs of compliance (and to a lesser extent, costs of administration) should have been reduced by this measure for the whole population of registered traders. The other accounting simplifications introduced (see p. 139 above) should also have made a favourable impact on compliance cost levels. In the follow-up interviews, 73 per cent of interviewees found the new VAT return easier to complete than the old one, with agreement spread throughout all size ranges. However, it was noticeable that agreement was substantially lower in the primary sector (at 55 per cent) than in any other category. Most of these traders were farmers whose outputs were all zero-rated, and it is probable that they had experienced few difficulties with the old return. Despite this general welcome, 62 per cent of respondents asserted that the new return had not resulted in an appreciable reduction in costs of compliance (and, indeed, 3 per cent were experiencing transitional difficulties), and said that initially they found the new form *more* difficult to use. The deletion of the partial exemption section from the return form did, in fact, mean increased compliance costs for the remaining partly exempt traders, as in future they would be expected to work out their own annual adjustments instead of merely providing the figures for Customs & Excise to work out.

Bad Debts

The provision enabling traders to reclaim VAT owed to them by formally insolvent debtors will have involved an increase in administrative costs. Compliance procedures for recovering VAT in such a case may also involve a certain amount of time and effort, so it is likely that this measure will have increased costs of operating VAT. Its justification is of course the inequity of the previous state of affairs, under which a trader stood to lose not only the payment owed to him, but also the tax on that payment. Again this change was welcomed by interviewees.

Summary of the effect of changes in VAT on operating costs

	Compliance costs	Administrative costs and other Exchequer costs
Increase in VAT rate	Benefit to trader in good credit position increased substantially, some traders adversely affected.	Cost of 'loan' to community increased.
Increase in interest rate		
Unification of positive rates	Reduced for some traders after temporary increase for most.	Reduced.
Partial exemption liberalisation	Reduced for some traders. Increased for the few remaining partly exempt traders.	Reduced.
Shortened return form and literature simplification	Reduced.	Reduced.
Other accounting simplifications	Reduced for some traders.	Probably not affected.
Bad debts provision	Increased for traders wishing to avail themselves of the provision.	Increased.

The Effect of Main Changes on Net Compliance, Administrative and Operating Costs

In this section we seek to take account of the changes in VAT since NAS and up-date the figures to 1979/80.

Compliance Costs

Between 1977/8 and 1979/80 the number and size distribution of registered VAT traders changed. The number of traders in each size range for 1979/80 was not available at the time of writing and hence the 1978/9 figures had to be used to approximate the 1979/80 distribution. The most appreciable difference between 1977/8 and 1978/9 was a fall in the number of traders in the smallest size range from 271,000 to 171,000. As labour costs are the largest component of compliance costs, the 1977/8 mean compliance costs appropriate to the revised distribution of traders were inflated by the rise in average wage rates from 1977/8 to 1979/80; the saving from abolition of the higher rate was similarly inflated, giving a figure of total (gross) compliance costs for 1979/80 of £474 million.

Administrative Costs

The cost of VAT administration may be expected to have risen in a similar way to compliance costs, with one notable exception – the saving (compared with 1978/9) of 400 man-years from VAT simplifications. Allowing for a reduction in administrative costs in proportion to the man-years saved, the administrative costs for 1979/80 were estimated to total £105 million.

Additional Exchequer Costs

The revenue from VAT in 1979/80 was £8,000 million which, on past evidence would break down into about £11,600 million paid by net payment traders and £3,600 million repaid to net repayment traders. The size of the VAT 'loan' from Customs & Excise (on the basis of our assumptions about the timing of payments and repayments) would then be $5/24 \times 11,600 - 3,600 \times 1/8$ giving a total 'loan' of £1,967 million. The cost to the Exchequer at an interest rate of 14.9 per cent (average MLR in 1979/80) would then be £293 million. The aggregate net benefit accruing to traders from this sum was estimated to be some £234 million, assuming the 'loss' to retail credit customers and non-registered traders was of a similar proportion to that in 1977/8.

Managerial Benefits

The value of managerial benefits was inflated by the change in the retail price index from 1977/8 to 1979/80 (less that part of the increase due to the rise in VAT rates in 1979). Following the same procedure used with compliance costs, the inflated means for each size range were aggregated by reference to the number

Table 14.1 Alternative estimates of aggregate operating costs of VAT 1979/80

	Basic estimate NAS (£m)	Alternative A (£m)
Traders		
Compliance costs	747	747
		− 235
		− 69
		170
		105
		+ 293
		398
		568

ERRATUM

Page 145, Table 14.1. *Traders compliance costs* should read (£m) 474 in both columns.

Note: These figures produce for the year 1979/80 a net compliance cost to revenue ratio of 3.0 per cent (and 2.1 per cent for alternative A) and a ratio of 8.0 per cent (7.1 per cent for alternative A) of total operating costs to revenue. When the new rate of VAT has applied in a full year the ratios should fall further.
^a Not measured.

of traders in each size range for 1978/9. The estimate for managerial benefits in 1979/80 was £69 million.

Table 14.1 gives two estimates of compliance and operating costs with and without measuring managerial benefits.

Ratio of Cost to Revenue

The effect of these changes, principally the rise in VAT rates, is to reduce markedly the ratio of compliance costs to tax revenue and reduce to about 8 per cent the proportion which total operating costs have to tax revenue in 1979/80. When the full revenue effects of the changes are felt the proportion will be much more heavily cut.

15　Conclusions and Implications for Policy

Introduction

In this chapter we seek to draw together the various threads of our study and assess their relevance for policy. We begin by recalling the main aspects of the study and its limitations and then review the principal findings. We look briefly at the significance which the effective incidence of compliance cost may have for government policy. We examine the relevance of tax operating costs for policy on demand management. Then we concentrate on the findings which bear on policies to minimise net compliance costs and Exchequer costs. From the evidence of our study we consider one or two ways in which traders might minimise net compliance costs.

Scope of Research and Summary of Findings

It was widely recognised that the operating costs of a value added tax would be high, and this study is the first major attempt at quantifying such costs. Data on administrative costs were obtained largely from published sources, but substantial field work was required to gather information on compliance costs. A national survey by mail questionnaire was undertaken in late 1978, followed up by telephone and personal interviews, and by discussions with individuals and organisations offering advice on VAT (Chapters 1 to 3).

The questionnaire sample was drawn from the official VAT register, and because of Customs & Excise obligations to maintain confidentiality, the research team only knew the names and addresses of those in the sample who completed the questionnaire and chose to identify themselves. Consequently no follow-up of non-respondents was possible. 2,857 of the 9,094 questionnaires despatched were returned, and response was biased towards larger businesses. The quality of response was generally high, and the large sample size ensured that the response was adequate to test most of the hypotheses formulated. Information subsequently provided by Customs & Excise made it possible to gross up the results for the whole population of registered traders in a reliable way (Chapter 3).

Total measurable compliance costs were estimated at £392 million for 1977/8; this estimate was subjected to a number of checks and tests of reliability, which supported the general accuracy of the figure. Alternative estimates were made on somewhat different principles including two based on the charges of specialist VAT advisory bureaux: the lowest estimate of total compliance costs on this hypothetical basis was £327 million. However the figure of around £400 million

(£392 million) was considered to be the best estimate that could be made from the data available. When this cost was added to the official administrative costs of £85 million, a total operating cost of around £480 million was obtained for 1977/8 which was just over 11 per cent of VAT revenue in that year. These estimates did not include some psychic and social costs which, though important, were not susceptible to measurement (Chapter 4).

The distribution of compliance costs across firms of different sizes and sectors revealed a very clear pattern. Although the compliance costs of traders rose fairly consistently with size, the rise was much less than proportional. Expressed as a percentage of taxable turnover the average compliance costs of traders of less than £20,000 turnover was estimated at some thirty or forty times that of traders with over £1 million taxable turnover. The ratio between the small firms and the very largest firms (over £5 million or over £50 million taxable turnover) was much bigger still. Whilst little reliance can be placed on precise figures, there is no doubt that the compliance costs of VAT are exceptionally regressive in their incidence. As between sectors, the lowest costs were in primary industry with its preponderance of zero-rated farmers and the highest in financial and business services, which contained a high proportion of partly exempt traders amongst the financial firms (Chapter 5).

It also seems likely that administrative costs tend, proportionally, to be concentrated on the smaller firms, partly because firms starting up are usually small and new firms require additional administrative effort to ensure that they are correctly registered, understand the tax system and set up a satisfactory accounting system. With continuing businesses, administrative effort increases in line with the size and complexity of the business. If this distribution of compliance and administrative costs was approximately correct for 1977/8 the total resources used in collecting VAT from the 80 per cent of traders with taxable turnover of less than £100,000 may have been little less than the revenue collected from them. It must be remembered, however, that such figures are strongly affected by the inclusion of repayment traders whose output is zero-rated for social reasons. If the zero rate were made positive the picture would change markedly (Chapter 5).

The above figures of compliance costs have been 'gross' costs, taking no account of any benefits accruing to traders as a result of VAT; nor have they allowed for any additional costs which might fall on the Exchequer. The main benefit to traders in aggregate is, in effect, a net 'loan' from Customs & Excise arising primarily from the cash flow benefit of VAT collected and held by traders before being passed to the revenue authorities. The other side of this coin is, however, a cost to the Exchequer (Chapter 2). On the basis of certain assumptions about the timing of payments and repayments and using a 7 per cent rate of interest (the average MLR for 1977/8) the net value of the 'loan' from Customs & Excise (and hence the net cost to the Exchequer) was estimated at £73 million in 1977/8. The distribution of the net benefit depended not only on whether traders were net payment or repayment traders (who usually made a 'loan' *to* Customs & Excise) but also on the operation of commercial credit. Nearly a quarter of the benefit, through the operation of commercial credit, found its way to non-registered traders and the general public; but at least £55 million could be regarded as an offset to traders' compliance costs (Chapter 8).

Many traders, especially the smaller ones, recognised managerial-type benefits from VAT mainly arising from better record-keeping, but few felt able to put a positive value on such benefits (Chapter 9).

If we take the cash flow benefit and include a rather high (and somewhat dubious) estimate of these managerial benefits, the total compliance costs for 1977/8 are reduced to around £285 million and the total operating costs to £450 million. A 'lower limit' on the hypothetical basis of using, where possible, the charges of one of the specialist VAT advisory bureaux, reduced the figure of total operating cost to £366 million (Chapter 10).

Although the managerial benefits accrued mainly to the smaller firms, the cash flow benefit, as modified by commercial credit periods, predominantly favoured the large firms. As a result, the regressive pattern of net compliance was even more pronounced than that of (gross) compliance costs (Chapter 10).

Factors influencing the level of (gross) compliance costs included the number of invoices processed and the mix of VAT rates; those traders involved with the higher rate reported higher costs than those not so involved. Repayment traders tended to have lower costs than payment traders. The operation of the higher rate also increased administrative costs. The status of the person completing VAT returns influenced costs significantly, and among the smaller firms, those trained in book-keeping reported lower costs than those without such training (Chapter 6).

Recurring difficulties with VAT included understanding VAT instructions and the number of arithmetical calculations. Difficulties were most frequently reported by users of retail schemes, and by those in the construction sector, where the borderline between zero-rated new construction and standard rated repairs often caused headaches (Chapter 7).

The comparatively small number of special problems with VAT were concentrated among the largest businesses, especially in manufacturing. Import and export paperwork, administrative errors and delays, and input tax invoices gave rise to such problems, and construction industry borderlines again figured as a difficulty (Chapter 7).

Respondents were in general slightly antipathetic to VAT; just under 10 per cent were strongly anti-VAT. Again construction and retail figured among the most anti-VAT sectors. As we should expect, the number of difficulties experienced with VAT appeared to influence attitudes adversely and the number of benefits perceived had a favourable effect on attitudes. Compliance costs of anti-VAT respondents were noticeably higher than costs of pro-VAT respondents. In all these instances the causal relationship between attitudes on the one hand and difficulties, perception of benefits and costs, on the other hand, could have worked both ways (Chapter 11).

Use of official sources of advice on VAT increased with size of firm; the VAT booklets and visiting officers were the most widely used sources. It was apparent that although the booklets were used most, visiting officers and the local VAT office were more consistently helpful. The better educated respondents were happier with the booklets than others; readability tests gave some substance to complaints of traders and accountants about the difficulties in understanding VAT booklets.

VAT officers visits were generally helpful, but a minority of respondents (especially small traders in the distribution and services sectors) were critical of the officers (Chapter 12).

It is clear from the study as a whole that net compliance costs are affected by a large number of factors, many of which – like size of firm; sector; payment or repayment situation; liability to the rules for partly exempt traders or to higher rate tax; the impact of interest rates; conditions of commercial credit and inflation on the size and distribution of the cash flow – are largely outside the control of individual traders. Consequently the net compliance costs are very arbitrarily spread across the trading community (most chapters, but especially 13).

An attempt was made to update the survey findings to give an approximate estimate of operating costs in 1979/80. Various changes, notably the abolition of higher rate and the easement in the rules for partly exempt traders had reduced both compliance and administrative costs. Taking these changes into account as far as possible led to an estimate of compliance costs for 1979/80 of around £474 million and of administrative costs of £105 million. However, the offsetting benefit of the 'loan' to the trading community had been very much accentuated firstly by the increased VAT rates and secondly by the higher interest rates. Taking the value of the net 'loan' into account reduces the figure of compliance costs from £474 million to £239 million; if (more doubtfully) the value of managerial benefits is included the net compliance cost falls to £170 million. However the additional cost of the 'loan' puts up Exchequer costs (including administrative costs) to nearly £400 million.

Even so there is an improvement in the operating cost to revenue ratio (from 11.3 to 8.0 per cent) and a much more marked fall in (gross) compliance costs as a proportion of the revenue (from 9.3 to 5.9 per cent). The full effects of the revenue changes were delayed to the 1980/1 fiscal year when the ratios should become very much more favourable.

In the sections which follow, the attempt is made to draw out the policy implications of the study, especially for the government. The object of the research was to provide a basis of fact about the compliance and operating costs of VAT which would make for improved policy-making. It was not the purpose of the study to make particular policy recommendations to meet problems and situations highlighted by the study. However desirable that might be, it would go beyond the competence of the study and of the research team. The most that can be done is to suggest possible courses of action, especially those which relate most closely to the study, and to point out such of their implications as the study has revealed. This we try to do.

Incidence of Compliance Costs

The concept relevant to the incidence of compliance costs is net compliance cost, i.e. compliance cost less benefits. Our study showed that (gross) compliance costs were very regressive and net compliance cost, after allowing for the effect of cash benefits modified by commercial credit, even more so; indeed, whilst in 1977/8 small traders had net compliance costs which were substantial as a percentage of taxable turnover, many large payment traders had net compliance costs which were negative, i.e. value of the cash benefit exceeded the compliance costs, often by a very substantial sum. In so far as managerial benefits could be brought into the reckoning the relative disadvantage of small firms was slightly reduced, but not sufficiently to change the picture significantly; the majority of traders did not perceive such benefits and of those who did, few felt able to put a value on them. Since 1978 the increase in VAT rates and higher interest rates has increased the benefit of most payment traders, increased the burden on most repayment traders, and accentuated the differences between the small and the large traders. The question to be asked is: 'Who really pays the compliance cost? – where does the effective incidence of compliance cost ultimately lie?'

It is natural to assume that compliance costs enter into costs of production and are passed on to the consumer. This may well be so in trades where competition is between firms with similar levels of compliance cost in relation to turnover. But where large and small firms are competing, and the large have net benefits compared with positive costs for the small, small firms may have to absorb all of their own compliance costs plus an additional margin to remain competitive. In other words the differential incidence of compliance costs must have the effect of reducing the profitability of firms with high compliance costs, in general the small firms, thus increasing the pressures squeezing them out of existence.

One sector where compliance costs fall most markedly with size is retail (Table 10.4). A recent article (Bamfield 1980) highlights the changes which have taken place in that industry. Since 1961 the number of retail outlets has fallen by almost 30 per cent, the decline having taken place mainly amongst the independents and co-operatives which have suffered a big loss in their share of trade to the multiples. To quote Bamfield: 'The major factors producing the fall in shop numbers seems to have been especially important in recent years, as four-fifths of the total decline (1961–78) has occurred since 1971'. And again: 'The fall in shop numbers is mainly, though not entirely, accounted for by the decline of small shops.'

Bamfield explains this decline partly in terms of the vulnerability of small shop-keepers to increases in working costs. Not surprisingly, in view of the lack of previous evidence, he does not mention the compliance costs of VAT as a cause of their decline, but there can be little doubt that the costs of VAT have added to the pressures forcing out the small retailer, and it may not be coincidental that the decline has accelerated since the tax was introduced.

Another possible effect of the differential burden of compliance may be to push the proprietors of small firms towards tax evasion and the black economy. If they feel that the State has itself directly created conditions of unfair competition between them and their bigger rivals they may become less scrupulous about ways of redressing the balance. (One respondent commented that the VAT system 'attacks moral principles by encouraging dishonesty. For example, contractors to private householders are tempted to say "pay me in cash and I will deduct VAT"'.) It should be recalled that, although the attitude survey showed, overall, only slight antipathy to VAT, there was a core of some 10 per cent of respondents who were very anti-VAT and they amount to a sizeable number across the total population of registered traders.

The effect of the differential incidence of compliance costs on small firms cannot fail to be a matter of concern to a government dedicated to encouraging them. What courses of action are open to the Government?

One approach would be for the Government to seek to compensate smaller firms by action entirely outside the VAT mechanism, e.g. by an easement restricted to small firms in non-domestic rates. Such an approach goes well beyond this study and we comment on it no further.

A second approach would be to take up the suggestion of some of the NAS correspondents and seek to compensate firms for their compliance costs by paying them an offsetting sum. Small firms would, proportionately, receive more than large – or the payment might be restricted to firms below a particular size. In our view this procedure bristles with difficulties. The net compliance costs of firms even of the same size vary so much according to sector and a host of other factors (many of which have been explored in this book) that we cannot envisage any method of compensation that would be both fair and simple.

The third, and most obvious approach, is to pursue measures designed to reduce compliance costs in general and particularly the costs of small firms. This approach we examine below.

A further possibility is to take action to improve the competitiveness of small firms by removing some of the benefit gained by large firms, notably by requiring large payment traders to make payments more frequently, thus reducing their cash flow benefit. We examine this point below in the context of reducing Exchequer costs.

Compliance Costs and Demand Management

Some incidental evidence relating to government policy on demand management emerged from the study. At the time of its introduction, it was argued in favour of VAT that its broader base made it less discriminatory than purchase tax and consequently superior as an instrument for regulating demand. Those presenting this view often took little account of the compliance costs of change. We have already discussed the temporary compliance costs arising from the unification of VAT rates (Chapter 14). Whilst the experience of the June 1979 rate changes were still fresh in the memory, the researchers were prompted to include in the follow-up interviews (FOL(P)) a general question on the difficulties of changes in VAT rates (Q7). The responses are recorded in Tables 15.1(a) and (b).

It can be seen that the percentage who would find changes more difficult and much more difficult increases with the frequency of change. As indicated in Chapter 14, the main area of extra work is the repricing required in the distribution and service sectors.

Table 15.1 Difficulties associated with changes in VAT rates

(a) *Would it make VAT work more difficult if VAT rates were changed:*

	Percentages (n = 44)		
	Every year	Every 6 months	Every 3 months
More difficult	61	68	68
No more difficult	36	30	30
Not applicable	2	2	2
	100	100	100

(b) *Those who replied 'More difficult' were asked: Would it make VAT work much more difficult if VAT rates were changed:*

	Percentages		
	Every year	Every 6 months	Every 3 months
More difficult	74	63	50
Much more difficult	26	37	50
	100	100	100
	(n = 27)	(n = 30)	(n = 30)

Other comments made by several respondents were that changes at the end of a month or at the end of a quarter were very much easier to cope with than changes in the middle of a month, as happened in 1979 (Chapter 14). It was further stressed that a return to multiple positive rates would make changes particularly burdensome.

The existence and importance of temporary compliance costs means that, to quote a recent EEC document: 'Adjusting VAT rates would not seem to be a particularly flexible instrument for managing demand' (EEC Report 1980). Perhaps, with fine-tuning out of fashion, this is not a serious disability. But it is clearly important for a government using VAT as a regulator to do so in a way which, compatible with the needs of demand management, minimises the inevitable temporary increase in compliance costs.

A second influence which a change in VAT might have in regulating the economy should be mentioned. Any changes in the timing of payments or repayments would affect the cash flow of firms and hence their borrowing requirements and their demand on resources. We discuss below the possibility of a change in the timing of payments. However, whilst there may be a case for a change in payment periods, which would have a once-and-for-all effect too important to be ignored, administrative disruption to firms and Customs & Excise caused by frequent changes in payment and repayment periods must rule it out as a serious policy instrument for demand management.

Government Policies to Minimise Compliance and Exchequer Costs

Policies to minimise temporary compliance costs have already been discussed in the context of demand management policy: a simple rate structure; infrequent changes; and the implementation of changes at convenient times for traders are the main considerations. Let us turn to the more difficult problem of reducing regular compliance costs.

Simple Rate Structure

A suggestion from some of the respondents to NAS (p. 118), likely to slash compliance and administrative costs, is to have a standard rate across all goods and services save exports, like the Danish tax (p. 163). Obviously, if it were introduced it would need to be accompanied by an up-rating of all social security payments to offset the effect for the lower income groups of the abolition of the zero rate on 'necessities'. To make the change at this point of time would cause a major upheaval in incomes and prices with effects on inflation which would be difficult to gauge. The original decision to go for a wide range of zero-rated goods was political, and we do not think the political judgement has changed; this possibility is therefore not pursued further.

However, we can stress from the evidence of our study the cost of an additional positive rate of tax. When NAS was undertaken a higher rate was in existence for a fairly narrow range of goods. The statistical evidence is clearly that it had a significant effect on compliance costs (Table 6.7). We estimate that the existence of a higher rate added some £32 million to compliance costs out of a total of £392 million in 1977/8. At the prices of April 1980 £32 million would rise to about £42 million. The views of many of the NAS respondents who had experienced the higher rate (FOL(T) and (P)) and the invariable views of accountants (ADV) were that the unification of positive rates was a valuable and cost saving simplification. There can also be little doubt that the abolition of the higher rate was the main element in administrative savings of 400 man-years which the Minister of State attributed to all the simplifications which became effective in 1979/80 (*Hansard*, W.A. 141, 24 June 1980). At 1980 prices 400 man-years equates to about £4 million. In *very* round terms the abolition of the higher rate may well have saved £45 million of today's resources. The additional compliance and administrative costs of adding a second positive rate must depend on the range of goods it covers, on how far it may be confined to a small number of firms and so on. But it is clear that there is a high price in resource costs to be paid for whatever political, social or economic advantages an additional rate of VAT may be thought to bring. Lord Barber's maxim of keeping VAT simple (Johnstone 1975) had much to commend it.

The view has recently been strongly argued (e.g. Holland 1980) that the retail schemes could be simplified by a drastic reduction in their number. We cannot say that our study produced any strong evidence either of significant differences in compliance costs associated with different schemes or of any general dissatisfaction with the schemes – hence we do not pursue this theme.

Compliance Costs of Small Firms

The outstanding finding of the study is the big disproportion between the amount of revenue collected from the smaller firms and the cost of acquiring it. This generalisation remains true even if we look at payment traders only and even after allowing for the effect of the 1979 rise in VAT rates on the ratio of operating cost to revenue. Compliance costs are the major component of operating costs for the smaller firms and, despite an offset from cash flow and managerial benefits for some firms, for most of them compliance costs remain a very real burden. If we omit the very lowest size range (consisting mainly of voluntary registrations) the average compliance cost of traders with a turnover of £10,000–£20,000 in 1977/8 was £184, some £3.50 per week, and in three sectors: manufacture and utilities; financial and business services; and professional and scientific services – it was well over £5 per week. For the next size range (£20,000–£50,000) the average was £5 per week with the highest sector showing £9 per week (Table 5.3). At 1980/1 prices the comparable averages for these size ranges would be around £5.25 and £7.50. Using specialist firms would have cost less. Even the specialist firms (Appendix F3) however charged between £2 and £3 per week in 1978 for firms with a turnover of up to £50,000 and to that sum has to be added a relatively heavy postage charge and further miscellaneous expenses. (Such charges are deductible for income tax, so the cost to the trader is somewhat less, but the resource cost to the community is not diminished.)

These findings emphasise the need for action to cut the compliance costs of small traders, a need reinforced by the effect of these costs on traders' competitiveness (discussed above).

The most obvious answer would be to raise the turnover exemption limit. But the obvious is not necessarily the right and there are grave problems about so doing. First Britain is restrained by EEC regulations from revising the threshold except to keep pace with inflation. Even without this restriction however, it is very doubtful if in the interests of fair competition such a policy would be right, especially as the 1979 rise in the standard rate of VAT has accentuated the difference between those just above and those below the limit. The higher the limit the more firms below it who have an incentive to restrict expansion (or cover it up) to stay below; and the more above who may be encouraged to cut back (or hide part of their activities) to get below it.

Whilst there is good reason for raising the limit regularly to keep pace with inflation, the answer would seem to lie not in excluding traders from the VAT system, but modifying the system to reduce the burden that falls on them.

This is much easier said than done. There would appear to be no simple solution. Of the various possibilities which have been suggested two approaches seem to be worth pursuing.

First, the scheme put forward by the Conservative Party VAT Task Force for annual accounting for small traders (though we would suggest a lower limit than the £1 million turnover indicated in that scheme) (p. 140). The scheme has its difficulties and does not appeal to many traders, but its implementation would be voluntary, as the Report proposed. An experiment within one region would seem to be worthwhile.

Second, a thorough examination of the schemes for small traders in the EEC and other countries which have introduced VAT. Most countries make such concessions, often in the form of 'tapering' provisions (see Appendix A, Table A3) which may be regarded as an approximate measure of compensation for the regressiveness of compliance costs.

Customs & Excise Service to Traders

One small but not unimportant way in which Customs & Excise could help small traders, especially the less well educated, is by a further simplification of the VAT booklets. The incomprehensibility of the booklets was stressed by many respondents (NAS), by accountants (ADV) and confirmed by the measures of readability (Chapter 12). It is easy for the academic to pontificate and, in fact, much has been done. Moreover the problem is not easy to solve; the readability of material is necessarily related to the complexity of the information to be communicated, and some aspects of VAT are far from simple. There is also the particular problem of reconciling simplicity in wording with the exact legal requirement of the tax. But further improvement would meet a real need. Encouragement to tackle this task may be found from the growing recognition, exemplified in the recent publication 'Gobbledegook' by the National Consumer Council (1980), of the need for improving government publications and the possibilities of so doing. There is a growing literature on the subject (for example, Wright and Barnard (1975), Hartley (1978), Lewis (1979)) and an increasing interest by government departments. The 122nd Report of Inland Revenue devoted seven paragraphs to comments on improvements in communications with the public and to an account of the results of survey work investigating the response of the general public to new forms and guides. The Inland Revenue have set themselves the target of major improvements in communication. Customs & Excise might be encouraged to nail their flag publicly to the same mast.*

One complaint amongst NAS respondents which appeared in the follow-up interviews (FOL(P)) and still more amongst accountants (ADV) was the lack of book-keeping training amongst VAT officers. There was a clear implication that with such training they could both do their job better and help traders more. This is also a view to be drawn to the attention of Customs & Excise.

Finally, whilst the majority of traders found VAT officers helpful the minority who complained or who worried about VAT officer visits was not small. If it were made clear that VAT officers would allow an accountant to be present to support his client on control visits, psychic costs would be reduced; and, indeed, anything which would improve the image of the VAT officer would have this effect.

Special Problem Areas

One way of reducing compliance and administrative costs as a whole, with benefits to traders in all size ranges, is to eliminate or reduce causes of special difficulty in particular sectors. A considerable improvement has been made with partial exemption. The biggest outstanding area of difficulty would appear to be in the

---

*Inland Revenue publications have been the subject of similar readability tests to those applied to Customs & Excise literature (pp. 124–5) by Lewis (1979).

construction industry, over the borderline between standard and zero-rated work. All our evidence emphasised the frequency and costliness of such problems. The construction industry made the most use of VAT officers and the local office (Chapter 12). The construction industry was clearly top of the list with common difficulties and problems (Table 7.1). Overall compliance costs in the industry were above average despite the low compliance costs of those firms which enjoyed full zero rating.

Clearly, the borderline problems would diminish if not completely disappear if all building work were subject to the same rate of tax, whether zero or standard. From our study we can indicate that it seems likely that compliance costs would be reduced by some £42 million at 1979/80 prices and administrative costs by an unknown but substantial sum, if all building were zero-rated. Our data do not enable us to give a numerical estimate for the reduction in compliance costs if all building work were standard rated, but it is clear that the saving would be less. Obviously the revenue implications are very different. Zero-rating would have caused a loss of revenue of £300 million in 1979/80 whilst standard-rating all building would have increased revenue by a similar sum. An extension of zero-rating, it should be added, would also run foul of EEC regulations.

Action to Minimise Administrative and Other Exchequer Costs
As indicated above, any measures to reduce borderline problems would be likely to save administrative costs as well as compliance costs, and measures which made VAT booklets easier to understand, if they had the effect of raising administrative costs in the short run, might be expected to lower them in the long run by reducing the demand on other Customs & Excise services.

Another possible way to reduce administrative costs is a tougher application of the Customs & Excise discretion in requiring traders who fall below the exemption limits to de-register, and removing from the register voluntary registrations where traders persistently default on their returns.

It is understood that Customs & Excise are reviewing their policy on visits to traders with a view to concentrating them more on those traders from whom the largest revenue is obtained. A reduction in visits to small traders would reduce the operating costs concentrated on them and so help to remove the present disproportion of costs to revenue at that level.

One method to reduce Exchequer costs associated with the administration of VAT would be to change the payment period for traders. The most obvious possibility to emerge from this study would be to transfer the large firms to a monthly payment basis. The study showed that many large payment firms obtained a substantial net benefit from VAT – the value of their cash benefit greatly exceeded their compliance costs. The changes since 1977/8 have increased this benefit enormously. If they were put onto a monthly payment basis, the rise in their compliance cost would be negligible (but not, of course, the rise in net compliance costs) and the saving to public funds would be considerable. On the basis of the 1979/80 revenue figures and assuming the same proportions of payments to repayments as in 1977/8, the reduction in 'loan' from Customs &

Excise (or the equivalent reduction in the PSBR) would be £725 million if all firms with taxable turnover over £1 million were put on a monthly payment basis or £531 million if the requirement were limited to firms over £10 million turnover. The estimate on 1980/1 revenue would be £1,129 million and £828 million respectively. Thus, for example, if all firms over £10 million taxable turnover were required to make monthly payments, at an interest rate of 17 per cent there would be a saving in Exchequer costs of £141 million, which would be paralleled by a rise in the net compliance costs of these firms.

Such a measure has the attraction that it would do something to redress the balance which VAT has tilted heavily against small firms (above). As we have noted, a change of this kind has its effect on the control of the economy and it is necessary to add that the present time of a slump would be singularly inappropriate for introducing such a measure. When the economy pulls up again, the possibility is worth serious consideration.

Trader Action to Minimise Net Compliance Costs

In conclusion a few of the points arising from the study might be brought to the attention of traders. It is clear that many traders could reduce their compliance costs by using a specialist bureau offering a VAT service or by hunting around for an accountant who specialises in VAT work. This can often be less costly in resource terms than doing it themselves, or be cheaper than employing an accountant who is not keen on such work. Such costs are, in practice, deductible for income tax as a business expense, whereas if the trader does the work himself, no deduction can be claimed.

It was also clear that many payment traders did not appreciate the cash benefit which they derived from VAT. They can reduce net compliance costs by maximising the loan from Customs & Excise by retaining their tax up to the due date and by making the money 'work' for them.

Repayment traders can minimise their disadvantage, and sometimes even obtain a positive advantage, by making purchases at the month end and submitting their claim forms with all speed, and correctly, to avoid delays in repayments. This way they can often recover the VAT before they have had to pay for the goods.

Finally, the point should be made that attitude to VAT is important. If more traders could think in terms of the managerial benefits of VAT, compliance would seem less of a burden and net compliance costs would fall.

Appendices

Appendix A   VAT in the European Economic Community

Introduction of VAT in the EEC

VAT was devised to meet the shortcomings of a simple tax on business turnover. Both France and Germany had general taxes on business turnover in the early 1920s. Each sale was taxed at low rates, and a 'cascade' element was thus incorporated. As the Richardson Committee (Cmnd 2300, 1964) put it:

> The defects of the cascade turnover tax all spring from the multiple application of the tax. This means that the tax gives an arbitrary encouragement to vertical integration and penalises specialisation, because a firm which reduces the proportion of materials or components which it buys from outside suppliers will carry less tax in its total production costs. For the same reason the tax is said to have given an artificial inducement to dispense with the services of the independent wholesaler. The multiple application also means that the tax penalises investment, because a firm which purchases new capital equipment from outside suppliers will have to bear the tax in the cost of its purchases, and because the tax element in costs is variable, it will be impossible to calculate precisely either the amount of tax which should be remitted on exports, or the amount of tax which should be imposed on imports in order that they may compete with domestic production on equal terms.

The main international impetus towards reform of sales taxes has been an increasing concern that sales taxation and subsidisation should not spill over into exports and thus distort the pattern of international competition.

The Tinbergen Committee, set up by the European Coal and Steel Community High Authority in 1953, emphasised that the refund for exports should exactly equal the turnover tax element of the price, and that the tax imposed on imports should be the same as the turnover tax on a similar domestic product. There was a considerable problem in estimating the turnover tax content of cascade taxes and it was widely believed, for example, that West Germany used this imprecision to give covert subsidies to exports (Tait 1962).

Attempts were made in France to improve the outlay tax system, firstly by trying out a single stage purchase tax, and secondly by a single stage production tax levied on a wide range of goods and on many raw materials. Under the 'regime suspensif', producers were exempted from tax on goods consumed in production, but capital goods and exports were taxed. From 1948 the taxpayer was permitted to offset the amount of tax paid on purchases against his own tax liability – which is the unique characteristic of a VAT. The tax was imposed up to the wholesale stage. From 1954, the tax content of capital goods was also allowed as an offset against tax liability; the tax was extended to the final, retail stage in 1968.

In 1959 an EEC Working Group was set up to examine possible turnover tax policy for the Community. Three sub-groups reported back to the Working Group. Sub-group A reported that the abolition of frontier controls while *continuing the existing separate taxes* was feasible, but that evasion and importers' compliance costs would increase. The disadvantages outweighed the advantages.

Sub-group B reported that a *single stage purchase tax* could result in evasion if tax rates in Member countries differed substantially. Spill-over effects would result from the taxing of capital investment and the goods and services assimilated into it. Purchase tax was therefore an unsound basis for harmonisation.

Sub-group C reported that a single stage production tax was open to similar objections to those applying to a purchase tax, and a multiple stage production tax did not exempt capital goods and had distortive effects. A VAT was better for avoiding competitive distortions if levied at all stages of production including the final retail sale. The EEC philosophy of taxation had always stressed the principle of neutrality, as stated by Reugebrink (1965):

> according to the welfare principle taxation should disturb price conditions as little as possible – apart from cases where it is necessary to take legislative action for political or other reasons. The usual function of the price mechanism is to control the allocation of finished products and factors of production.... Assisted by the price conditions ruling on the market, and with their limited incomes, consumers will endeavour to purchase those goods which give the maximum satisfaction. If these price conditions are disturbed by taxes, the result will be distortion of the optimum allocation of productive resources to the detriment of the welfare principle.

It is noteworthy that the Working Group did not consider a single stage retail sales tax in any detail as an alternative to the value-added tax. Since it is intended that the VAT should be fully shifted forward on to the final consumer, the incidence and burden of VAT and a single stage retail tax are identical, and the single stage tax is 'engagingly simple' (Tait 1972) compared with VAT.

Why then was a single stage retail tax not considered? According to Tait 'the answer lies partly in the peculiar history of the development of VAT, and partly in some of the more far-fetched claims made for it'. It seems that the major reasons for selecting value-added tax were the continental tradition of multiple stage turnover taxes and concern about the evasion possibilities of a retail sales tax.

The Neumark Committee of the EEC, which reported in 1962, recommended the introduction of VAT throughout the Community on the indirect subtractive method of calculation, which is especially suitable for use in an economic community operating on the country of destination principle, and helps to qualify the tax for rebate under the General Agreement on Tariffs and Trade. The Committee also recommended that VAT rates, allowances and exemptions should be similar in all member countries.

In the long term, the EEC has declared its intention to opt for the 'country of origin' principle (Article 4, First Directive on Value Added Tax), under which commodities would be sold throughout the Community at the rates of taxation imposed in the country of production. It is argued that this method has less distortive effects on intra-Community trade than the 'country of destination' principle (under which the domestic tax is rebated on exports, and the domestic country's tax rates are imposed on imports), because the countries of destination can apply high tax rates to goods which are predominantly imported. The destination principle would continue to apply to exports outside the Community except where reciprocal arrangements had been made.

Little progress has in fact been made towards switching to the origin principle. The main obstacle is that it would not be mutually acceptable to countries with widely varying VAT rates, as those with the highest rates would be at a competitive disadvantage. The differences in rate levels in turn stem from the varying significance of the tax as a revenue-raiser in different countries. Those countries most dependent on VAT have the highest rates and would be unwilling to acquiesce in the change. It is therefore probable that there will have to be a concerted Community effort to harmonise VAT rates and coverage before the adoption of the origin principle.

Features of VAT in EEC Countries

The structure of VAT amongst the nine countries of the EEC is remarkable more for diversity than similarity. Table A.1 shows considerable differences between countries as to the number and levels of rates. Apart from the zero-rating for exports, which all Members have, only the UK and the Republic of Ireland apply a zero rate internally. At the extremes Italy has five rates (and until recently had eight) whilst Denmark is the only country with just one. Most countries have substantial categories of exemption for activities such as cultural, educational and medical services, financial services and renting land and property.

Table A.1   VAT rates in EEC countries, as at 24 July 1980 (percentages)

	Reduced rate	Standard rate	Intermediate rate	Higher rate
Belgium	6	16	—	25
Denmark	—	22	—	—
Federal Republic of Germany	6.5	13	—	—
France	7	17.6	—	$33\frac{1}{3}$
Republic of Ireland[a]	0 and 10	25	—	—
Italy	2 and 8	15	18	35
Luxembourg	2 and 5	10	—	—
Netherlands	4	18	—	—
United Kingdom	0	15	—	—

Source: *Hansard*, W.A., col 381, 24 July 1980.
[a] 35 and 40 per cent rates are applied in Ireland at the manufacturing and importing stage to passenger vehicles, radios, TVs, record players and records. Subsequent sales of these items are subject to VAT at 10 per cent and input tax is only deductible at 10 per cent throughout.

In several Member states there has been a tendency for the number of rates to be reduced, e.g. France and Belgium have abolished intermediate rates and Ireland and the UK have abolished higher rates. Rate levels have tended to increase in six of the Member states during the past decade.

The respective coverage of standard, reduced (including zero) and higher rates varies considerably between countries, so that nominal rates provide no adequate basis for comparing the weight of VAT. Table A.2 attempts such a comparison by expressing tax yield as a percentage of national final consumption (at current prices) for the period 1974–7.

Table A.2 Revenue from VAT as a percentage of national final consumption

	1974	1975	1976	1977
Belgium	9.5	8.5	9.3	9.3
Denmark	7.2	6.8	6.8	6.9
Federal Republic of Germany	9.4	8.7	8.5	10.1
France	11.9	11.2	11.4	10.8
Republic of Ireland	6.0	5.7	6.7	7.2
Italy	6.5	5.4	6.3	6.9
Luxembourg	6.1	6.5	6.3	6.6
Netherlands	8.7	8.7	9.1	9.6
United Kingdom	3.8	3.9	3.8	3.8

Source: *Report from the EEC Commission to the Council on Scope for Convergence of Tax Systems in the Community*, 27 March 1980.

The differences are substantial, but one of the biggest, that between the UK and the rest, will have been substantially narrowed by the changes in UK rates of VAT of June 1979. As a result of these changes the UK figure for 1981 can be expected to rise to around 6½ per cent, which would still leave the UK the lowest, but at a level only marginally below the most recent levels of Italy and Luxembourg.

Another feature of importance is the treatment accorded to small businesses. Differences between countries are again considerable and the details are too complex to permit an easy summary, but, because of their importance for policy, an account of the concessions to small firms in each country is recorded in Table A.3. It is particularly interesting that 'tapering' provisions, under which small traders are given some relief from VAT, apply in several countries. These provisions may in effect be regarded as a measure of compensation for the regressiveness of compliance costs.

Table A3 Summary of treatment of small traders for VAT in EEC countries

Country	Simplified calculations (Type of firm and max. turnover)	Simplified documentation (Type of firm and max. turnover)	Exemption thresholds and tapering provisions	Other schemes
Belgium	Certain retailers up to £150 000 can have an assumed turnover assessed according to the type of firm. This assessment is called the 'fixed tax base'.	Up to £50 000 traders may have a simplified quarterly return instead of a monthly one.		Equalisation tax. Small retailers (up to £50 000 in food or £30 000 turnover otherwise) exempted from VAT, and their suppliers charge them a supplementary tax.
Denmark (as at Feb 1980)			Exemption below £780 turnover.	
France	Non-corporate traders up to £52 000 (or £16 000 for services other than hotels), pay an assessment (called the *forfait*), negotiated between the trader and the authorities.	Traders between £52 000 and £104 000 (or £16 000 and £31 000 in services other than hotels) can have a shortened return for VAT and income tax, and make estimated payments with an annual adjustment.	If *forfait* is less than £140, no payment is required. If *forfait* is £140–£560, one third of the difference between £560 and the assessment is abated.	
Germany	Certain traders and professionals, including traders up to £60 000, may be assessed on a receipts basis instead of an invoice basis.		If turnover below £4800, exempt. £4800 to £4900, liability is reduced by 80 per cent. £4900 to £14 000, the reduction in liability is decreased by 1 per cent for each additional £120 of turnover.	

Table A3 (*cont.*)

Country	Simplified calculations (Type of firm and max. turnover)	Simplified documentation (Type of firm and max. turnover)	Exemption thresholds and tapering provisions	Other schemes
Republic of Ireland			Exemption below £3000 if 90 per cent of turnover is in goods *and* 50 per cent or more is at the lower rate; below £1500 if 90 per cent is in goods; below £500 otherwise.	
Italy	If turnover under £1000 lump sum payment of £10.	If turnover under £185 000 quarterly returns instead of monthly.	If turnover is less than £3000 there is a flat rate deduction, varying with type of trade, for certain traders.	Average rating scheme for retailers.
Luxembourg			If turnover below £1500 generally exempt. If turnover below £1600, £80 is deducted from liability. If turnover £7600–£15 000, deduction of 1 per cent of the shortfall from £15 000. If liability below £80, it is waived. If it is between £80 and £230, half the difference between the liability and £230 is abated.	

Netherlands
(as at Feb 1980)

Most traders selling to the general public may be assessed on a receipts basis instead of an invoice basis.

For non-corporate taxpayers. If liability is less than £450, exempt. If liability is £450–£550, £450 may be deducted from the payment. If tax due is between £550 and £900, the difference between the liability and £900 may be deducted. Temporary deductions are made during the year, with an annual adjustment.

Special schemes (similar to some UK schemes) for multiple rated retailers.

---

[a] Information relates to 1979 unless otherwise stated. Conversions to sterling are made on the basis of rates obtained on 1 August 1980 and rounded. All turnover and liability figures are given in annual terms.

Appendix B Methods of Calculating VAT

The Additive Method

Tax is levied on the amount of wages and profits derived from the activity of the firm, i.e. on the value added by the firm. This method identifies the tax more as an imposition on payroll and profits rather than a tax on sales, and, as such, it may not qualify for rebate on exports under the GATT.

Problems may arise with defining taxable profits, and it is almost essential that the tax is levied at a single rate. (Different firms can in principle be taxed at different rates, but it would then be difficult to measure the tax content of any individual transaction.) The additive method is advantageous for use in industries where inputs and outputs are difficult to measure, e.g. banking and finance.

The Direct Subtractive Method

Tax is again levied on the value added by the firm, but in this case it is calculated by subtracting the total inputs of the firm from its total outputs. The tax is thus more clearly identified with sales.

Again this method is most suitable for operation at a single rate.

The Indirect Subtractive Method (Invoicing Method)

This is the method which is in general use. The value added by the firm is *not* calculated; the tax content of inputs and outputs is shown on each invoice, and the firm's tax payment equals the amount of tax collected from customers less the amount of tax paid to suppliers.

It is always possible to identify the tax content of any sale precisely and the tax is identified with sales, ensuring its eligibility for rebate on exports (except where there are short-cut schemes, e.g. the UK special retail schemes).

It is easier to apply different tax rates to different commodities under this method. However, a firm which does not trade entirely in standard rated goods and services will then be making tax payments which are *not* proportional to the value added by it (see Table B.1); the tax has ceased to be a true tax on value added.

Table B.1 Comparison of calculation of VAT by different methods

	Tax exclusive price (£)	Tax rate (%)	Additive method	Direct subtractive method	Indirect subtractive (invoicing) method
...uts			Calculated on the basis of the Value Added by the Firm (£3500). 15 per cent of £3500:	Calculated on the basis of the tax exclusive prices of inputs and outputs. Outputs are £6500, inputs are £3000. £6500 minus £3000 equals £3500. 15 per cent of £3500:	Calculated on the basis of the tax applied to outputs and inputs. Tax applied to outputs is £975 (£6500 × 15 per cent, and tax applied to inputs is £300 (£2000 × 15 per cent – there is no tax applied to inputs of fuel) £975 minus £300:
...terials	2000	15			
...el	1000	0			
...lue added					
...ages and					
...ofits	3500	15			
...tputs					
...nished goods	6500	15			
...t tax due			£525	£525	£675

...te: It may be seen that where two rates are imposed at one stage and only one rate at the next, the ...invoicing' method yields a different net tax due at that stage from either of the alternative methods, ...as the tax relief at the previous stage is recouped at the next.

Appendix C A Summary of Previous Research Studies on Compliance Costs

1 Corporate Taxation

Title	Authors	Reference	No. of responses	Response rate (%)	Respondents	Findings
1 The cost to business concerns of compliance with tax laws	R. M. Haig	*Management Review* November 1935, 232–333	160	10	Large US corporations with annual average sales of $17m.	Total compliance costs were 2.3% of tax liability. Size of costs was influenced by the number of states traded in. High compliance costs possibly imply low administrative costs.
2 Costs of tax administration Examples of compliance expenses	J. W. Martin	*Bulletin of the National Tax Association*, April 1944, 194–205	5	100	Large and medium sized US corporations	Compliance costs were highly variable, being influenced by the type of business, type of tax, state policy and level – federal, state or local – and possibly by size and efficiency of firm. There was a floor to compliance costs, so they were proportionately higher for small

3 The tax on taxes	J. B. May and G. C. Thompson	*Conference Board Business Record,* April 1950, 130–3	125	?	US manufacturing companies	Compliance costs were 1½% of tax liability and 0.1% of sales. Differences between state tax laws cause high costs.
4 The high cost of compliance	S. M. Mathes and G. C. Thompson	*Business Record,* August 1959, 383–8	222	?	US manufacturing companies	Compliance costs appeared to be increasing and this trend was likely to continue.
5 Compliance costs and the Ohio axle mile tax	C. V. Oster and A. D. Lynn	*National Tax Journal,* April 1955, 209–14	11	61	Ohio trucking companies	Compliance costs of this tax were 10% of tax liability. They were highly variable with the predictability of operations, low costs being incurred where operations were very predictable and vice versa.
6 *The cost of tax compliance*	M. H. Bryden	*Canadian Tax Foundation* Paper 25, July 1961	125	25	Corporate supporters of CTF–nearly 50% manufacturers	Compliance costs were highly variable even between similar firms. They were proportionately higher for small firms. Costs of minor taxes were very high compared to liability.
7 *Corporations' federal income tax compliance costs*	K. S. Johnston	Ohio University Bureau of Business Research Monograph 10, 1961	6	100	Firms in Colombus, Ohio	There were economies of scale in compliance procedures – they are proportionately higher for small firms.
8 Administrative and compliance costs of state and local taxes	J. H. Wicks and M. N. Killworth	*National Tax Journal,* September 1967, 309–15	74	?	Employers in Montana	Employers' costs of withholding income tax averaged 8.3% of taxes withheld.

2 Business Taxation Excluding Corporate Taxation

Title	Author	Reference	No. of respondents	Response rate (%)	Respondents	Findings
9 A measurement of the cost of collecting sales tax monies in selected retail stores	M. P. Matthews	Salt Lake City: Bureau of Economic & Business Research, University of Utah, 1956	7	100	Utah retail stores	Compliance costs were highly variable, with selling costs higher than administrative costs. Average transaction size is the principal determining factor, but store financial policy also had an influence. Compliance weighed heaviest on small firms.
10 Retailers' costs of sales tax collection in Ohio	J. C. Yocum	Ohio University Bureau of Business Research, 1961	526	?	Ohio retail stores over $50 000 in second half of 1959	Compliance costs were influenced by size of firm, average transaction size, and ratio of taxable to gross sales. They were proportionately greater for small firms.
11 The burden of compliance	F. J. Muller	Seattle Bureau of Business Research, 1963	198 by questionnaire – 80% Interview follow-up of 75 – 25%		Small businesses in Washington State	Economies of scale existed in sales tax compliance costs, particularly in administering the system. Indirect costs were also significant, and costs in stress were often high. Payroll taxes were also investigated, with similar findings.

12 The disguised tax burden. Compliance costs of German businessmen and professionals	B. Strumpel	*National Tax Journal*, January 1966, 70–77	1009	?	German businessmen with less than 100 employees each	Owners spent an average of 18 hours per month on tax work and their employees a further 4 hours. Cost of tax advice was 60 Dm per month. Compliance costs were regressive; other taxpayers did not incur significant costs.
13 German Added Value Tax – 2 Years After	R. J. Niehus	*Taxes*, September 1969, 554–66	?	?	?	66–70 per cent of German businesses surveyed said the VAT law caused more book work, often much more than a ten per cent increase.
14 Value Added Tax, the cost to the businessman	P. A. Barker	*Journal of Accountancy*, September 1972, 75–9	6	100	Selected Indiana Firms	Compliance costs of a hypothetical VAT are related to the number of sales and purchases invoices handled, and to average transaction size. Manufacturers handle the greatest number of invoices and incur the highest costs.
15 VAT – compliance costs to the independent retailer	M. Godwin	*Accountancy*, September 1976, 48–60	29	44	Independent Bath retailers	Compliance costs were related to the scheme of accounting selected for VAT, and this in turn depends on the rating of goods sold. Frequent changes in the tax increase compliance costs.

Title	Authors	Reference	No. of responses	Response rate (%)	Respondents	Findings
16 Compliance costs of the Value Added Tax	S. K. Parker	*Taxes*, June 1976, 369–80	6	—	Non-retail businesses	Indicated that a hypothetical VAT on either the invoice or the accounts basis could be operated without major accounting changes in any of the surveyed firms. Total compliance costs amounted to less than 1 per cent of sales. Compliance costs were regressive.

3 Personal Taxation

Title	Authors	Reference	No. of responses	Response rate (%)	Respondents	Findings
17 Taxpayer compliance costs from the Montana personal income tax	J. H. Wicks	*Montana Business Quarterly*, Fall 1965, 36–42	106	33	Parents of economics undergraduates	Compliance costs were a function of occupation. A few respondents reported very high costs. Response was biased towards higher cost taxpayers – low compliance cost taxpayers did not reply.
18 Taxpayer compliance costs from personal income taxation	J. H. Wicks	*Iowa Business Digest*, August 1966, 16–21	118	31	Parents of college students	Similar to the above. The self-employed incurred the highest compliance costs. Costs were not related to income or to size of tax payment.

| 19 | Administrative and compliance costs of state and local taxes | J. H. Wicks and M. N. Killworth | *National Tax Journal*, September 1967, 309–15 | 421 | 42 | Montana income taxpayers | Average compliance cost of the Montana income tax to the personal taxpayer was 20.7% of liability. |
| 20 | *The hidden costs of taxation* | C. T. Sandford | Institute for Fiscal Studies, 1973 | 2773 for short questionnaire, 137 follow-up | 78 for questionnaire 41 for follow-up | UK personal taxpayers, with re-survey of those paying for tax advice or spending at least 8 hours pa on tax work | UK personal taxpayers' costs increased between 1965 and 1970. The self-employed constitute half of the high cost taxpayers. Compliance costs were inequitable and regressive. Total operating costs of personal direct taxation were between 3.8 and 5.8% of revenue, whereas administrative costs were less than 1.5%. |

Appendix D The Questionnaire and Interview Schedules

**University of Bath
Centre for Fiscal Studies
1978**

Value Added Tax
A Survey of Costs and Benefits to Businesses

HOW TO FILL IN THIS QUESTIONNAIRE

Please follow the questionnaire through in sequence from question 1 to question 36.

There are two main types of question. The first simply asks you to tick one or more boxes. For example, if you have been visited by a VAT officer, you would answer question 28a by ticking the YES box as follows:

28a   Have you been visited by a VAT officer?   YES √

NO

The second type of question asks you to write an answer in the space provided. Directions in the question will explain the type of answer wanted. For example, if you are the proprietor of a business, and you work full-time in it, and during the financial year 1977/78 you employed an average of 3 people full-time and 2 people part-time, you would answer question 6 as follows:

6   How many people were employed in the business on average in the financial year 1977/78?

(a)   Full-time employees (count a proprietor or partner as one employee)   4

(b)   Part-time employees (employed for less than 21 hours a week). If there are no part-time employees, please write "O"   2

There are also some diagrams to show you which sections to fill in. For example, if your company has 5 directors, you would answer question 20 by ticking the boxes shown and following the directions to question 23:

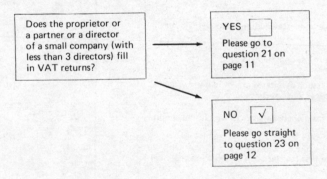

Does the proprietor or a partner or a director of a small company (with less than 3 directors) fill in VAT returns?

YES   Please go to question 21 on page 11

NO √   Please go straight to question 23 on page 12

You will see various numbers, letters and boxes in the right hand margins. Please ignore them – they are there to help us classify your answers.

Where a question asks for information about the financial year 1977/78, please take your last 12 months of completed VAT periods if that is more convenient.

If you wish to add further comments, please feel free to do so.

For ALL traders

Col.

1   Please indicate, by ticking the appropriate box,
    your main business activity (please tick one).

☐☐☐☐☐ 1 1–6
         (QNUM)
☐☐☐☐ 7–10
         (DATE)

Agriculture, forestry, fishing, mining or quarrying . . . . ☐   1   11

Manufacturing . . . . ☐   2

Construction . . . . ☐   3

Gas, electricity, or water supply . . . . ☐   4

Garages, motor vehicle distributors and repairers . . . . . ☐   7

Transport and communication . . . . ☐   5

Wholesale distribution . . . . ☐   6

Retailing . . . . ☐   6

Dealers and merchants (excluding motor vehicle dealers) ☐   6

Financial or professional services . . . . ☐   7

Other services, such as entertainment, catering
services, laundries and hairdressers . . . . ☐   7

2   What are the main goods or services which you supply?

Code

☐   12–13

. . . .

3   When did you first register for VAT? (please tick one)

1972–3 . . . . ☐   1   14
(introduction of VAT)

1974 . . . . ☐   2

1975 . . . . ☐   3

1976 . . . . ☐   4

1977 . . . . ☐   5

1978 . . . . ☐   6

3

For ALL traders

For office use only —
please do not write in this margin

Col.

4a   Approximately what proportion of your outputs (sales
etc.) is classed in each of the following categories?
(please tick)

PROPORTION OF OUTPUTS

CATEGORIES	1 NONE	2 Up to ¼ of all outputs	3 ¼ to ½ of all outputs	4 ½ to ¾ of all outputs	5 ¾ or more (but not all outputs)	6 ALL
Standard rated						
Higher rated (rate a)						
Exports						
Zero rated (other than exports)						
Exempt from VAT						

Code

☐ 15

☐ 16

☐ 17

☐ 18

☐ 19

4b   And roughly what proportion of your inputs (purchases
etc.) is classed in each of the following categories?

PROPORTION OF INPUTS

CATEGORIES	1 NONE	2 Up to ¼ of all inputs	3 ¼ to ½ of all inputs	4 ½ to ¾ of all inputs	5 ¾ or more (but not all inputs)	6 ALL
Standard rated						
Higher rated (rate a)						
Zero rated						
Exempt from VAT						

Code

☐ 20

☐ 21

☐ 22

☐ 23

For ALL traders

5   What was your VAT payment for the financial year
1977/78 or for the last **12 months of completed VAT
returns?**

Col.

		For the Whole Year 1977/78	For your Final Quarter in 1977/78		
(a)	Total tax due (Part A, Box 5 on your VAT returns)	£	£	*Punch*	24- 31, 32- 39
(b)	Total tax deductible (Part A Box 9 on your VAT return)	£	£	*Do not punch*	
(c)	Net VAT payment made	£	£	*Punch Positive*	40- 47, 48- 55
(d)	Or net VAT repayment received	£	£	*Punch Negative*	40- 47, 48—55

(e)   Do you usually qualify for
a net repayment of VAT?   YES ☐   1

NO ☐   2   56

6   How many people were employed in the business on average in
the financial year 1977/78?

(a)   Full-time employees (count a proprietor or
partner as one employee)   ☐   57– 62

(b)   Part-time employees (employed for less
than 21 hours a week). If there are
no part-time employees, please write "O"   ☐   63- 66

5

For ALL traders

Please tick the turnover band(s) representing the business's
approximate size in the financial year 1977/78.

Col.

	Taxable turnover for 1977/78	Total turnover for 1977/78 (if different from taxable turnover)	Punch lead zeros			
Less than £7,500	☐	.... ☐	001	001	67- 69	70–72
£7,500 up to £10,000	☐	.... ☐	002	002		
£10,000 up to £20,000	☐	.... ☐	003	003		
£20,000 up to £50,000	☐	.... ☐	004	004		
£50,000 up to £75,000	☐	.... ☐	005	005		
£75,000 up to £100,000	☐	.... ☐	006	006		
£100,000 up to £150,000	☐	.... ☐	007	007		
£150,000 up to £250,000	☐	.... ☐	008	008		
£250,000 up to £500,000	☐	.... ☐	009	009		
£500,000 up to £1 million	☐	.... ☐	010	010		
£1m up to £5m	☐	.... ☐	011	011		
£5m up to £10m	☐	.... ☐	012	012		
£10m up to £50m	☐	.... ☐	013	013		
£50m up to £100m	☐	.... ☐	014	014		

code

If £100m or more please
state approximate amount   £ ☐ m .... £ ☐ m   ☐ ☐

8a	Are you partly exempt from VAT?	YES ☐	1	73
		NO ☐	2	

8b   If "YES", which method of calculating
partial exemption do you use?

	Method 1 ☐	1	74
	Method 2 ☐	2	
	Any other method ☐	3	

End of Card 1

For ALL traders

For office use only —
please do not write in this margin

9   About how much in value does a customer usually buy at one time from you, counting the total of all items on a single bill as one sale? (For example, if most customers buy 6 items at a time price £5 each, an average sale totals £30, and you would tick the box £10 up to £100).

Col.

| | | | | |2| 1–6

New Card

Up to £10 . . . . ☐	1
£10 up to £100 . . . . . . ☐	2 7
£100 up to £1,000. . . . ☐	3
£1,000 or more . . . . . . ☐	4

10   About how many invoices do you process in a year?

Number of Invoices	Purchases Invoices	Sales Invoices	P	S	
1 – 500	☐	☐	1	1	8, 9
501 – 1,000	☐	☐	2	2	
1,000 – 10,000	☐	☐	3	3	
10,000–100,000	☐	☐	4	4	
Over 100,000	☐	☐	5	5	

Please tick here if sales invoices are **not** issued . . . . ☐   6

11   Excluding bad debts, approximately what percentage of purchases and sales invoices are settled within each of the following periods after invoicing?

Punch 99 for 100

Invoices settled:	Percentage of Purchases Invoices	Percentage of Sales Invoices	
Within 1 week		. . . .	10–11, 12–1
Between 1 week and 1 month		. . . .	14– 15, 16–1
During the second month		. . . .	18–19, 20–2
During the third month		. . . .	22–23 24–2
During the fourth month		. . . .	26–27, 28–2
More than four months after invoicing. .		. . . .	30–31, 32–3

7

For ALL traders

Col.

12 In what form are your accounting records kept?
(please tick one)

Ledgers all written up by hand .... ☐ 1   34

Kalamazoo type system .... ☐ 2

Machine accounting system .... ☐ 3

Fully computerised system .... ☐ 4

13 About how much time within the business was spent
entirely on VAT work in the financial year 1977/78?

	Number of Hours	**Approximate value of this Time**		
(a) By the proprietor, or by partners in the business	☐	£ ☐	Punch	35–38, 39–43
(b) By directors of the company	☐	£ ☐		41–47, 48–52
(c) By qualified accounting staff employed in the business	☐	£ ☐		53–56, 57–61
(d) By other staff	☐	£ ☐		62–65, 66–70
(e) TOTAL	☐	£ ☐		71–74, 75–79

End of Card 2

For ALL traders

Col.

| | | | | | 3 | 1–6

New Card

14   Approximately what percentage of your costs of
accounting (excluding fees to outside advisers)
are the costs of accounting solely for VAT?

Of all accounting costs,
VAT accounting costs are about . . . . [   ]

per cent

Punch 99 for 100   7–8

15   Who normally fills in most or all of your VAT
return forms? (Please tick one)

(a)   The proprietor, or a partner in the business . . . . [   ]   1   9

(b)   A director of the company . . . . [   ]   2

(c)   Company secretary . . . . [   ]   3

(d)   A qualified accountant employed in the business . . . . [   ]   4

(e)   An accountant in private practice . . . . [   ]   5

(f)   A member of your book-keeping staff . . . . [   ]   6

(g)   Any other person (please describe). . . . . [   ]   7

. . . .

16   How often do you submit VAT returns?
(Please tick one)

Quarterly   [   ]   1   10

Monthly   [   ]   2

17   During the autumn of 1978, Customs & Excise are
introducing a new VAT 100 return form. Have you
used this new return form yet?

YES   [   ]   1   11

NO   [   ]   2

9

For ALL traders

18   Please tick the answers which apply to you and follow
      the directions.

Col.

Start here:

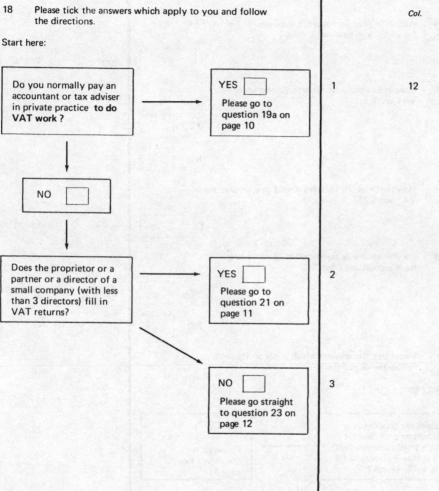

| Do you normally pay an accountant or tax adviser in private practice **to do VAT work ?** | → | YES ☐ Please go to question 19a on page 10 | 1 | 12 |

NO ☐

| Does the proprietor or a partner or a director of a small company (with less than 3 directors) fill in VAT returns? | → | YES ☐ Please go to question 21 on page 11 | 2 |

| | → | NO ☐ Please go straight to question 23 on page 12 | 3 |

ONLY for traders who normally employ an accountant in private practice to do VAT work

For office use only –
please do not write in the margin

Col.

19a   What was your accountant's total fee for the last 12 months for which you have been billed?

£ [   ]   *Punch*   13–16

19b   Does your accountant charge you separately for VAT work?

YES [   ]   1   17

NO [   ]   2

19c   How much of the total fee would you say was for VAT work?

£ [   ]   *Punch*   18–21

19d   Do you incur any significant VAT costs apart from accountant's fees?

YES [   ]   1   22

NO [   ]   2

20   Please tick the answers which apply to you and follow the directions.

Start here:

Does the proprietor or a partner or a director of a small company (with less than 3 directors) fill in VAT returns?

YES [   ]   1   23
Please go to question 21 on page 11

NO [   ]   2
Please go straight to question 23 on page 12

11

ONLY for proprietors, partners and directors of small
companies (less than 3 directors) who fill in their own
VAT returns

21   Has the person responsible for filling in VAT returns
had any formal book-keeping training? (please tick one)

            Yes, qualified
            accountant   ☐   1   24

            Yes, other
            book-keeping
            training   ☐   2

            No, self taught   ☐   3

22a   How old was the person responsible for
filling in VAT returns at the end of their
last year of full-time education?

            Age: ☐   *Punch*   25–26

22b   How many years of part-time education
did the person responsible for filling
in VAT forms have after age 15?
(if none, please write "O")

            Years after age 15:   ☐   *Punch*   27–28

For ALL traders

23a   Do you have any difficulties with
VAT which keep cropping up?   YES ☐   1   Col.
29

NO ☐   2

If "NO" please go straight to Question 24a

23b   If "YES", what are the main causes of these
difficulties? (Please tick)

The number of arithmetic calculations .... ☐   1   30

The number of rates of VAT .... ☐   1   31

The volume of invoices processed .... ☐   1   32

Understanding VAT instructions .... ☐   1   33

Partial exemption .... ☐   1   34

Second hand schemes .... ☐   1   35

Import paperwork .... ☐   1   36

Export paperwork .... ☐   1   37

Changes in VAT rates .... ☐   1   38

Self-billing . . . . ☐   1   39

Liability borderlines .... ☐   1   40

Any other reasons for difficulty .... ☐   1   41
(please explain below)

. . . .

. . . .

. . . .

. . . .

13

For ALL traders

Col.

24a Have you had any **special** problems with
VAT in the last 12 months?

YES ☐ 1   42

NO ☐ 2

If "NO" please go straight to Question 25

24b If "YES", please describe them briefly

24c How much did these **special** problems cost in time
and money?

	Total number of hours	Total value of this time in £		
Proprietor's or partner's time	☐	£ ☐	*Punch*	43–45, 46–49
Time of company directors	☐	£ ☐		50–52, 53–56
Accounting staff time	☐	£ ☐		57–59, 60–63
Other staff time	☐	£ ☐		64–66, 67–70
Cost of fees to tax advisers		£ ☐		71–75
Other costs (journeys, phone etc)		£ ☐		76–79

24d Did you include these costs in your
answer to question 13?

YES ☐ 1   80

NO ☐ 2

End of Card 3

For ALL traders

25   Please indicate, by ticking the appropriate boxes, your attitude to the following statements:

	1 Agree strongly	2 Agree	3 Un-certain	4 Disagree	5 Disagree strongly	
VAT is a simple method of collecting tax						7
Pressure of VAT work means that other aspects of the business suffer						8
Most other taxes work more efficiently than VAT						9
I do not mind doing VAT work						10
As it stands, VAT is unreasonably complicated						11
Keeping VAT accounts helps to control purchases and sales efficiently						12
VAT works satisfactorily for all concerned						13
Considering how much VAT I pay, I spend too much time on VAT accounts						14
	1	2	3	4	5	

26   In order to save you the trouble of preparing VAT returns within the business, about HOW MUCH would you be willing to pay an adviser (or do you pay an adviser) to prepare one year's VAT returns from existing records?

£ ☐

Punch   15—19

15

For ALL traders

For office use only —
please do not write in this margin

Col.

27 Please indicate, by ticking the boxes, whether you have used the following sources of advice on VAT, and how helpful you found them.

	Have you used this Source?		How Helpful was this Source?				
			Very Helpful	Helpful	Neither Helpful nor Un-helpful	Un-helpful	Very Un-helpful
	YES	NO					
Official VAT booklets							
Other tax guide books and journals							
Your accountant							
Local VAT Office							
Visiting VAT Officer							
Your Trade Association							
VAT Headquarters							
Other sources you use (please describe below)							
	1	2	1	2	3	4	5

Y/N HELP

20 21
22 23
24 25
26 27
28 29
30 31
32 33
34 35

. . . .

28a Have you been visited by a VAT officer?   YES ☐   1   36

NO ☐

If "NO" please go straight to Question 29

If "YES"

28b When was your last visit from a VAT officer? (please tick one)

During the last 3 months ☐   1   37

3 – 6 months ago ☐   2

6 – 12 months ago ☐   3

More than 12 months ago ☐   4

28c How long did the visit last?   Hours: ☐   *Punch*   38–40

28d Do you have any comments on this visit?   End of Card 4

For ALL traders

Col.

| | | | | | |5| 1–6

New card

29   The VAT system may have both advantages and disadvantages for your business. Please tick whether you agree or disagree with the following statements and where possible estimate the value of the benefit in the past financial year.

	1 Agree	2 Dis- agree	Value in the past Financial Year	A/D Code	Value	A/D
My purchases records are better kept since VAT came in	☐	☐	£	☐	7–11,	12
My sales records are better kept since VAT came in	☐	☐	£	☐	13–17,	18
Useful extra cash is collected during each VAT period	☐	☐	£	☐	19–23,	24
I claim discounts more frequently	☐	☐	£	☐	25–29,	30
I save money by doing more of my own accounts, and giving my accountant less work to do	☐	☐	£	☐	31–35,	36
Losses from bad debts are reduced	☐	☐	£	☐	37–41,	42
Stock control is improved	☐	☐	£	☐	43–47,	48
Other advantages (please explain below)	☐	☐	£	☐	49–53,	54

. . . . £ . . . .

. . . .

. . . .

17

For ALL traders

For office use only —
please do not write in this margin

Col.

30   Please tick the boxes which apply to you and follow
      the instructions

Start here:

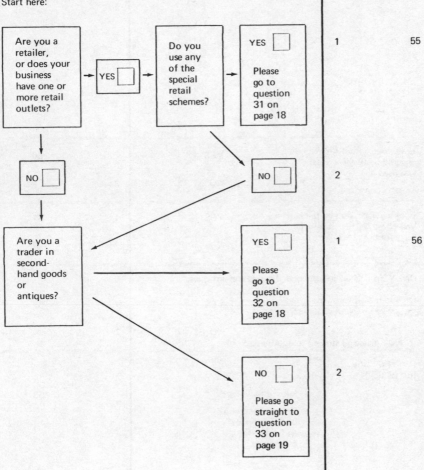

1	55
2	
1	56
2	

ONLY for users of special retail schemes

31a   Which special retail scheme(s) do you use?
(please tick)

		Col.
A ☐ F ☐	1 6	57–59
B ☐ G ☐	2 7	
C ☐ H ☐	3 8	
D ☐ J ☐	4 9	
E ☐	5	

31b   Is all your output tax
covered by the scheme(s)
you use?

YES ☐   1   60

NO ☐   2

31c   Looking back, do you think
you chose the best scheme(s)
for your business?

YES ☐   1   61

NO ☐   2

ONLY for traders in secondhand goods and antiques

32a   Do you use either of the
special secondhand schemes?

YES ☐   1   62

NO ☐   2

If "NO" please go straight to question 33

32b   If "YES" which?
(please tick)

Second-hand cars ☐   1   63

Second-hand works
of art, antiques
and scientific
collections ☐   2

19

For ALL traders

Col.

33   If you could have claimed from the Customs and Excise
     for time and money spent on VAT accounting in the
     financial year 1977/78, about how much would you have
     claimed?

£ _____

Punch   64–68

34   Do you have any comments on the VAT system?

Code   69

Please turn over

For ALL traders

35   Please indicate who has completed this questionnaire
(tick one)

Proprietor or partner . . . . ☐   1   70

Company director . . . . ☐   2

Company secretary . . . . ☐   3

Qualified accountant employed
in the business . . . . ☐   4

Book-keeper . . . . ☐   5

Other (please describe) . . . . ☐   6

. . . .

. . . .

36   If you are willing to answer any queries that arise from this
questionnaire, or would like a summary of the results, please
state your name, address, and telephone number, and tick
the box(es):

Name . . . .

Address . . . .

. . . .

. . . .

. . . .

Telephone . . . .

I would be willing to answer
some further questions . . . . ☐   1   71

I would like a summary of
the results . . . . ☐   1   72

THANK YOU AGAIN FOR COMPLETING THIS
QUESTIONNAIRE. WE HOPE YOU HAVE
ENJOYED FILLING IT IN AND NOT FOUND
IT TOO TIME-CONSUMING. PLEASE POST IT
IN THE REPLY PAID ENVELOPE AS SOON
AS POSSIBLE.

End of Card 5

The research team cannot identify you from the number on the questionnaire; but if you wish to make doubly sure that you will remain completely anonymous please cut off the business reply card below and return it separately from the questionnaire. No one will then be able to link the card with your questionnaire, but the receipt of the card will ensure that you are not bothered by reminders.

Postage
will be
paid by
licensee

Do not affix Postage Stamps if posted in
Gt. Britain, Channel Islands or N. Ireland

BUSINESS REPLY SERVICE
Licence No. BA 683

Professor C. T. Sandford
Director for the Centre for Fiscal Studies
School of Humanities and Social Sciences
University of Bath
Claverton Down
BATH BA2 4TQ

|2|

D2 The Letter Accompanying the NAS Questionnaire

University of Bath

Special Telephone Advisory Service until 17 November 1978: Bath (0225) 63887	CENTRE FOR FISCAL STUDIES Claverton Down, Bath BA2 7AY Telephone: Bath (0225) 6941 Director: Telex: 449097 Professor C T Sandford

20 September 1978

Dear Sir or Madam

                              STUDY OF COSTS OF VAT

I am writing to ask you to be kind enough to answer the enclosed questionnaire.
It is particularly about the time and money spent by traders in complying with
VAT regulations.   We aim to discover the way VAT is working so that it may be
improved.   Your answer will help to influence Government policy.

The survey is independent of Government, civil service and political party, but
there is no doubt that the Government will take notice of the results.
Treasury Ministers have authorised Customs and Excise to cooperate with the
research team and have expressed the hope that traders will also help (see
over); how *much* influence the results will have on policy-making now depends
on the number of traders who reply and the accuracy of their answers.   Your
business has been chosen as part of a scientifically-designed sample and your
reply is needed to make the results representative.   So please help us and
help yourself.

Replies will be treated in strict confidence and will be seen only by the
University research team.   Your reply can only be identified if you choose to
give us your name and address.   We hope you will feel able to do so, because
then we can send you a summary of the results if you would like one, and it is
also possible for us to contact you for any further information if you are
willing to give it;   but the choice is yours.   If you wish to be doubly sure
that your reply will be completely anonymous, please cut off the numbered reply
card on the back cover and return it separately from the questionnaire.   No
one will then be able to link the card with the questionnaire but we will know
that you have replied.   In any case, we will ensure that it is not possible
for individual businesses to be identified in any publication resulting from
this survey.

The questionnaire is not as long and difficult as it may appear.   About one
third of the space is for office use; most answers simply require ticks; and
many of the questions only apply to certain kinds of businesses.   However, it
may take you as long as an hour to complete.   You will appreciate that a
shorter questionnaire would not be sufficient to cover all the issues.   If you
are having any problems with completing the questionnaire, please do not
hesitate to call Research Officer Michael Godwin at our special advisory
service number, Bath (0225) 63887.   You may reverse the charges.

Because of the crucial importance of the survey for policy-making, we urge you
to find the time to fill in and return the questionnaire, in the reply paid
envelope, as soon as you can.

Thank you for your help.

Yours faithfully

C. T Sandford.

Reply by the Financial Secretary to the Treasury (on behalf of the Chancellor of the Exchequer) to a Parliamentary Question about the Bath University study of the Costs to Traders of Value Added Tax.

Value Added Tax
Mr Cartwright asked the Chancellor of the Exchequer to what extent his Department will be involved in the proposed studies at the University of Bath of the expense in time and money to businesses in making VAT returns.

Mr Robert Sheldon: I understand that some preliminary work has been done and that a research team led by Professor C T Sandford is planning to make a major survey of VAT compliance costs. Customs & Excise have been authorised to give the help sought from them in mounting this survey. In particular, Customs & Excise will select a suitable statistical sample of registered traders and co-operate in the addressing and dispatch of questionnaires under secure conditions. I should make it clear that the University will not be told the names and addresses of persons to whom questionnaires have been sent; that persons receiving a questionnaire will be under no legal obligation to reply to it, though I hope they will do so; and that the services provided by Customs & Excise will be paid for by the University of Bath.

Reported in *Parliamentary Debates* (House of Commons) 20 April 1977, Vol. 930, No. 1071, col. 96.

D3 The Interview Schedules used in Follow-up Interviews

(a) *Telephone Interview Schedule*

CODE NUMBER: TURNOVER BELOW £50,000? YES —— NO ——

NAME: PARTLY EXEMPT? YES —— NO ——

PHONE NUMBER: VAT RATES OPERATED: ——

Did the alteration of VAT rating on 18 June cause you any transitional difficulties, such as repricing goods and services? Nature of difficulty:

YES | NO

How many hours of man work were involved? hours

Is the new VAT 100 Return Form, introduced in October 1978, easier to use than the old VAT Return?

YES | NO

Does this mean that time spent on VAT work within the business has been cut?

Then it has not cut the time spent on VAT work at all?

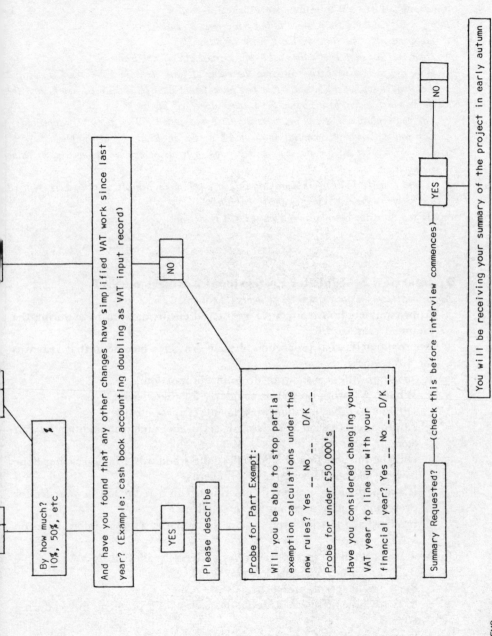

By how much?
10%, 50%, etc

And have you found that any other changes have simplified VAT work since last year? (Example: cash book accounting doubling as VAT input record)

NO

YES

Please describe

Probe for Part Exempt:

Will you be able to stop partial exemption calculations under the new rules? Yes __ No __ D/K __

Probe for under £50,000's

Have you considered changing your VAT year to line up with your financial year? Yes __ No __ D/K __

Summary Requested? ———— (check this before interview commences)

YES

NO

You will be receiving your summary of the project in early autumn

FMG
July 1979

(b) *The Personal Interview Schedule*

The personal interviews began with the telephone interview questions, and the following additional questions were asked as well:

In the mail questionnaire returned to the University of Bath:

1. *How was the time spent on VAT work calculated?*
2. *How was the proprietor's time valuation arrived at? (if applicable).*
3. *Why are there discrepancies between the value of time spent on VAT work done, and the amount you would be willing to pay an external adviser to do VAT work, and the claim which would be made for VAT work done? (if applicable).*
4. *Can you explain any special problems you have had with VAT in detail? (if applicable).*
5. *Can you explain your comments on the VAT system in detail? (if applicable).*
6. *Did you answer the question on credit periods in terms of number of invoices, or value of invoices?*
7. *Would it make VAT work more difficult, or much more difficult, if rates were changed every year; every 6 months; or every 3 months?*
8. *Do you have any other comments on the VAT system?*

D4 Interview Schedule for Professional Advisers on VAT

Professional advisers were asked the following questions:

1. Approximately how many VAT registered clients did you have during the financial year 1977/8?
2. Approximately what proportion of your firm's fee income in that year was for VAT work?
3. Is this a growing, constant, or declining proportion?
4. a. What VAT work do you do regularly for these clients?
   b. Do you do other taxation work for all of these clients?
   c. Approximately what VAT costs does the client incur in addition to your fee?
5. a. Did the introduction of VAT effect the standard of book-keeping done by your clients? How? And which clients?
   b. If standards have improved, has this led to a reduction in your fee for preparing annual accounts for these clients?
   c. From what source do you obtain the majority of your information on VAT?
6. Are any particular types of trader very adversely affected by VAT?
   a. By virtue of heavy regular costs?
   b. By virtue of special problems?
   c. Roughly how many clients brought special VAT problems to you during 1977/8?
   d. Please describe.
   e. Is the number of special problems increasing or decreasing?
7. a. How many problems involved disputes with Customs & Excise?
   b. Is the appeals procedure satisfactory?

8. a. Generally, how efficient have you found Customs in administering VAT?
   b. How long do Customs take to make repayments?
   c. In what respects does the accountant's relationship with Customs differ from the relationship with Inland Revenue?
9. Are there any particular traders who gain considerable benefits from operating the VAT system?
10. How successful are the retail and secondhand schemes?
11. Were there any difficulties with the change of VAT rates on 18th June 1979?
12. In what ways would frequent changes (every 12, 6, or 3 months) in VAT rates cause difficulties?
13. Is the single positive VAT rate an improvement?
14. Is the new VAT return form, issued late 1978, an improvement? Could it be further simplified?
15. Has the liberalisation of partial exemption rules made a big improvement?
16. Do you now advise clients to line up their financial and VAT years?
17. Are there ways in which VAT could be further simplified?
18. Advisers were also given a list of a selection of businesses and their characteristics (output VAT rates, approximate taxable turnover, approximate annual number of invoices, special scheme used if any, and frequency of VAT returns) and asked:–
    Approximately what fee would you charge for preparing one year's VAT returns, (a) in 1978, (b) in 1980, in each of the following cases, assuming the clients supply you with all necessary records maintained to a reasonable standard?

Appendix E Technical Aspects of the National Survey

E1 Summary of the VAT Trade Classification

This list is not comprehensive; the *VAT Trade Classification* (VAT 41) gives full details.

Primary includes agriculture, forestry, fishing, mining and quarrying.

Manufacture and utilities includes all manufacturing industry, plus supply of gas, electricity and water.

Construction includes all building contractors and specialists, and opencast coal mining.

Transport and communication includes rail, road, air and sea transport, post and telecommunications, shipping agents, travel agents, driving instruction, storage, operation of car parks, toll roads and bridges.

Retail includes all retail distribution.

Wholesale and dealers includes all wholesale distribution, dealers in industrial and waste materials, machinery, and livestock; merchants in coal, oil, agricultural and builders' supplies, and leasers of machinery.

Financial and business services includes insurance, banking, stockbroking, unit trusts, property management, advertising, valuers, auctioneers, computer services, management consultancy, employment and other business agencies, and other business services.

Professional and scientific services includes accountancy, educational, legal, medical and research services, surveyors, architects, consultant engineers, artists, writers and composers.

Miscellaneous and public services includes entertainment, sport, gambling, hotels, restaurants and take-aways, pubs and clubs, hairdressers, laundries, garages and car dealers, national and local government services.

E2 Comparison of Eligible and Total Populations, 1977/8

Sector	Eligible traders	Total traders	Eligible as percentage of total traders
(a) By sector			
Primary	171 512	179 926	95.3
Manufacture and utilities	106 765	120 800	88.4
Construction	157 635	179 153	88.0
Transport and communication	48 495	56 353	86.1

Sector	Eligible traders	Total traders	Eligible as percentage of total traders
Retail	244 010	280 212	87.1
Wholesale and dealers	76 617	87 677	87.4
Financial and business services	37 042	44 019	84.2
Professional and scientific services	55 047	63 154	87.2
Miscellaneous and public services	227 106	262 884	86.4
(b) By taxable turnover (£ooos p.a.)			
0– 9.9	200 007	270 000	74.1
10– 19.9	238 721	270 000	88.4
20– 49.9	312 163	341 000	91.5
50– 99.9	166 588	178 000	93.6
100–499.9	153 919	161 000	95.6
500–999.9	23 422	24 000	97.6
1000 and over	29 409	30 000	98.0
Total	1 124 229	1 274 178	88.2

E3 Estimated Response Rates by Size within Sector (percentages)

Taxable turnover (£000 p.a.)	Primary	Manufacture and utilities	Construction	Transport and communication	Retail	Wholesale and dealers	Financial and business services	Professional and scientific services	Miscellaneous and public services	Overall
0– 9.9	34.7	22.1	21.2	19.0	22.5	23.1	35.1	28.9	14.9	26.3
10– 19.9	26.5	22.7	25.7	26.7	25.6	20.0	29.2	35.7	21.4	25.1
20– 49.9	29.1	22.4	19.6	24.7	22.2	18.9	39.7	33.7	18.1	22.4
50– 99.9	45.7	33.9	29.6	18.4	31.7	22.5	43.3	57.4	30.4	32.2
100–499.9	65.9	44.1	35.1	38.8	34.3	27.0	60.5	53.5	33.0	37.7
500–999.9	83.3	77.3	76.5	37.5	69.2	78.0	42.9	75.0	36.0	63.1
1000 and over	46.7	47.4	56.1	53.8	66.7	44.3	37.5	46.7	48.8	44.3
Overall	34.8	39.0	27.3	29.4	29.0	33.2	41.8	37.8	24.3	30.8

Note: Customs & Excise were not willing to reveal the precise details of the sample structure. Consequently, the response rates had to be estimated from information provided by Customs & Excise on total number of registered traders and rates of eligibility by size and by sector, applying the appropriate sampling fractions. The approximations made are more reliable for the size totals and sector totals than for the individual cells.

E4 Possible Reasons for the Low Response

(a) The undertakings given to Customs & Excise included the full quotation of an answer to a Parliamentary Question about the survey which stressed its voluntary nature, and made particular mention of the co-operation given by the Customs & Excise Department.

(b) The address labels on the undelivered questionnaires returned to the University which were in any case rather illegible, were evidently prepared by the Customs & Excise Central Unit computer, which cast doubts in some addressees' minds about the independence and confidentiality of the research. The fact that the mailing firm was located outside Bath also meant that the material was not postmarked from its apparent source, which again generated a certain amount of suspicion.

(c) 98 questionnaires which should not have been in the sample were returned marked 'gone away' or 'ceased trading'. It is possible that there were more out of frame respondents whose blank questionnaires were not returned to the University; but because of confidentiality restrictions it was not possible to follow up non-respondents to investigate this conjecture.

(d) Because the introduction of a new VAT 100 return form was imminent, the survey was brought forward from early 1979 to late 1978, thus enabling the researchers to investigate compliance costs before the new form was introduced. (Changes in compliance costs brought about by the use of the simplified form were investigated during follow-up interviews.) Bringing the survey forward was the only method open to the researchers of differentiating between the costs before the new form came in and after, because any later investigation would have picked up many respondents whose year had involved both old and new style VAT returns. In fact, only 14 per cent of respondents had seen the new return. The earlier survey date caused a rush in notification of the survey to the press and to trade associations. Had favourable publicity been more widespread before distribution of the questionnaires, the response might have been increased significantly.

(e) There was some criticism of the length of the questionnaire. Originally it had been intended to differentiate between the larger, more sophisticated firms and the small traders, and to send a simplified version only to the smaller traders. Unfortunately, the sampling procedure finally agreed did not permit identification of the small traders.

(f) Problems with the post apparently arose in several cases. At least 34 questionnaires were either not delivered or severely delayed in the post.

(g) It may be seen that response was biased towards the larger businesses. This may help to explain the difference between response to the pilot survey, which was over 46 per cent, and response to the national survey at 31 per cent. The pilot sampling frame used was the Bristol area Yellow Pages telephone directory, and it is probable that many of the smaller traders do not ensure that their names appear in the Yellow Pages, and even that some of them are not on the telephone. It therefore seems that the pilot sample was biased (by omissions) towards the traders who proved most likely to reply. Another possible reason for the difference in response to the pilot and the national survey is that the Bristol area could be unusually co-operative in comparison with the national average, either because the survey was being undertaken by a local university and therefore appealed particularly to a sense of civic duty, or because of some other undefined characteristics of the area.

E5

Table E5.1 Comparison of the size distributions of respondents to NAS with the total population of registered traders 1977/8 (percentages)[a]

Taxable turnover (£000 p.a.)	Primary	Manufacture and utilities	Construction	Transport and communication	Retail	Wholesale and dealers	Financial and business services	Professional and scientific services	Miscellaneous and public services	Overall
0– 9.9	29.3	8.2	22.6	16.7	7.8	8.9	23.0	24.0	12.0	16.3
	(32.0)	(14.7)	(30.0)	(26.1)	(10.2)	(12.8)	(29.8)	(35.1)	(19.7)	(21.2)
10– 19.9	17.5	8.9	25.3	29.2	19.1	7.7	16.8	22.7	22.2	18.6
	(22.7)	(13.7)	(24.9)	(28.2)	(20.1)	(11.3)	(22.3)	(23.4)	(23.1)	(21.2)
20– 49.9	23.2	12.9	17.0	18.8	31.1	12.4	20.4	18.2	24.8	21.7
	(26.9)	(19.6)	(21.4)	(19.0)	(37.2)	(18.6)	(19.3)	(19.1)	(30.0)	(26.8)
50– 99.9	14.9	14.6	12.3	7.3	24.5	11.8	11.5	17.5	18.8	16.6
	(10.8)	(14.6)	(10.2)	(9.6)	(20.4)	(14.8)	(10.0)	(10.8)	(13.5)	(13.9)
100–499.9	13.7	30.7	15.3	19.8	14.3	26.0	20.4	14.9	17.0	18.0
	(6.8)	(23.3)	(10.6)	(12.4)	(10.9)	(26.7)	(12.3)	(9.7)	(11.1)	(12.6)
500–999.9	1.2	12.1	4.3	3.1	1.8	18.9	2.7	1.9	2.3	4.6
	(0.4)	(5.4)	(1.4)	(2.1)	(0.7)	(7.0)	(2.3)	(0.9)	(1.4)	(1.9)
1000 and over	0.3	12.4	3.0	5.6	1.5	14.3	4.0	1.3	2.7	4.1
	(0.3)	(8.9)	(1.4)	(2.6)	(0.6)	(8.9)	(4.1)	(0.8)	(1.2)	(2.4)
Total	100	100	100	100	100	100	100	100	100	100

[a] Total population of registered traders in brackets.
Note: in the NAS figures allowance has been made for the different sampling fraction of traders with a taxable turnover over £1 million.
Source: NAS and Customs & Excise.

Table E5.2 Significance of differences between the size distribution of
the population of registered traders and of respondents to the national survey

Sector	Chi-squared	Degrees of freedom	Significant difference at 95% level
Primary	12.09	7	No
Manufacture and utilities	20.00	9	Yes
Construction	13.17	8	No
Transport and Communication	13.11	8	No
Retail	7.33	8	No
Wholesale and dealers	33.94	9	Yes
Financial and business services	9.30	9	No
Professional and scientific services	11.75	7	No
Miscellaneous and public services	11.24	8	No
All sectors	10.65	9	No

Note: these tests of significance were performed on a finer breakdown than is presented here. The degrees of freedom may thus be greater than the preceding tables indicate.

Table E5.3 Cumulative size distribution of the total population
of registered traders (percentages)

Taxable turnover (£000 p.a.)	Primary	Manufacture and utilities	Construction	Transport and communication	Retail	Wholesale and dealers	Financial and business services	Professional and scientific services	Miscellaneous and public services	Overall
Under £10 000	32.0	14.7	30.0	26.1	10.2	12.8	29.8	35.1	19.7	21.2
Under £20 000	54.7	28.4	54.9	54.3	30.3	24.1	52.0	58.5	42.8	42.4
Under £50 000	81.6	48.0	76.3	73.2	67.5	42.6	71.4	77.7	72.8	69.1
Under £100 000	92.4	62.6	86.6	82.8	87.9	57.5	81.4	88.4	86.3	83.1
Under £500 000	99.3	85.8	97.2	95.2	98.8	84.2	93.6	98.1	97.3	95.7
Under £1 million	99.7	91.2	98.5	97.3	99.5	91.1	95.9	99.1	98.8	97.6
All traders	100	100	100	100	100	100	100	100	100	100

Table E5.4 Cumulative size distribution of respondents to NAS
by sector and range of taxable turnover

Taxable turnover (£000 p.a.)	Primary	Manufacture and utilities	Construction	Transport and communication	Retail	Wholesale and dealers	Financial and business services	Professional and scientific services	Miscellaneous and public services	Overall
Under 10 000	29.3	8.2	22.6	16.7	7.8	8.9	23.0	24.0	12.0	16.3
Under 20 000	46.8	17.1	47.3	45.9	26.9	16.6	39.8	46.7	34.2	34.9
Under 50 000	70.0	30.0	64.9	64.7	58.0	29.0	60.2	64.9	59.0	56.6
Under 100 000	84.9	44.6	77.2	72.0	82.5	40.8	71.7	82.4	77.8	73.2
Under 500 000	98.6	75.3	92.5	91.8	96.8	66.8	92.1	97.3	94.8	91.2
Under 1 million	99.8	87.4	96.8	94.9	98.6	85.7	94.8	99.2	97.1	95.8
All traders	100	100	100	100	100	100	100	100	100	100

Note: Allowance has been made for the different sampling fraction of traders with a taxable turnover over £1m.

Appendix F Estimation of Total Compliance Costs

F1 Estimation of Total Compliance Costs from NAS

Mean estimates of compliance cost for each range of taxable turnover within each sector were obtained from NAS. Compliance costs were defined as:

Total value of time within the business spent entirely on regular VAT work in the financial year 1977/8.

Plus Total fee to an accountant in private practice for regular VAT work.

Plus Total value of time and other costs arising due to special problems with VAT.

In terms of the NAS questionnaire the compliance cost of a respondent was calculated as:

Q13(e) + Q19(c) + Q24(c) (if Q24(d) = No)

The number of usable responses for grossing up purposes was 2,396 and the distribution of these by sector and range of taxable turnover is shown in Table F1.1. Many of the cells contained fewer than ten cases; such cells were combined with adjacent ones within the same sector, and a grouped mean obtained for the combined cells. Such combinations are also shown on Table F1.1.

The mean compliance cost figures obtained from NAS for the various cells are shown in Table F1.2. Total grossed up compliance costs can be estimated from the mean figures using the formula:

$$\text{Total compliance cost} = \sum_{i=1}^{n} \sum_{j=1}^{9} F_{ij} \bar{\chi}_{ij}$$

Where i = range of taxable turnover (n $\leqslant$ 10); j = sector of business; F_{ij} = number of traders of taxable turnover range i in sector j on the VAT Register of Traders as at 31 March 1978. $\bar{\chi}_{ij}$ = sample mean estimate of compliance cost of taxable turnover range i in sector j obtained from respondents to NAS. Table F1.4 gives the distribution of VAT registered traders by sector and range of taxable turnover as at 31 March 1978.

The total estimated gross compliance cost obtained on this basis from NAS was £392 million as shown in Table F1.5 but some of the means have high standard errors (Table F1.3). Relatively high standard errors can be expected given the low response, but the cross-checks on the NAS estimate reported in

Table F1.1 Number of respondents to NAS showing cell groupings to obtain at least 10 respondents in each cell

Taxable turnover (£000 p.a.)	Primary	Manufacture and utilities	Construction	Transport and communication	Retail	Wholesale and dealers	Financial and business services	Professional and scientific services	Miscellaneous and public services	Total
0– 9.9	101	18	61	14	30	14	25	35	40	338
10– 19.9	59	21	69	26	73	10	19	31	71	379
20– 49.9	87	31	48	16	129	18	23	27	82	461
50– 99.9	57	38	34	16 ⎱ 23	103	19	12	27	56	353
100– 499.9	47	76	45	7 ⎰	64 ⎱ 71	42	22 ⎱ 25	19	56 ⎱ 64	389
500– 999.9	4 ⎱	32	11	18	7 ⎰	30	3 ⎰	3 ⎱	8 ⎰	101
1000– 4999.9	5	85	27 ⎱	3	22 ⎱	57	14 ⎱	5	29	260
5000– 9999.9	1 ⎰ 11	19	4	16 ⎱	0	15	3 ⎱ 18	0 ⎰ 10	4 ⎱	47
10 000–49 999.9	0	25 ⎱ 31	4 ⎰ 35	1 ⎰ 21	5 ⎰ 28	12 ⎱ 13	1	1	3 ⎰ 10	54
50 000 and over	1	6 ⎰	0	3	1	1 ⎰	0	1	3	14
Total	362	351	303	105	434	218	122	149	352	2396

Table F1.2 Mean compliance cost (£) from NAS by sector and range of taxable turnover (cells combined to provide a minimum of 10 respondents in NAS)

Taxable turnover (£000 p.a.)	Primary	Manufacture and utilities	Construction	Transport and communication	Retail	Wholesale and dealers	Financial and business services	Professional and scientific services	Miscellaneous and public services
0—9.9	54	118	107	80	165	74	179	123	121
10—19.9	86	272	196	199	150	211	302	266	203
20—49.9	95	279	278	256	237	353	354	474	314
50—99.9	141	294			318	317	665	363	607
100—499.9	392	440	592	763	535	606	437	1183	584
500—999.9	1392	700	478		4714				
1000—4999.9		845		1923		636	3786	1714	1922
5000—9999.9		485	656			720			
10 000—49 999.9		3661	2109			1095			1040
50 000 and over						2024			

Table F1.3 Standard errors of the mean estimates of compliance cost (£) from NAS

Taxable turnover (£000 p.a.)	Primary	Manufacture and utilities	Construction	Transport and communication	Retail	Wholesale and dealers	Financial and business services	Professional and scientific services	Miscellaneous and public services
0— 9.9	6	23	12	21	36	24	47	21	17
10— 19.9	13	82	17	64	27	93	107	50	33
20— 49.9	9	58	37	59	33	91	59	292	39
50— 99.9	18	56	180		34	78	281	60	194
100— 499.9	84	55	78	198	70	112	83	465	103
500— 999.9		165	124			216			
1000— 4999.9	1093	192	527	577	3541	113	1809	664	558
5000— 9999.9		98				415			
10 000—49 999.9		1942				918			438
50 000 and over									

Note: the standard error of an estimate indicates the degree of variation likely between repeated samples.

Table F1.4 Distribution ('000s) of VAT registered traders by sector and range of taxable turnover in parent population at 31 March 1978 (cells grouped to provide at least 10 respondents in NAS)

Taxable turnover (£000 p.a.)	Primary	Manufacture and utilities	Construction	Transport and communication	Retail	Wholesale and dealers	Financial and business services	Professional and scientific services	Miscellaneous and public services	Total
0– 9.9	57.6	17.7	53.8	14.7	28.6	11.2	13.1	22.2	51.8	
10– 19.9	40.8	16.6	44.6	15.9	56.3	9.9	9.8	14.8	60.8	
20– 49.9	48.4	23.7	38.4	10.7 } 16.1	104.1	16.3	8.5	12.1	78.8	
50– 99.9	19.5	17.6	18.3	5.4 }	57.2	13.0	4.4	6.8	35.4	
100– 499.9	12.3	28.1	19.0	7.0 } 8.2	30.9 } 32.5	23.4	5.4 } 6.4	6.1	32.9	
500– 999.9	0.8	6.5	2.5	1.2 }	1.6 }	6.1	1.0 }	0.6 } 1.1	2.6	
1000– 4999.9	1.3 }	7.7	2.5 }	1.4	1.7 }	6.3 }	1.8 }	0.5 }	0.6 }	
5000– 9999.9	}	1.4 } 1.6	}		}	0.8 }	}		}	
10 000– 49 999.9	0.5 }	}				0.7 }				
50 000 and over	}									
Total	179.9	120.8	179.2	56.4	280.2	87.7	44.0	63.2	262.9	1274.2

Source: HM Customs & Excise.

Table F1.5 Total estimated compliance cost by sector and range of taxable turnover (£ million)

Taxable turnover (£000 p.a.)	Primary	Manufacture and utilities	Construction	Transport and communication	Retail	Wholesale and dealers	Financial and business services	Professional and scientific services	Miscellaneous and public services	Total
0— 9.9	3.11	2.09	5.76	1.18	4.72	0.83	2.34	2.73	6.27	29.0
10— 19.9	3.51	4.52	8.74	3.16	8.45	2.09	2.96	3.94	12.34	49.7
20— 49.9	4.60	6.61	10.68	2.74	24.67	5.75	3.01	5.74	24.74	88.5
50— 99.9	2.75	5.17	10.83	1.38	18.19	4.07	2.93	2.47	21.49	69.3
100— 499.9	4.82	12.36	9.08	4.12	17.4	14.18	2.80	7.22	19.21	105.5
500— 999.9	1.11	4.55	1.64	6.26		3.88		1.03	5.00	49.9
1000— 4999.9	0.70	6.51	5.27	2.69	8.01	4.54	6.81	0.86	0.62	
5000— 9999.9		0.68				0.88				
10 000— 49 999.9		5.86				1.42				
50 000 and over										
Total	20.6	48.4	52.0	17.4	81.4	37.7	20.9	24.0	89.7	392

Mean 308

Chapter 4 confirm the general accuracy of the estimated total. If the cells had not been grouped to obtain at least 10 respondents per cell the estimated total gross compliance cost would have been £400 million.

Two checks were carried out on the sensitivity of the estimated means to extreme values occurring in NAS data. Firstly, the lowest and highest 10 per cent of reported values were excluded from each range of taxable turnover within each sector (except the open-ended uppermost range, where the top 10 per cent are likely simply to be associated with the largest firm and could in no sense be regarded as 'outliers'). Secondly, extreme values were weighted to allow for the positive but decreasing probability of their occurrence, the further away from the mean they lay.

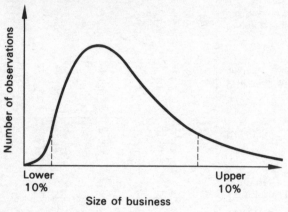

Figure F1.1   Illustration of skewed size distribution of VAT registered traders overall, and in many size/sector ranges

Removing the extreme 10 per cent of values in all but the upper band of taxable turnover reduced the estimate of total compliance cost by 24 per cent from £392 million to £296 million, as shown in Table F1.6. However, the size distribution of VAT registered traders is positively skewed, (see Figure F1.1.) and compliance cost and taxable turnover are positively correlated.* Thus ignoring the top and bottom 10 per cent of values in each cell removes a greater range from the top end than from the bottom, resulting in an underestimate of total compliance costs.

A modification to the above procedure for dealing with extreme values is to apply weights to observations in inverse proportion to the distance they lie away from the mean of the relevant sector and taxable turnover range cell. A weight of *unity* was applied to observations lying within two standard deviations from the cell mean, *zero* if the observation was more than three standard deviations away from the mean, and a weight of (3 − [number of standard deviations away from the mean]) if they lay between two and three standard deviations away, i.e. a weight of between one and zero. Figure F1.2 illustrates the procedure.

The rationale for the weighting system is that if the observations were *normally*

* Coefficient of correlation between compliance cost and taxable turnover is 0.84.

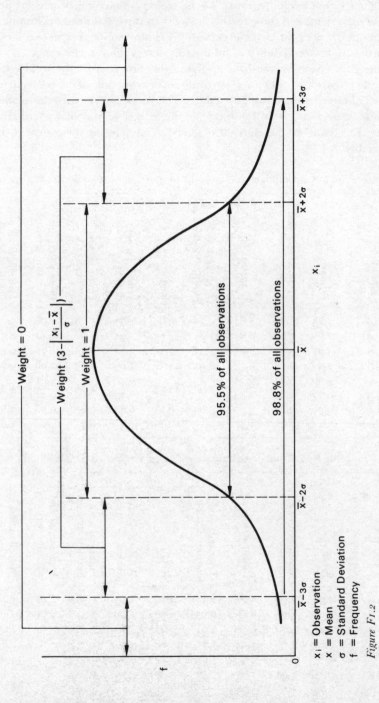

Weight = 0

Weight $\left(3 - \left|\dfrac{x_i - \overline{x}}{\sigma}\right|\right)$

Weight = 1

95.5% of all observations

98.8% of all observations

$\overline{x} - 3\sigma$ $\overline{x} - 2\sigma$ $\overline{x}$ $\overline{x} + 2\sigma$ $\overline{x} + 3\sigma$ x_i

x_i = Observation
$\overline{x}$ = Mean
σ = Standard Deviation
f = Frequency

Figure F1.2

distributed within a cell, the range x̄ ± 2σ would contain a little over 95 per cent of the observations, and those further away than three standard deviations would form about 0.2 per cent of the observations. Thus the weights were allocated in proportion to the probability of finding an observation in the range.

Table F1.7 gives the results of applying this procedure – the total estimated gross compliance cost falls to £307 million, a reduction of 21 per cent on the estimate obtained using unweighted data. This procedure, as with the unweighted exclusion of outliers, is still subject to the effects of the skewed distribution (Figure F1.1) and is therefore also likely to underestimate compliance costs appreciably.

Table F1.6 Total compliance cost (omitting top and bottom deciles) (£ million)

Taxable turnover (£000 p.a.)	Primary	Manufacture and utilities	Construction	Transport and communication	Retail	Wholesale and dealers	Financial and business services	Professional and scientific services	Miscellaneous and public services	Total
0– 9.9	2.25	1.82	4.84	0.90	3.69	0.77	1.39	2.06	5.75	23.5
10– 19.9	2.61	3.20	8.03	1.80	5.63	1.34	1.82	3.12	8.57	36.1
20– 49.9	3.97	5.10	8.95	1.93	17.18	5.54	2.35	1.77	19.54	66.3
50– 99.9	2.30	3.68	6.13	0.97	14.36	2.99	2.13	2.08	9.84	44.5
100–499.9	3.00	9.64	6.71⎫	4.98⎫	13.23	10.76⎫	1.85	3.61⎫	14.28⎫	75.5
500–999.9	0.27	2.87	1.43⎭	⎭		2.15⎭		0.74⎭	⎭	
1000 and over	0.70	13.05	5.27	2.69	8.01	6.84	6.86	0.86	5.62	49.9
Total	15.1	39.4	41.4	13.3	62.1	30.4	16.4	14.2	63.6	296

Table F1.7 Total compliance costs using *weighted* data (£million)

Taxable turnover (£000 p.a.)	Primary	Manufacture and utilities	Construction	Transport and communication	Retail	Wholesale and dealers	Financial and business services	Professional and scientific services	Miscellaneous and public services	Total
0– 9.9	2.36	2.05	5.22	1.13	3.89	0.59	1.78	2.18	5.44	24.6
10– 19.9	2.98	3.60	8.25	2.05	6.76	1.43	2.04	3.33	9.36	39.8
20– 49.9	4.11	5.00	9.10	2.32	19.47	4.60	2.58	1.57	20.65	69.4
50– 99.9	2.42	4.08	7.94	1.50	15.84	3.30	2.33	2.18	14.37	54.0
100–499.9	3.70	10.09	7.64	5.45	13.46	10.83	2.06⎫	5.56	14.20⎫	85.1
500–999.9	0.21	3.45	1.62	0.34	1.00	2.75	0.60⎭		2.10⎭	
1000 and over	0.79	10.01	3.94	2.13	2.01	5.65	4.12	0.99	4.29	33.9
Total	16.57	38.28	43.71	14.92	62.43	29.15	15.51	15.81	70.4	307

F2 Comparison of NAS Time Values with New Earnings Survey (NES) Data

Tables F2.1–4 show the hourly valuations of time reported by respondents to NAS. With the exception of 'other staff' (Table F2.4) there is a generally increasing valuation of time as the size of the business increases. Table F2.5 shows NES data for comparable staff categories as at April 1978.

Proprietors

The mean hourly valuation of the proprietors' time (as given in NAS) varied from £3.00 in the primary sector, to £13.00 in the professional and scientific services sector with an overall mean of £4.60. It is interesting to note that the sectors with most respondents – namely retail, primary, miscellaneous and public services, and construction all showed mean valuations in the range £3.00–£3.80, which compared very favourably with the mean figure for top management in the NES of £3.74 per hour. Indeed, if we add an allowance of 13.5 per cent of gross pay to cover National Insurance (up to a limit of £135 per week) then the NES figure would rise to £4.24 per hour.

Of the other sectors, transport and communication fall below NES levels up to a turnover of £100,000 p.a. – and the high figures thereafter are based on a very small number of respondents. Figures for manufacture and utilities and wholesale and dealers are similar to the upper quartile top management mean in NES (£4.74 per hour, or £5.24 allowing for National Insurance), leaving only the two most specialist sectors, financial and business services and professional and scientific services outside this range. These are sectors which have a high proportion of high earners among the self-employed (Cmnd 7679, 1979), and thus there seems little reason to fear serious exaggeration among NAS respondents.

Directors

Average reported hourly rates for directors (from NAS) varied from £4.60 for primary sector to £10.60 in professional and scientific services sector, with an overall mean of £7.10. Allowing for National Insurance contributions, the NES for the top management upper decile mean was £7.17 per hour. Only the transport and communication, wholesale and dealers, professional and scientific services and financial and business services sectors show higher figures, influenced largely by high figures in a few cases.

Accounting Staff

The overall mean (from NAS) was £5.00 per hour, with only the wholesale and dealers and professional and scientific sectors (at £6.40 and £7.70 respectively) showing any marked deviation. This is however well above the NES mean figure for accountants of £2.69 (£3.05 allowing for National Insurance) but it is likely that 'accountants' in the NES will also include book-keepers. The overall consistency of estimates between sectors lends weight to the view that no significant exaggeration is present.

Other

Again there was a consistent picture (from NAS) between sectors, with only the financial and business services and professional and scientific services sectors (at £4.00 and £4.10 respectively) differing markedly from the overall mean of £2.70. This compares well with the figure of £2.14 (£2.42 allowing for National Insurance) reported in the NES for the upper quartile mean for clerical and related staff.

Overall Conclusion

There is no evidence that respondents have exaggerated the value of the time spent on VAT.

Table F2.1 Mean hourly time valuations reported by respondents to NAS (£) – 1. *Proprietors*

Taxable turnover (£000 p.a.)	Primary	Manufacture and utilities	Construction	Transport and communication	Retail	Wholesale and dealers	Financial and business services	Professional and scientific services	Miscellaneous and public services	Sample mean
0– 9.9	2.5 (86)	5.8 (11)	3.5 (52)	3.1 (11)	3.2 (25)	4.1 (11)	4.6 (16)	8.2 (26)	3.6 (28)	3. (26
10– 19.9	2.5 (56)	4.4 (17)	3.9 (56)	3.7 (21)	2.8 (68)	6.4 (8)	7.8 (14)	10.8 (25)	3.7 (54)	4. (31
20– 49.9	2.9 (65)	4.0 (14)	3.7 (32)	3.8 (9)	3.2 (107)	2.9 (12)	8.9 (12)	15.9 (20)	3.6 (48)	4. (31
50– 99.9	4.4 (34)	6.3 (7)	4.2 (16)	4.1 (3)	3.4 (78)	5.7 (8)	10.0 (8)	18.0 (19)	3.6 (32)	5. (20
100–499.9	4.7 (19)	8.0 (14)	5.3 (6)	14.8 (3)	4.1 (32)	5.5 (13)	9.1 (7)	13.5 (11)	3.9 (17)	6. (12
500–999.9	— (0)	— (0)	5.0 (1)	— (0)	— (0)	10.0 (1)	— (0)	25.0 (1)	— (0)	13. (
1000 and over	5.0 (1)	10.0 (1)	4.0 (1)	20.0 (1)	10.0 (1)	8.8 (4)	10.0 (1)	25.0 (2)	10.0 (1)	11. (1
Sample mean	3.0 (261)	5.6 (64)	3.8 (164)	4.6 (48)	3.3 (311)	5.1 (57)	7.6 (58)	13.1 (104)	3.7 (180)	4. (124

Figures in parenthesis are the number of respondents.

Taxable turnover (£000 p.a.)	Primary	Manufacture and utilities	Construction	Transport and communication	Retail	Wholesale and dealers	Financial and business services	Professional and scientific services	Miscellaneous and public services	Sample mean
0– 9.9	— (0)	6.0 (1)	3.0 (3)	— (0)	2.5 (2)	12.5 (1)	1.5 (2)	9.3 (6)	10.0 (2)	6.6 (17)
10– 19.9	2.5 (1)	4.1 (2)	4.3 (2)	— (0)	1.8 (2)	5.0 (1)	— (0)	6.3 (6)	3.3 (3)	4.4 (17)
20– 49.9	5.3 (3)	5.4 (13)	2.9 (10)	2.3 (5)	4.1 (9)	4.3 (4)	9.8 (5)	3.8 (2)	4.8 (15)	4.7 (66)
50– 99.9	2.6 (4)	3.9 (10)	5.5 (11)	— (0)	5.7 (13)	6.8 (9)	— (0)	19.5 (2)	4.0 (8)	5.5 (57)
100–499.9	4.5 (8)	8.3 (30)	7.7 (20)	8.8 (9)	4.8 (20)	7.0 (14)	12.2 (6)	6.8 (3)	6.1 (17)	7.2 (127)
500–999.9	6.4 (1)	6.8 (15)	9.1 (4)	24.0 (2)	11.6 (3)	6.3 (13)	10.0 (1)	12.5 (1)	7.4 (5)	8.2 (45)
1000 and over	8.1 (2)	8.9 (30)	8.0 (14)	6.9 (3)	9.5 (13)	10.0 (31)	10.6 (2)	50.0 (1)	8.5 (15)	9.4 (111)
Sample mean	4.6 (19)	7.3 (101)	6.4 (64)	8.4 (19)	6.0 (62)	8.0 (73)	9.8 (16)	10.6 (21)	6.2 (65)	7.1 (440)

Table F2.3 Mean hourly time valuations reported by respondents to NAS (£) – 3. *Accounting staff*

Taxable turnover (£000 p.a.)	Primary	Manufacture and utilities	Construction	Transport and communication	Retail	Wholesale and dealers	Financial and business services	Professional and scientific services	Miscellaneous and public services	Sample mean
0– 9.9	7.2 (4)	— (0)	5.0 (1)	— (0)	6.6 (4)	5.0 (1)	3.7 (2)	8.8 (2)	2.0 (2)	5.9 (16)
10– 19.9	4.0 (1)	1.5 (1)	3.2 (5)	2.0 (1)	4.3 (2)	— (0)	3.3 (2)	7.5 (1)	3.6 (4)	3.5 (17)
20– 49.9	4.7 (6)	1.5 (4)	3.0 (2)	3.0 (1)	5.2 (8)	3.0 (1)	3.7 (3)	6.1 (3)	7.1 (9)	4.9 (37)
50– 99.9	7.9 (9)	4.9 (8)	3.0 (1)	6.8 (3)	2.2 (7)	1.6 (2)	5.3 (3)	6.0 (3)	1.5 (4)	4.8 (40)
100–499.9	3.8 (12)	3.8 (19)	4.1 (8)	5.3 (4)	3.5 (13)	3.1 (8)	6.5 (7)	3.7 (4)	4.1 (16)	4.0 (91)
500–999.9	3.1 (1)	3.1 (18)	4.1 (6)	3.0 (1)	3.8 (3)	5.7 (11)	5.0 (2)	2.0 (1)	2.1 (4)	3.8 (47)
1000 and over	7.9 (2)	5.0 (97)	5.1 (23)	4.2 (11)	4.6 (14)	7.3 (55)	7.3 (12)	11.8 (7)	4.6 (24)	5.8 (245)
Sample mean	5.6 (35)	4.5 (147)	4.4 (46)	4.6 (21)	4.2 (51)	6.4 (78)	5.9 (31)	7.7 (21)	4.3 (63)	5.0 (493)

Table F2.4 Mean hourly time valuations reported by respondents to NAS (£) –
4. *Other staff*

Taxable turnover (£000 p.a.)	Primary	Manufacture and utilities	Construction	Transport and communication	Retail	Wholesale and dealers	Financial and business services	Professional and scientific services	Miscellaneous and public services	Sample mean
0– 9.9	2.9 (8)	2.8 (7)	3.6 (14)	1.5 (3)	1.4 (4)	1.4 (1)	4.7 (6)	2.3 (6)	1.7 (11)	2.8 (60
10– 19.9	4.4 (3)	3.4 (3)	1.7 (18)	1.4 (8)	1.8 (11)	2.0 (1)	4.4 (4)	3.4 (9)	3.2 (19)	2.6 (76
20– 49.9	3.0 (16)	1.9 (9)	2.4 (13)	2.5 (4)	2.1 (24)	2.8 (5)	4.5 (8)	2.7 (12)	2.6 (16)	2.6 (107
50– 99.9	2.1 (20)	2.7 (22)	2.1 (14)	1.0 (2)	2.5 (21)	3.7 (5)	2.4 (7)	4.0 (17)	1.9 (21)	2.5 (129
100–499.9	1.9 (19)	2.2 (50)	2.1 (32)	2.1 (11)	2.3 (24)	3.2 (24)	3.8 (11)	5.4 (13)	1.9 (27)	2.5 (211
500–999.9	2.3 (2)	2.3 (22)	3.4 (8)	— (0)	1.5 (4)	2.9 (18)	3.0 (3)	4.1 (2)	1.9 (5)	2.6 (64
1000 and over	2.3 (5)	3.1 (105)	2.8 (30)	2.6 (17)	2.9 (19)	2.9 (61)	4.6 (15)	7.5 (6)	2.4 (34)	3.1 (292
Sample mean	2.5 (73)	2.7 (218)	2.5 (129)	2.1 (45)	2.3 (107)	3.0 (115)	4.0 (54)	4.1 (65)	2.3 (133)	2.7 (939

Figures in parenthesis are the number of respondents.

Table F2.5 Hourly wage rates in April 1978 derived from *New Earnings Survey*
(full-time men aged 21 and over)

Category	Hourly wage rate (£)
Top management –	
Mean	3.74
Upper Quartile	4.74
Upper Decile	6.67
General management	3.74
Accountants	2.69
Clerical and related staff –	
Upper Quartile	2.14

Source: *New Earnings Survey* 1978 Part D (Analysis by Occupation).

F3 Estimates of Compliance Costs Incorporating the Charges of Specialist Firms

Two firms specialising in VAT work were consulted as a cross-check on the reliability of compliance cost estimates of small firms. Charges were based on turnover, but neither firm supplied information on charges to firms with a turnover greater than £100,000 p.a. The charges made in 1978 were:

Firm A: turnover up to £100,000 p.a.: £132 p.a.

Firm B: turnover up to £50,000 p.a.: £104 p.a.

turnover £50,000–£65,000 p.a.: £156 p.a.

turnover £65,000–£80,000 p.a.: £182 p.a.

turnover £80,000–£100,000 p.a.: £312 p.a.

Note: for Firm B a mean figure of £182 p.a. was taken for the whole turnover range £50,000–£100,000 p.a.

Although the charges are expressed in terms of total turnover, no serious problems arise in stating this as *taxable* turnover as few respondents reported any difference. The two firms concentrate their activity in the retail and

Table F3.1 Comparison of compliance costs derived from NAS in individual sectors with those incorporating the charges of specialist firms

Taxable turnover (£000 p.a.)	NAS data total (£m)	Firm A				Firm B			
		Regular (£m)	Special & other (£m)	Total (£m)	As % of NAS	Regular (£m)	Special & other (£m)	Total (£m)	As % of NAS
a) Retail sector									
0– 9.9	4.7	3.8				2.3			
10–19.9	8.5	7.4	12.2	44.6	80	5.9	12.2	41.5	74
20–49.9	24.7	13.7				10.8			
50–99.9	18.2	7.6				10.4			
oo and over	25.4	23.8	1.6	25.4	100	23.8	1.6	25.4	100
Total	81.4	56.3	13.8	70.0	86	53.2	13.8	66.9	82
b) Services sectors[a]									
0– 9.9	11.3	11.5				9.1			
10–19.9	19.2	11.3	12.2	54.3	60	8.9	12.2	48.6	53
20–49.9	33.5	13.1				10.3			
50–99.9	26.9	6.2				8.1			
100 and over	43.7	38.7	5.0	43.7	100	38.7	5.0	43.7	100
Total	134.6	80.8	17.2	98.0	73	75.1	17.2	92.3	69

[a] Including financial and business, professional and scientific, miscellaneous and public services

service sectors, but their charges have been used as a cross-check on *all* firms with a taxable turnover of less than £100,000 p.a. Table F3.1 looks at the effect on the retail and services sectors alone, and Table F3.2 looks at the effect on *all* firms with a taxable turnover less than £100,000 p.a. It is interesting to note that the NAS data for the smallest firms, most of which will be voluntary registrations, give an estimated figure *lower* than that for Firm A, and approximately equal to that for Firm B. The tables indicate a substantial reduction in compliance costs as a result of using specialist firms in the services sectors, but overall the figures are consistent with the NAS estimates.

Table F3.2 Comparison of compliance costs derived from NAS (all sectors) with those incorporating the charges of specialist firms

Taxable turnover (£000 p.a.)	NAS data total (£m)	Firm A				Firm B			
		Regular (£m)	Special & other (£m)	Total (£m)	As % of NAS	Regular (£m)	Special & other (£m)	Total (£m)	As % of NAS
0–9.9	29.0	35.7 ⎫				28.1 ⎫			
10–19.9	49.7	35.6 ⎪	48.0	187.8	79	28.0 ⎪	48.0	171.9	73
20–49.9	88.5	45.0 ⎬				35.5 ⎬			
50–99.9	69.3	23.5 ⎭				32.3 ⎭			
100 and over	155.4	142.8	12.6	155.4	100	142.8	12.6	155.4	100
Total	392	282.6	60.6	343	88	266.7	60.6	327	83

F4 Response to Question 26 of NAS
Question 26 of the NAS asked:

> *In order to save you the trouble of preparing VAT returns within the business, about how much would you be willing to pay an adviser (or do you pay an adviser) to prepare one year's VAT returns from existing records.*

The objective behind this question was to obtain a measure of the opportunity cost of VAT work which would allow for the alternative use (if any) to which the time taken to do VAT work could be put and would take in at least some psychic costs. In retrospect it is easy to see the deficiencies in the question.

The number of respondents to the questionnaire who failed to reply to this particular question was abnormally high at over 17 per cent. Of the 2,316 who did reply 1,221 (52 per cent) answered 'zero'. The remainder mainly gave a figure which was less than compliance cost or claim.

A particular point was made of probing the meaning of the replies in interviews (FOL(P)). The question was seen as separating the completion of the return from the work necessary to complete it, and it was stressed by interviewees that the burden of the tax was in the maintenance of the necessary records rather than simply filling in the returns. Others maintained that they were unwilling to pay anything to an outside agent because they needed to do the work themselves to keep in touch with the business (which links with the advantages perceived from the VAT system). A further frequent response 'written in' on the NAS questionnaire was that the business simply could not afford to pay an adviser for this work; this comment was repeated in FOL(P) especially by sole proprietors.

It is clear from this analysis that the question was not answered in a way which could be meaningfully used in analysis.

Appendix G Effect of Different Measures of Size on the Distribution of Compliance Costs

G1 Total Turnover Compared with Taxable Turnover

A comparison of the size distribution of respondents to NAS measured by taxable turnover with that measured by total turnover was carried out for all sectors, but only in the financial and business services sector were the distributions substantially different – 11 per cent of respondents changed size ranges between the two measures. Table G1 gives details of the comparison together with that of compliance costs.

The overall regressive nature of compliance costs is evident using both measures but it is interesting to note the relatively higher burden of compliance costs for those whose taxable *and* total turnover fell into the smaller range, compared with those whose *taxable* turnover fell into that range, irrespective of total turnover. This suggests that there are some determinants of compliance cost dependent upon *total* rather than just *taxable* turnover (e.g. the accounting system used).

Table G1 Financial and business services sector – comparison of estimates of compliance cost using taxable turnover and total turnover

Size (£000 p.a.)	(a) Using taxable turnover			(b) Using total turnover		
	Number of cases	Mean compliance cost (CC) (£)	CC as per cent of taxable turnover (% mean)	Number of cases	Mean compliance cost (CC) (£)	CC as per cent of total turnover (% mean)
0– 9.9	25	179	2.84	22	184	3.38
10– 19.9	19	302	2.01	18	299	2.00
20– 49.9	23	354	1.01	24	344	0.98
50– 99.9	12	665	0.88	12	665	0.88
100–499.9	22	416	0.23	20	419	0.25
500–999.9	3	595	0.08	3	178	0.02
1000 and over	18	3786	0.06	23	3079	0.04

G2 Employment as a Measure of Size

Table G2 shows the distribution of respondents to the NAS classified by sector and level of employment (the proprietor was also classed as an 'employee' of the business, and part-time employees were given a weight of 0.5). As can be seen, the distribution for each sector is highly skewed – more so even than the distribution by taxable turnover; thus employment is a poor discriminator.

Tables G3 and G4 show compliance costs, and compliance costs as a percentage of taxable turnover, classified by sector and level of employment. Although not too much reliance should be placed on the figures in the middle and upper size ranges (because of the small number of cases on which they are based), it is clear that the same sharply regressive pattern emerges as obtained when using taxable turnover as the basis of size classification.

No overall mean figures are provided in Tables G3 and G4 because the distribution of the parent population of registered traders by number of employees in unknown, and thus no weighting system can be applied. Similarly, no allowance can be made for the higher sampling fraction for firms with a taxable turnover greater than £1 million.

Table G2 Percentage distribution of respondents to NAS by employment within sector

Number of employees	Primary	Manufacture and utilities	Construction	Transport and communication	Retail	Wholesale and dealers	Financial and business services	Professional and scientific services	Miscellaneous and public services	Overall
0– 5	80.5	17.6	55.6	55.9	75.3	40.2	49.1	60.5	53.9	56.2
– 10	12.1	12.1	12.9	12.7	12.7	15.1	11.6	17.0	21.8	14.4
– 25	3.7	20.0	13.3	12.7	4.5	17.1	14.3	10.9	11.3	11.0
– 50	2.8	8.8	4.7	2.9	2.4	11.1	9.8	4.1	5.0	5.3
– 100	0.3	9.7	6.8	5.9	1.8	9.0	5.4	2.7	3.6	4.6
– 500	0.6	20.3	5.7	7.8	2.0	6.5	7.1	3.4	2.8	5.9
–1000	0	6.1	0.4	0	0.4	0.5	0.9	0	0	1.1
1000 and over	0	5.5	0.7	2.0	0.9	0.5	1.8	1.4	1.7	1.6
Total	100	100	100	100	100	100	100	100	100	100
No. of respondents	354	330	279	102	449	199	112	147	362	2334

Note: missing cases equal 465 or 16.6 per cent; these respondents failed to supply data either on employment or compliance costs.

Table G3 Mean compliance costs (£) by sector and number of employees

Number of employees	Primary	Manufacture and utilities	Construction	Transport and communication	Retail	Wholesale and dealers	Financial and business services	Professional and scientific services	Miscellaneous and public services
0– 5	88	262	235	291	249	339	773	304	245
– 10	236	332	470	696	424	815	372	290	569
– 25	561	384	440	419	551	826	502	967	751
– 50	591	740	633	379*	600	669	474	238*	1154
– 100	70*	697	1155	1403*	957*	868	3163*	1740*	1546
– 500	6500*	810	2567	951*	848*	1858	776*	1662*	1644
–1000	—	809	3800*	—	800*	180*	70*	—	—
Over 1000	—	5704	3365*	4508*	27352*	2700*	6188*	2605*	1382*

—no cases occurred in the sample
* Fewer than 10 respondents in cell

Table G4 Compliance costs as a percentage of taxable turnover by sector and number of employees (means)

Number of employees	Primary	Manufacture and utilities	Construction	Transport and communication	Retail	Wholesale and dealers	Financial and business services	Professional and scientific services	Miscellaneous and public services
0– 5	0.55	1.19	1.31	0.92	0.73	0.71	1.69	1.67	1.06
– 10	0.22	0.45	0.81	1.59	0.75	0.19	0.93	0.47	0.89
– 25	0.34	0.27	0.32	0.19	0.28	0.10	0.73	0.88	0.32
– 50	0.16	0.14	0.10	0.06*	0.10	0.03	0.23	0.17*	0.13
– 100	0.01*	0.06	0.06	0.05*	0.05*	0.02	1.16*	0.41*	0.13
– 500	0.01*	0.08	0.08	0.01*	0.03*	0.02	0.20*	0.12*	0.05
–1000	—	0.01	0.05*	—	..*	..*	0.06*	—	—
Over 1000	—	0.01	0.01*	0.01*	0.01*	..*	0.11*	0.01*	0.05*

—no cases occurred in the sample.
.. less than 0.005.
* Fewer than 10 respondents in cell.

Appendix H   Retailers' Special Schemes of VAT

Scheme	Percentage of all scheme users in the population (n = 348,247)	Percentage of scheme users in NAS (n = 399)	Description	
F	26	31	Goods analysed into VAT categories at point of sale.	
A	36	23	*Single Rate Only*. VAT calculated directly on takings.	
B	5	11	No more than two rates, one of which must contribute more than 50% of total. *Purchases* at the lower rate are recorded, and their expected selling prices are totalled. The balance is assumed to have been contributed by goods liable at the higher of the two rates.	
C	3	4	Maximum turnover £50,000. *Purchases* at positive rates are recorded. Customs & Excise standard mark-up for the type of business is added on to get the assumed outputs.	
D	22	22	Maximum turnover £125,000. *Purchases* at all rates are recorded for the quarter. The purchases proportions derived are applied to takings to determine VAT. An annual adjustment, based on a year's figures, is carried out to correct any distortions arising from fluctuations in trading patterns.	Assumed mark-ups applied
G	2	2	*Purchases* at all rates are recorded for the quarter. The current and three preceding quarters are added together to determine proportions of purchases at each rate. The purchases proportions derived are applied to the takings for the quarter. VAT is	

calculated on this basis, and then an uplift is applied to take account of different mark-ups on goods liable at different rates of VAT. For the first 3 quarters in which the scheme is used, the apportionment must take into account opening stock as well as goods received.

E   4   4   *Expected selling prices* of positive rated goods are recorded. The retailer must pay VAT on existing stock at commencement of use of Scheme E. He must also record total takings, but VAT is determined directly from the total of expected selling prices.

H   1   3   *Expected selling prices* of goods are recorded. Expected selling prices of goods liable at each rate of tax are recorded. The current and 3 preceding quarters are added together to derive proportions at each rate. VAT is calculated on this basis for the quarter's takings.

Expected selling prices applied

J   1   2   *Expected selling prices* at all rates are recorded for the quarter. The proportions derived are applied to takings to determine VAT. Then expected selling prices at all rates are recorded for the *year*. The more accurate proportions derived are applied to calculate an annual adjustment of VAT paid which also takes into account opening and closing stock for the year.

Appendix I Mean Costs of Special Problems

Table I.1 Costs are in £, the number of cases is given in brackets.

Taxable turnover (£000 p.a.)	Primary	Manufacture and utilities	Construction	Transport and communication	Retail	Wholesale and dealers	Financial and business services	Professional and scientific services	Miscellaneous and public services	Overall
0– 9.9	26 (4)	— (0)	23 (3)	12 (1)	25 (1)	— (0)	528 (2)	36 (1)	63 (2)	102 (14)
10– 99.9	49 (4)	232 (6)	95 (11)	5 (1)	77 (11)	113 (2)	83 (2)	— (0)	73 (14)	96 (51)
100–999.9	16 (2)	303 (6)	100 (5)	98 (3)	157 (3)	249 (5)	40 (1)	101 (4)	110 (5)	158 (34)
1000 and over	— (0)	278 (19)	2950 (2)	78 (2)	2908 (3)	193 (6)	2389 (4)	290 (3)	167 (3)	765 (42)
Overall	33 (10)	274 (31)	358 (21)	67 (7)	559 (18)	202 (13)	1202 (9)	164 (8)	92 (24)	311 (141)

Appendix J Further Aspects of Credit Periods and Loans from and to Customs & Excise

Table J.1 Mean time (in days) taken to settle purchases invoices

Taxable turnover (£000 p.a.)	Primary	Manufacture and utilities	Construction	Transport and communication	Retail	Wholesale and dealers	Financial and business services	Professional and scientific services	Miscellaneous and public services	Overall
0– 9.9	22	22	27	22	17	26	22	23	20	22
10– 19.9	25	36	27	25	20	28	26	27	21	24
20– 49.9	26	36	29	30	22	29	28	25	22	25
50– 99.9	28	43	36	31*	26	33	23	27	27	30
100–999.9	32	43	43	42	27	32	29	31	29	35
1000 and over	28*	46	45	37	39	33	32	37*	37	39
Overall	25	38	31	28	23	30	26	26	23	27

* Less than 10 respondents in cell.

Table J.2 Mean time (in days) taken to receive payment on sales invoices

Taxable turnover (£000 p.a.)	Primary	Manufacture and utilities	Construction	Transport and communication	Retail	Wholesale and dealers	Financial and business services	Professional and scientific services	Miscellaneous and public services	Overall
0– 9.9	16	36	35	21	10	39	28	32	19	24
10– 19.9	13	37	28	36	8	30	29	36	10	19
20– 49.9	15	47	37	48	8	30	34	44	12	20
50– 99.9	17	49	45	39*	10	30	45	52	13	24
100–999.9	27	51	46	49	17	40	39	48	21	35
1000 and over	32*	48	38	40	26	39	36	55*	33	41
Overall	16	46	36	37	10	35	33	39	14	24

* Less than 10 respondents in cell.

Table J.3 Value of mean loans (£) to traders from Customs & Excise (scaled data)

Taxable turnover (£000 p.a.)	Primary	Manufacture and utilities	Construction	Transport and communication	Retail	Wholesale and dealers	Financial and business services	Professional and scientific services	Miscellaneous and public services	Overall mean
0– 9.9	−2	2	..	2*	2	3*	2	4	2	1
10– 19.9	−3	5	1	5	5	2*	2	10	10	3
20– 49.9	−6	17	−2	8	4	5	27	20	20	6
50– 99.9	−11	35	3	20*	3	20	57*	51	24	14
100–999.9	−6	125	16	63	45	41	139	174	−31	48
1000 and over	−5750*	4638	−611	−163*	5727	500	281	1043*	−226	1964
Overall mean	−21	456	−7	10	43	62	45	8	2	58

* Fewer than 10 respondents.
.. Positive but less than £0.50.
Derived by applying rate of interest of 7.0 per cent to scaled down mean 'loans' from Customs & Excise.

Table J.4 Value of mean loans to traders after allowing for commercial credit periods (scaled data)

Taxable turnover (£000 p.a.)	Primary	Manufacture and utilities	Construction	Transport and communication	Retail	Wholesale and dealers	Financial and business services	Professional and scientific services	Miscellaneous and public services	Overall mean
0– 9.9	−2	1	..	..*	2	2*	2	2	2	1
10– 19.9	−2	2	†	†	4	−2*	5	6	8	2
20– 49.9	−3	4	−2	2	8	1	14	8	11	5
50– 99.9	−6	5	−5	4*	11	8	15*	12	32	11
100–999.9	1	32	4	16	28	−9	16	63	−10	12
1000 and over	−33*	2258	−222	−20*	12 368	23	9	1240*	1264	1648
Overall mean	−2	211	−3	2	84	..	9	22	23	44

* Fewer than 10 respondents.
.. Positive but less than £0.50.
† Negative but greater than − £0.50.
Derived by applying rate of interest of 7.0 per cent to scaled down mean loans from Customs & Excise after allowing for commercial credit periods.

Table J.5 Mean size of loans (£) to payment traders from Customs & Excise (NAS)

Taxable turnover (£000 p.a.)	Primary	Manufacture and utilities	Construction	Transport and communication	Retail	Wholesale and dealers	Financial and business services	Professional and scientific services	Miscellaneous and public services
0– 9.9	51	88	63	76	51	59	76	96	79
10– 19.9	140	127	96	124	77	58	212	195	150
20– 49.9	164	319	181	245	115	186	499	415	225
50– 99.9	311	694	518	483	210	508	1052	999	467
100–999.9	1588	2974	1319	1690	1239	1577	3181	3528	1463
1000 and over	—	123587	11028	8242	142190	18614	10107	34036	22440

Table J.6 Mean size of loans (£) from repayment traders to Customs & Excise (NAS)

Taxable turnover (£000 p.a.)	Primary	Manufacture and utilities	Construction	Transport and communication	Retail	Wholesale and dealers	Financial and business services	Professional and scientific services	Miscellaneous and public services
0– 9.9	40	35	40	43	37	—	109	27	77
10– 19.9	72	160	80	118	36	146	64	7	32
20– 49.9	137	56	178	208	29	79	—	18	38
50– 99.9	259	224	261	332	251	40	—	300	35
100–999.9	651	1206	1066	230	462	1056	1069	415	29444
1000 and over	105778	40939	14110	13436	5106	11076	3034	54653	145936

Appendix K Multiple Benefits Analysed by Sector (Including 'Extra Cash' Benefit)

Table K.1 Primary (percentage of NAS respondents)

| Number of benefits | Taxable turnover (£000 p.a.) | | | | | | | |
	0 to 9.9	10 to 19.9	20 to 49.9	50 to 99.9	100 to 499.9	500 to 999.9	1000 and above	Total
0	6.8	7.1	10.1	7.1	6.5	0.6	1.8	40.2
1	4.8	2.4	3.3	1.8	4.2	0.3	0	16.7
2	6.0	3.6	5.1	3.0	2.4	0	0.3	20.2
3	4.5	1.8	2.1	1.8	0.3	0	0	10.4
4	2.7	2.1	1.5	0.3	0.3	0	0	6.8
More than	1.8	0.6	0.6	1.5	1.2	0	0	5.7
Total	26.5	17.6	22.6	15.5	14.9	0.9	2.1	100

(n = 336)

Table K2 Manufacture and utilities (percentage of NAS respondents)

| Number of benefits | Taxable turnover (£000 p.a.) | | | | | | | |
	0 to 9.9	10 to 19.9	20 to 49.9	50 to 99.9	100 to 499.9	500 to 999.9	1000 and above	Total
0	2.7	3.3	2.7	4.7	12.7	6.5	21.9	54.4
1	0.9	0.6	2.4	2.7	2.7	2.4	12.4	24.0
2	0.6	1.5	1.2	0.9	3.6	0.6	2.1	10.4
3	0.9	0.9	0.9	0.9	2.1	0	1.8	7.4
4	0	0	0.6	0.3	1.2	0	1.8	2.4
More than 4	0	0.3	0.6	0.3	0.3	0	0	1.2
Total	5.0	6.5	8.3	9.8	22.5	9.5	38.5	100

(n = 338)

Table K3 Construction (percentage of respondents)

Number of benefits	Taxable turnover (£000 p.a.)							Total
	0 to 9.9	10 to 19.9	20 to 49.9	50 to 99.9	100 to 499.9	500 to 999.9	1000 and above	
0	6.5	7.5	6.5	5.7	7.2	2.2	9.3	44.8
1	4.3	6.5	2.5	1.8	3.2	1.4	1.1	20.8
2	3.2	2.2	3.9	1.4	2.2	1.1	1.1	15.1
3	2.9	2.5	1.8	0.7	0.4	0	0.4	8.6
4	3.2	2.5	1.1	0.7	0.7	0	0	8.2
More than 4	0	1.1	0.4	0	1.1	0	0	2.6
Total	20.1	22.2	16.1	10.4	14.7	4.7	11.8	100

(n = 279)

Table K4 Transport and communication (percentage of respondents)

Number of benefits	Taxable turnover (£000 p.a.)							Total
	0 to 9.9	10 to 19.9	20 to 49.9	50 to 99.9	100 to 499.9	500 to 999.9	1000 and above	
0	3.5	7.0	5.8	4.7	7.0	2.3	16.3	46.5
1	1.2	9.3	2.3	1.2	3.5	0	3.5	20.9
2	4.7	7.0	2.3	0	1.2	1.2	1.2	17.4
3	0	0	1.2	0	3.5	0	1.2	5.8
4	1.2	0	0	0	1.2	0	0	2.3
More than 4	0	3.5	2.4	1.2	0	0	0	7.1
Total	10.5	26.7	14.0	7.0	16.3	3.5	22.1	100

(n = 86)

Table K5 Retail (percentage of respondents)

Number of benefits	Taxable turnover (£000 p.a.)							
	0 to 9.9	10 to 19.9	20 to 49.9	50 to 99.9	100 to 499.9	500 to 999.9	1000 and above	Total
0	3.1	9.7	13.0	11.8	7.5	1.4	3.1	49.5
1	1.9	1.9	6.1	3.5	2.6	0	2.4	18.4
2	0.7	2.6	4.5	3.3	1.9	0.7	0.5	14.2
3	0.7	2.6	2.4	1.9	0.9	0	0.2	8.7
4	0.2	1.2	1.7	1.4	0.2	0	0	4.7
More than 4	0	0.9	0.9	1.7	0.9	0	0	4.5
Total	6.6	18.9	28.5	23.6	14.2	2.1	6.1	100

(n = 424)

Table K6 Wholesale and dealers (percentage of respondents)

Number of benefits	Taxable turnover (£000 p.a.)							
	0 to 9.9	10 to 19.9	20 to 49.9	50 to 99.9	100 to 499.9	500 to 999.9	1000 and above	Total
0	3.3	2.4	2.8	2.8	9.0	7.6	26.1	54.0
1	0.9	1.4	3.3	2.4	6.6	2.8	10.9	28.4
2	0.5	1.4	1.4	0.9	3.3	1.9	2.4	11.8
3	0.9	0.5	0	0.9	0	0.5	0	2.8
4	0	0	0.5	0	0	0	0.9	1.4
More than 4	0	0	0.5	0	0	0	0.9	1.4
Total	5.7	5.7	8.5	7.1	19.0	12.8	41.2	100

(n = 211)

Table K7 Financial and business services (percentage of respondents)

Number of benefits	Taxable turnover (£000 p.a.)							Total
	0 to 9.9	10 to 19.9	20 to 49.9	50 to 99.9	100 to 499.9	500 to 999.9	1000 and above	
0	11.9	6.9	7.9	3.0	11.9	2.0	14.9	58.4
1	4.0	3.0	6.9	5.0	3.0	0	1.0	22.8
2	3.0	0	1.0	0	2.0	1.0	0	6.9
3	0	1.0	0	2.0	1.0	0	0	4.0
4	0	2.0	1.0	0	0	0	0	3.0
More than 4	2.0	0	2.0	0	0	0	1.0	5.0
Total	20.8	12.9	18.8	9.9	17.8	3.0	16.8	100

(n = 101)

Table K8 Professional and scientific services (percentage of respondents)

Number of benefits	Taxable turnover (£000 p.a.)							Total
	0 to 9.9	10 to 19.9	20 to 49.9	50 to 99.9	100 to 499.9	500 to 999.9	1000 and above	
0	7.6	10.6	9.8	3.8	9.1	1.5	3.8	46.2
1	5.3	4.5	3.8	4.5	3.8	0.8	0.8	23.5
2	2.3	5.3	0	2.3	0.8	0	0	10.6
3	0.8	2.3	1.5	2.3	1.5	0	0.8	9.1
4	1.5	0.8	1.5	0.8	0.8	0	0	5.3
More than 4	3.8	0	0.8	0.8	0	0	0	5.3
Total	21.2	23.5	17.4	14.4	15.9	2.3	5.3	100

(n = 132)

Table K9 Miscellaneous and public services (percentage of respondents)

| Number of benefits | Taxable turnover (£000 p.a.) | | | | | | | |
	0 to 9.9	10 to 19.9	20 to 49.9	50 to 99.9	100 to 499.9	500 to 999.9	1000 and above	Total
0	4.0	9.2	9.8	6.8	5.2	0.6	5.2	40.9
1	2.2	4.6	2.5	6.2	4.6	1.8	3.1	24.9
2	2.2	2.5	5.2	3.1	3.4	0	0.9	17.2
3	1.2	2.2	3.1	0.6	0.9	0.3	0.9	9.2
4	1.2	0	1.2	1.2	1.2	0	0	4.9
More than 4	0	0.9	0.6	0.3	0.6	0	0.3	2.8
Total	10.8	19.4	22.5	18.2	16.0	2.8	10.5	100

(n = 325)

Appendix L Correlation of Attitudes with Other Variables

Table L1 shows very low correlation coefficients between the attitudes scale and the cost measures (though the coefficients are, in fact, significant). The cost measures divided by the taxable turnover show up much better, as indeed one would expect, as the 'burden' of VAT work is being taken into account. The larger the firm, generally, the lower the 'burden'. A partial correlation, taking turnover into account, has the result of raising to -0.16 the correlation coefficient of the attitude score to compliance cost – a substantial improvement, which puts the level of association in line with that of compliance cost divided by taxable turnover.

Table L1 Correlation coefficients of attitude score with other variables

Sector	Number of difficulties	Number of benefits	Compliance cost as a percentage of taxable turnover	Compliance cost
Primary	-0.23	0.35	-0.12	-0.03
Manufacture and utilities	-0.35	0.22	-0.21	-0.10
Construction	-0.45	0.28	-0.23	-0.11
Transport and communication	-0.24	0.28	-0.19	-0.19
Retail	-0.32	0.34	-0.12	-0.03
Wholesale and dealers	-0.37	0.11	-0.21	-0.13
Financial and business services	-0.38	0.31	-0.11	-0.24
Professional and scientific services	-0.38	0.27	-0.25	-0.25
Miscellaneous and public services	-0.38	0.29	-0.15	-0.15
Overall	-0.36	0.27	-0.19	-0.07

Appendix M Correlation of Sources of Advice

The correlation matrix indicates that there is a strong tendency for those who use the official VAT booklets as a source of advice also to use the local VAT office and visiting officer. However, users of official VAT booklets who also use other tax guidebooks are unlikely to use visiting VAT officers. Those who use their accountant as a source of advice tend not to use other sources, and vice versa.

Correlation matrix of percentages of respondents in each sector using the particular sources of advice

	Official VAT booklets	Visiting VAT officer	Local VAT office	Accountant
Visiting VAT officer	0.68			
Local VAT office	0.83	0.82		
Accountant	−0.59	−0.47	−0.24	
Other tax guidebooks	0.59	0.05	0.37	−0.27

References

Bamfield, J. A. N. (1980). 'The changing face of British retailing', *National Westminster Bank Quarterly Review* May 1980, pp. 33–45.

Barker, P. A. (1972). 'Value Added Tax, the cost to the businessman', *Journal of Accountancy* September, pp. 75–9.

Barr, N. A., James, S. R. and Prest, A. R. (1977). *Self assessment for income tax*. London, Heinemann Educational Books/IFS/ICAEW.

Beesley, M. E. (1965). 'The value of time spent in travelling', *Economica* May.

Bryden, M. H. (1961). *The cost of tax compliance*. Toronto, Canadian Tax Foundation.

Buehler, A. G. (1960). 'The state and local tax structure and economic development' in McCracken, *Taxes and economic growth in Michigan*. Kalamazoo, Upjohn Institute for Employment Research.

Carter (1966). *Report of the Royal Commission on taxation*. Ottawa, QPCS.

Carter (1967). *Report of the Royal Commission on taxation*. Ottawa, QPCS.

Chown, J. (1972). *VAT explained*. London, Kogan Page.

Clyne, P. (1973). *The disadvantaged adult, educational and social needs for minority groups*. London, Longman.

Cmnd 4621, 1971. *Value Added Tax*. London, HMSO.

Cmnd 4929, 1972. *Value Added Tax*. London, HMSO.

Commission of the European Communities, 1980. *Report from the Commission to the Council on the scope for the convergence of tax systems in the Community*. Brussels.

Conservative Central Office, March 1977. *Report of the VAT Task Force*. London.

Consultative Committee of Accountancy Bodies, 1977. *Annual accounting for VAT*. London.

Dean, P. N. (1976). 'Costs, productivity and efficiency in the Inland Revenue', *Accountancy and Business Research* Winter, pp. 17–35.

Ferber, R. (1954). 'How aware are consumers of excise tax changes?', *National Tax Journal* **7**, 7 December, p. 358.

Flesch, R. E. (1948). 'A new readability yardstick', *Journal of Applied Psychology* **32**, pp. 221–33.

Fry, E. A. (1968). 'A readability formula that saves time', *Journal of Reading* **11**, pp. 513–16, 575–8.

Godwin, M. (1976). 'VAT compliance costs to the independant retailer', *Accountancy* September, pp. 48–60.

Haig, R. M. (1935). 'The cost to business concerns of compliance with tax laws', *Management Review* November, pp. 232–3.

Hartley, J. (1978). *Designing instructional text*. London, Kogan Page.

Holland, C. (1980). 'Simplifying VAT for the retailer', *Accountancy* January, pp. 57–8.

Interview with the Chancellor of the Exchequer, *The Observer* 23 March 1980.

Johnston, K. S. (1961). *Corporations' federal income tax compliance costs*. Columbus, Ohio University Bureau of Business Research.

Johnstone, D. (1975). *A tax shall be charged*. London, HMSO.

Lewis, A. (1979). 'The comprehensibility of government forms and pamphlets with special reference to means tested benefits', *Policy and Politics* vol. 7, no. 4, pp. 377–85.

Martin, J. W. (1944). 'Costs of tax administration – examples of compliance expenses', *Bulletin of the National Tax Association* April, pp. 194–205.

Mathes, S. M. and Thompson, G. C. (1959). 'The high cost of tax compliance', *Business Record* August, pp. 383–8.

Matthews, M. P. (1956). *A measurement of the cost of collecting sales tax monies in selected retail stores*. Salt Lake City, University of Utah Bureau of Economic and Business Research.

May, J. B. and Thompson, G. C. (1950). 'The tax on taxes', *Conference Board Business Record* April, pp. 130–3.

Mcloughlin, G. H. (1969). 'Smog grading – a new readability formula', *Journal of Reading* May, pp. 639–46.

Møller, M. E. (1967). 'On the Value Added Tax in Denmark and the European Economic Community and the renaissance of tax neutrality', *Bulletin for International Fiscal Documentation* **21**, pp. 431–50.

Muller, F. J. (1963). *The Burden of Compliance*. Seattle, Seattle Bureau of Business Research.

NEDO (1969). *Value Added Tax*. London, HMSO.

NEDO (1971). *Value Added Tax* (second edition). London, HMSO.

Niehus, R. J. (1969). 'German Added Value Tax – two years after', *Taxes* September, pp. 554–6.

Oppenheim, A. N. (1979). *Questionnaire design and attitude measurement*. London, Heinemann Educational Books, pp. 133–42.

Oster, C. V. and Lynn, A. D. (1955). 'Compliance costs and the Ohio Axle Mile Tax', *National Tax Journal* April, pp. 209–14.

Parker, S. K. (1976). 'Compliance costs of the Value Added Tax', *Taxes* June, pp. 369–80.

Prest, A. R. (1963). *Reform for Purchase Tax* (second edition). London, Institute of Economic Affairs.

Public Accounts Committee (1976). *5th Report Session 1975/6, Para. 2075*. London, HMSO.

Reddaway, W. B. (1970). *The effects of Selective Employment Tax, first report, the distributive trades*. London, HMSO.

Reddaway, W. B. (1973). *The effects of Selective Employment Tax final report*. Cambridge, CUP.

Report from the EEC Commission to the Council on the scope for convergence of tax systems in the Community 27 March 1980.

Report of the Commissioners of HM Customs & Excise for the year ended 31 March 1978, 1979, HMSO.

Reugebrink, J. (1965). 'Enkele beschouwingen over de neutraliteit de omzetbelasting' *Deventer* quoted in Møller (1967) op. cit.

Richardson (1964). *Cmnd 2300: Report of the Committee on Turnover Taxation*. London, HMSO.

Rolph, E. R. and Break, G. F. (1961). *Public finance*. New York, Ronald Press.

Royal Commission on the Distribution of Income and Wealth (1979), report no. 8, Cmnd 7679, Chapter 11.

Sandford, C. T., Godwin, M. R., Hardwick, P. J. W. and Butterworth, M. I. (1979). *Some preliminary findings on the compliance costs of VAT*. Bath, Bath University Centre for Fiscal Studies occasional paper no. 7.

Sandford, C. T. (1973). *The hidden costs of taxation*. London, Institute for Fiscal Studies.

Scott, C. (1961). 'Research on mail surveys', *Journal of the Royal Statistical Society* vol. 124, pp. 143–215.

Shoup, C. S. (1949). *Report on Japanese Taxation*. Tokyo.

Smith, A. (1776). *Wealth of Nations*. London, Everyman edition.

Strumpel, B. (1966). 'The disguised tax burden – compliance costs of German businessmen and professionals', *National Tax Journal* January, pp. 70–7.

Tait, A. A. (1972). *Value Added Tax*. Maidenhead, McGraw Hill.

Trimby, L. (1980). 'Small business versus Value Added Tax', *Accountancy* 17 January, pp. 52–4.

Vernon, T. (1980). *Gobbledegook*. London, National Consumer Council.

Wheatcroft, G. S. A. and Avery Jones, J. F. (1973) (updated regularly). *Encyclopaedia of Value Added Tax*. London, Sweet & Maxwell and Edinburgh, W. Green & Son.

Wicks, J. H. and Killworth, M. N. 'Administrative and compliance cost of state and local taxes', *National Tax Journal* September, pp. 309–15.

Wicks, J. H. (1965). 'Taxpayer compliance costs from the Montana personal income tax', *Montana Business Quarterly* Fall, pp. 36–42.

Wicks, J. H. (1966). 'Taxpayer compliance costs from personal income taxation', *Iowa Business Digest* August, pp. 16–21.

Wright, P. and Bernard, P. (1975). 'Just fill in this form – a review for designers', *Applied Ergonomics* vol. 6, no. 4, pp. 213–30.

Yocum, J. C. (1961). *Retailers' Costs of Sales Tax Collection in Ohio*. Columbus, Ohio University Bureau of Business.

Index